RTEEN DAY

Growing Old

ELAINE CUMMING
WILLIAM E. HENRY

Growing Old

THE PROCESS OF
DISENGAGEMENT

FOREWORD BY TALCOTT PARSONS

BASIC BOOKS · INC. · NEW YORK

Foreword

By TALCOTT PARSONS

This is an important book. Dr. Cumming, Dr. Henry, and their associates have both given us an impressively detailed empirical study of a sample of older people and made what is probably the most serious attempt so far to put forward a general theoretical interpretation of the social and psychological nature of the aging process in American society. It may be safely predicted that this study will serve as the most important focus of discussion of the problems on this level for some time.

The importance of these problems, both as a challenge to social science and in their practical urgency, scarcely needs underlining. The changing age composition of Western, including American, populations, bringing greatly increased proportions into the older age categories, is one of the central features of the demographic revolution of this century. The proportion having reached the magic line of 65 is already 8.7 per cent and is destined in another decade to reach about 9.5 per cent. These figures are to be compared with 3.4 per cent in 1880. Clearly, there has been an immense change not only in terms of simple longevity, but also in terms of state of health in the later years.

This demographic change presents a rather special challenge to American society, and through that to the social scientist concerned with the understanding of that society. This is, above all, because of the historical recency of the major American development and because, in accord with its instrumental and activist values, it seems to be a society to which a rather special "accent on youth" is appropriate. It has been common to regard the problem of the aged as a special Achilles' heel of the American system, in the sense that the only possible status for older people was that of "discards" who could not possibly have a positive significance in the system, but constituted mainly a kind of philanthropic burden.

In this connection it is particularly important that the Cumming-Henry study did not concentrate on the disabled minority, which to be sure is relatively larger than for other age groups, but studied people in good health who had by and large been able to maintain their positions of basic "independence." From the point of view of our social common sense their findings are in certain respects paradoxical, but it seems to be the kind of paradoxical complex which is capable of a certain kind of resolution through scientific analysis.

A first and major point is that, judged in terms of personal attitudes, by and large this group do not appear to be as drastically dissatisfied and frustrated as they might be expected to be. Though evidence is presented of something of a crisis of transition from middle to "old" age, once past that transition it seems probable that the states of subjective satisfaction of "normal" older people, even in this society, compare

favorably with those of other age groups. The suggestion is
that there is a process of adaptation to the conditions of later
life which, with all the variations among individuals, and for
example as interestingly analyzed by sex, has sufficient common
features to present a common pattern.

As indicated by their subtitle, the formula the authors suggest for this process is "disengagement." The point of reference
here is the involvement in role-obligations of the social system
as these are typically organized for the years of mature middle
age, notably occupational roles for men and family responsibilities for women, but various others as well. The thesis as
to the general character of this process is well formulated and
documented. There is, however, one question about it which I
should like to raise, which does not seem to me to be fully dealt
with in the study. This concerns the relative weight of two
principal components of interest or commitment which are alternatives to engagement in the social role sense, namely, on
the one hand interests primarily at the personality—and organic
—levels, and on the other hand those at the cultural levels.

The most obvious of the former is concern with problems
of ill health and disability. On the whole the evidence of the
study seems to be that these are less prominent than is generally supposed, as is the case, interestingly, for preoccupation
with death. There certainly are, however, important psychological preoccupations of a "self-centered" sort.

The other component is the cultural. This may of course
take a wide variety of forms—aesthetic interests, including
gardening, literature, science, history, and others. The important point is that cultural concerns are inherently somewhat
removed from the more immediate urgencies of concrete social
situations. Indeed, it is only through positive institutionalization, as in the case of research in universities, that their culti-
vation can be securely provided for in societies. It is at least
an interesting possibility that the relatively disengaged position

of the older groups may play an important part in this situation. If so one would expect those in the higher status groups to show this trend most clearly.

One reason why this possibility is such a suggestive one is that the general trend of development of American society can be shown to be one of institutionalization of progressively higher levels of cultural standard—though exactly in what respects and with what emphases represents a very complicated set of problems. At any rate, if this interpretation is correct it would be extremely likely that the trend would have a particularly important impact on the older age groups. Drs. Cumming and Henry have provided an admirable setting for further research into this problem as well as many others in this important field.

Preface

We are reporting here a portion of the findings from the Kansas City Study of Adult Life, a research project, supported by the National Institute of Mental Health,* which is investigating some aspects of the aging process. This report is organized around a social-psychological theory of aging. It does not begin to exhaust the data collected in the study, and other publications will follow.

Research can be reported so that the natural history of the operations coincides with the logical pattern of the inquiry.

* Grant No. M-9082 to the Committee on Human Development of the University of Chicago, W. E. Henry, Principal Investigator, with Bernice L. Neugarten, Robert J. Havighurst. The terminal phases of the analysis of the data, and the preparation of the manuscript for this book, were made possible by the co-operation of the staff of the Mental Health Research Unit of the Department of Mental Hygiene of the State of New York, and its director, Dr. John Cumming.

ix

In this exploratory research involving repeated waves of field work, however, a logical account does some violence to the natural history. This is a pity because the natural history provides a full view of those ragged edges which in any research contribute to the conceptual structure but seldom get reported. Natural-historical reporting, however, becomes cumbersome when, as in our case, the work extends over a period of years and major reformulations have taken place in the course of the inquiry. For this reason, this book is organized in a logical rather than a natural-historical form. However, we will here indicate briefly the processes that led to the portion of the research reported.

The inquiry began with the question *"What are healthy, economically secure old people like?"* From the answers of friends, colleagues, and a handful of very old people, we developed a set of hypotheses about the processes that might have produced the characteristics which these people described.

Later, new ideas, which certain unexpected findings generated, were tested, reformulated, and tested again. The theory we report was constructed, in other words, by shuttling back and forth between the data and the concepts. It is, therefore, an inductive theory, although in Chapter XIII we have articulated it with other sociological and psychological concepts.

This research followed a previous study of aging undertaken in the Kansas City Metropolitan Area,* and was one of a number of sister studies under the direction of the Committee on Human Development of the University of Chicago. The advisory committee for these studies greatly facilitated the establishment of our research. Robert J. Havighurst, Bernice L. Neugarten, Everett Hughes, and Richard H. Williams all deserve our thanks. W. D. Bryant and Homer Wadsworth

---

* By R. J. Havighurst and Bernice L. Neugarten; supported by the Carnegie Corporation and referred to throughout as the Carnegie Study.

were particularly helpful in making the study's entrance into Kansas City a smooth one. Martin Loeb acted as liaison between an earlier study and this one.

Many people have worked on this study, as is inevitable when a research project lasts as long as this one has. Some have had only passing contact, while others have made a sustained contribution. In particular we are indebted to Jacqueline Rosen and David L. Gutmann, upon whose work we have drawn heavily in Chapter VI. We are acknowledging in each chapter the people who have made direct contributions to the phase of the work reported there. Many of them have contributed to the whole book and not only to those chapters bearing their names; for example, Lois R. Dean, who appears as co-author of two chapters, supervised all the interviewing and was deeply involved in all aspects of the study, and Isabel McCaffrey gave invaluable help in supervising much of the statistical analysis. Rhondda Cassetta checked and corrected all the tabulated material, and David Newell has worked on all aspects of the research, interviewing, analysis, and writing. Bernice L. Neugarten and Robert J. Havighurst not only helped develop the initial study plan but have assisted in the preparation of all interview guides and supervised part of the analysis. We are particularly indebted to them for their stimulating critical interest throughout and for their careful review of various chapters of this book. In spite of the additional writers listed for some of the chapters, the authors take complete responsibility for all of the contents.

Many other people contributed greatly to the study, but in areas that are not the direct concern of this volume. Some of their contributions are listed in Appendix 6, an inventory of the articles and addresses given by the staff between 1957 and 1960. In particular, we are indebted to Dr. Hedda Bolgar, who was the first director of the study and who very successfully got it under way. Dan C. Lortie was an early member of the group, and his painstaking work in choosing the sample is reflected in our confidence in the representativeness of our study group. Bess Udell served the project for several years, first as an interviewer and later as a data analyst. Ione Price faithfully performed many tiresome tasks of tabulation and analysis; to her we owe also a religious-piety measure discussed in Chapter V. James D. Allegretto, Mary Newell, Ann Haendel, and Roxane Cohen assisted with the analysis of data. Carrie Conti and Erna Christensen helped with tabulations and the construction of the tables.

During the five waves of interviewing with which this book deals, many interviewers were employed. We offer our sincere thanks to Margaret Laughrey, Georgiana McLarnen, Blaine Pennington, Thomas Arthur, Clifton Wolfe, Olivia Pope, Peter Marsalla, Katherine King, Freda Newell, Iola Edgerton, Agnes Hall, Ann Montague, Opal Long, Eva Marx, Barbara Goldberg, Kathryn Rollert, and Minnie Loman. The difficult task of maintaining the clerical coherence of the study was performed throughout by Helen J. Erickson. She also gave valuable assistance to the staff, often outsiders, in interpreting the community and providing the project with continuity. Assisting her were Patricia Hanson and Jessie Lancaster. Margaret Whitmore, Antoinette Douglas, Helen Powless, and Margaret Williams have done painstaking work in typing and proofreading the manuscript and checking tables.

The administration of an away-from-base project is always difficult; we are very grateful to Alice Chandler and Mabel Frazier of the Committee on Human Development for relieving us of much of the administration of the project. We also received important help and stimulation from colleagues. Dr. James Davis assisted with the morale and alienation measures; Dr. David Schneider guided us in the collection of kinship data. The criticisms and suggestions of Dr. Thomas McPartland, Dr. John Cumming, and Dr. Richard Williams have been valuable to us.

Finally we wish to express our gratitude to our respondents, most of whom will never read these lines. We are particularly grateful to those people who, although weary of the incessant demands on their time, stuck with it because they had said they would, and because they felt that they were serving a good end. Every study stands or falls on the co-operation of its respondents, and we are deeply grateful to ours.

The authors gratefully acknowledge permission to reproduce tables and quotations granted by W. B. Saunders and Company, and the Institute for Sex Research, Inc. of Indiana University, The Free Press of Glencoe, Illinois, The American Sociological Association, the *Journal of Gerontology*, the *American Anthropologist*, and General Features Corporation. Specific references to the authors and publishers are made in the text and the list of references.

ELAINE CUMMING
Syracuse, New York

WILLIAM E. HENRY
Chicago, Illinois

September, 1960

Contents

xv

Growing Old

Growing Old

CHAPTER I

Introduction

EVERYDAY SPEECH is filled with references to age: "as old as you feel," and "young for your age," and "try to act your age." Furthermore, the stages of life lend themselves to metaphor, and often to symmetrical metaphor—the springtime of life and its winter, the green years and the golden ones, and, of course, December brides. But in spite of this preoccupation, how much can we really tell about a person if we know only how old he is? How much, indeed, does our own age mean to us when it is divorced from going to school, having babies, or getting jobs, all of which may accompany age but are not age itself? If we are told that the man we are about to meet is thirty-five years old, we can confidently predict that his skin is still unwrinkled; that if he lives in North America he is probably married; and that if he has children they are quite young. But can we predict anything about how he will relate to us? Will his handshake be firm or limp? Will his smile be broad or will it be absent? How will he view himself, and how will he view his fellow men—and women? Can any of these things be guessed from his age? If we hear that he is sixty-five years old, will we be able to know anything more than that his skin has lost its elasticity? Will being sixty-five affect the way he approaches, or does not approach, a stranger?

If there are ways in which we can estimate another's age, is it because there are changes in him that are intrinsic to the aging process, or is it because when we see signs of biological aging, we associate them with a hundred things we know about, that is, the whole precipitate of empirical detail which accompanies all the various stages of life? In brief, does the passage of time *alone* make some difference, or does time stand only for a variety of experience in a number of social systems? If both count, which is the more important, and how can we tell their effects apart?

Although these questions cannot all be answered, everyone *feels* that age makes a difference, and that this difference is more than simply biological. Throughout this book, we shall be reporting on that aspect of aging which is more than simply biological, although wherever physical aspects of aging are related to social and psychological aspects, we shall be indirectly concerned with them. Our focus will be upon interpersonal behavior. We will try to identify changes during middle and old age in attitudes, sentiments, and values, and such changes in the personality as express themselves in interaction with others, and hence in the performance of society's roles.

To begin with, everyday usage about age is often misleading. When we hear a friend say, "I wish I had more friends my own age," it sounds at first as if there were something about being a similar age that makes friendship more rewarding, but when this desire is probed, it may be that the speaker means friends who would also face the problems of a young profes-sional—finding baby-sitters, managing on a low income, and worrying about a new job. He does not mean that having friends his own age will guarantee gaiety rather than gloom, or, if he prefers it, seriousness rather than frivolity. He just means that they will share with him certain limitations upon action or certain preferences for action. But these are situa-tional considerations, not interpersonal ones. In short, when we say we want friends our own age, we may mean that we want friends in our own social stage. We may also have biologi-cal matters in mind; if we are young, we may not want to climb a mountain with a person too old to get to the top.

Yet when the shorthand uses of "age" that actually refer to biology, social structure, values, or the opportunities and limitations for action are put aside, we still have some meaning left. Between the ages of twenty-five and thirty-five, there may be very few changes in physical appearance, and yet something tells us there is a difference. Somehow we can guess one an-other's years more closely than biological cues alone would allow. And we demonstrate our confidence in our ability to make these judgments when we comment on the exceptions. Phrases like "he is a young forty" or "she was born old" betray the fact that we are holding some standard latent in our think-ing. Although a large number of references to age occur in everyday speech, we are certain of very little about the aging process, which is odd when we consider how much we know about the maturation of children.

In some ways our imbalance of knowledge is a function of a culture which, being young, has interested itself much more in youth than in age. When the population pyramid suddenly became top-heavy and America settled into the ranks of "older countries," our interest in the question of what happens be-tween adulthood and old age was aroused, and we can expect in the future an efflorescence of interest in the nature of the aging process.

Another reason for our past failure to explore the aging process is our difficulty in thinking about age by itself, divorced from the pageant of marriage, procreation, and work which accompanies us through time. It is hard enough to think about the passage of time without thinking of its effect on patterns of behavior. To ask a person how he experiences the passage of time is often as useless as to ask him how he experiences the circulation of his blood. We can describe how it feels to breathe because we have had short experiences with not breathing, but we cannot experience a sense of time *not* passing, and are at a loss in trying to confront the aging process at this most immediate level. We must, therefore, if we wish to describe it, resort to approaching it indirectly.

The people of all cultures have been preoccupied with one or another aspect of age. Plato, speaking from a culture which venerated wisdom, appreciated the advantages of extreme age. He reports a conversation between Cephalus and Socrates. Cephalus describes having, as a young man, asked Sophocles, "How does love suit with age—are you still the man you were?" to which he received the reply, "Peace, most gladly have I escaped from a mad and furious master." Cephalus continues, talking to Socrates:

His words have often occurred to my mind since, and they seem as good to me now as at the time when he uttered them. For certainly old age has a great sense of calm and freedom; when the passions relax their hold, then as Sophocles says, we are freed from the grasp not of one master only, but of many. The truth is, Socrates, that these regrets, and also the complaints about relations, are to be attributed to the same cause, which is not old age but men's characters and tempers; for he who is of a calm and happy nature will hardly feel the pressure of age, but to him who is of an opposite disposition, youth and age are equally a burden (55).*

* References will be found at the back of this volume.

Although this image of aging as a passage from a state of tyranny to a state of freedom gives us a certain sense of the process, it nevertheless says nothing about the details of making the shift, and refers to only one aspect of aging, the loss of sexual powers. Moreover, it explicitly says that differences in men's natures are more important than differences in age.

David Riesman (60, pp. 484-92) distinguishes "three ideal-typical outcomes" of the aging process: first, those autonomous people with creative resources who use them to advantage in old age; second, those who are adjusted and remain so—that is, preserved in old age; and finally, those who are neither, and so decay. This is clearly related to his well-known character types—inner-, outer-, tradition-directed, and autonomous (61). In talking of aging, Riesman supplies us with an end-point, but he does not attempt to delineate the process of aging itself. The end state seems logical enough, but the process remains a mystery.

Erik Erikson (23, pp. 231-33; 24, pp. 98-99), in contrast, has an approach toward maturation that focuses directly on process. He sees the individual developing both as an emergent biological organism and as a responsive social being. To mark this unfolding, he conceives of eight analytically distinct stages between birth and full maturity. His model is that of recurrent crises involving developmental dilemmas which can be resolved either by moving forward to a new stage or by remaining "frozen" at a level of incomplete development. However, his imaginative and useful formulation stops at the crisis of maturity, which he calls ego integrity—versus despair. The resolution of this last adult crisis marks completed development. Erikson has written a book about childhood, and he cannot be blamed for not writing one about old age, but it is a loss to us that he did not extend his analysis to include the responses of the retrenching organism. Nevertheless, the picture he draws of the mature person provides a good starting point, and we will return to it from time to time.

■ **Social Science Studies of Aging**

Although there seem to be no systematic theories of the aging process, there have been a number of empirical attempts to delineate it. Schaw and Henry (64) made a study of business executives, and concluded from their analyses of projective materials that there are shifts in orientation in the decades from thirty to sixty. They report that, in their thirties, these men have a minimum preoccupation with inner states and a maximum involvement with the active mastery of an outer world which to them seems amenable to conquest. However, in their forties there is the beginning of a move toward seeing the self as an experiencing entity. At the same time the world, which has been seen in simple terms, is seen now to be conflict-ridden. In their fifties, a good deal more turning inward has occurred, and these men have moved "away from the possibility of finding immediate and satisfactory resolutions . . . and their responses suggest a movement of energy into . . . [a] world of their own creation, governed by their own rules." In short, "the basic principle of change appears to be a movement from an active combative, outer-world orientation to an adaptive, conforming and abstract inner-world orientation." In a similar vein, Neugarten and Gutmann (48) have reported, using a related technique of analysis of projective materials, that a sample much like our own of middle-aged people perceive men as becoming more and more passive with the years. These authors report that the sample perceived older women as remaining actively dominant. These findings are important because they are couched in terms of process and suggest hypotheses for us.

Analyzing a British working-class population, Peter Townsend (74) gives us a vivid description of the way in which roles change with age among the people of Bethnal Green, a suburb of London. He shows us with great clarity the continuity with which women act out the roles of daughter, mother, and grandmother, shifting back and forth from helper to helped, in mutually dependent and closely knit relationships, throughout their life cycles. Only the emphasis changes as they slip from one generation to another. The men, on the other hand, depend upon their work for their role of household head and final authority in the home. Work also supplies them with the roles of friend and companion, because in Bethnal Green, although social life for women is determined by kinship, for men it is determined by working together. Compared to women, men are weakly bound to the kinship structure. The aging process is marked for them by a sharp and painful discontinuity. Compared to men, even the unmarried women, who are important as sisters and aunts in kinship networks, do not have much to lose upon retirement. This striking difference in pattern results in different reactions to aging among men and women. Later we will contrast the findings from our own study with Townsend's report in order to suggest differences in the aging process that arise from our different kinship pattern and our different values about authority in the home.

Besides these studies, there is little to be found in the literature about the aging process itself. On the other hand, there are numerous studies of the "adjustment" (34) of people at various ages, and comparisons of various types of "successful" aging. Although these studies do, of course, throw some light upon the aging process, they raise a very ticklish question; namely, what is adjustment and what is success? We will return to this troublesome matter in a later chapter.

Another group of studies has analyzed the characteristics of populations of old people (41). A great many useful findings have been made this way, contrasting the ambulant old with the institutionalized old, the foreign-born old with the native-born, and so on, but at no time can we be sure that these older people differ from younger ones, and furthermore, as Kutner has pointed out in his study, age itself does not seem to make a great deal of difference *within* these older populations.

We have been talking about the aging process, but, strictly speaking, the social sciences are not well equipped with concepts of the social-psychological process. What we can do fairly adequately is to describe both personality and social structure at short enough time intervals to allow some inferences about process. In just this way, biological science has progressed. The study of the structure of the embryo at different stages of maturation, for example, allowed inferences about growth and development long before the differentiation of tissues and organs, which is the actual process of development, was understood.

Using this technique of repeated "cross-sectional" observations, we have studied a panel of aging people over a period of time. We are reporting at this time comparisons of people of different ages, as well as some preliminary "panel-to-panel" comparisons we have completed. We have been able in our study to collect some empirical facts about aging people and to examine ideas of "successful" aging.

In this phase of the research, however, our primary goal has been to construct inductively a theory of aging. The purpose of this book is to report the "disengagement theory" of aging which we have developed and to present the data upon which it rests. Our theory is social-psychological, and it is offered as a bridge between personality theory on the one hand and social theory on the other. Its range includes the inner mental and emotional states of the respondents as they appear to the researchers, the self-perception of the respondents, their orientation toward other people in their world, and the nature of the network of social relationships surrounding them. We have not tried to exhaust all of these aspects of the lives of our respondents, but only to sample them. In other words, we are interested in how the individual relates to his environment. We are not directly interested here in the structure of personality or in the structure of society but, rather, in the interface between them. This, of course, demands that, in the interest of meaning, we take into account both personality and society, but we will hold our focus upon the interface as much as possible.

We are attempting, wherever possible, to use concepts and terms that describe both personality and interaction. Following Parsons (50), we view both personality and society as action systems and we view the interface between them as interpersonal behavior. Clearly, we have important antecedents in this, and thus heavy intellectual debts. Throughout this book we will lean upon general theories of human behavior developed by others, and upon substantive theories in areas other than aging.

All the authors have shared, except where one of us explicitly denies it, a number of assumptions. Probably the most important is an underlying model of human development. We are agreed that growth and development follow a pattern in which each phase is determined by the one which went before it rather than being primarily determined by any particular "crucial" phase. Specifically, we assume that the nature of old age is immediately derived from the nature of adulthood, which in turn depends upon the nature of adolescence, which is a product of childhood. In other words, we do not assume that all the phases of life are directly and irrevocably affected by childhood experiences but, rather, that childhood experiences are mediated in adulthood and old age by the intervening stages of development. This means that in our examination of aging we will concern ourselves directly with adulthood, and pay very little attention to childhood experiences.

A second important assumption is that the total social environment is the most important focus of study for human behavior. We are, of course, not studying the total environment but only selected parts of it, and the assumption itself may appear obvious. In short, it is one that everyone in an open society is bound to make. However, we believe it is important that we have *not* assumed that heredity, either biological or social, has much importance, or that any *specific* social institution—the church, the family, or the class or caste of origin—is almost totally responsible for behavior.

Finally, it is our assumption that the individual has access to the whole culture, directly or indirectly, and, furthermore, that he exercises some freedom of choice in selecting his contacts with its various values and institutions.

Two Theories of Aging

IN SCIENCE there is simply no way of disregarding theory. If we are not consciously using theory, we are inevitably employing instead groups of implicit assumptions, because we must have anchor points for our thinking and guidelines to show us what to look for in our data. The disengagement theory of aging which we are developing here is a common-sense theory, inasmuch as it arises from general observation and tends at first glance to appear rather familiar and obvious. However, it is by no means the only possible common-sense theory of the aging process, and indeed it differs rather radically in its implications from another common-sense theory, which we are calling the "implicit theory" of aging. The latter is a set of assumptions about old people which appears to us to underlie a good deal of the social-scientific writing and most of the popular literature on the subject of aging and old age.

It is quite possible for two radically opposed common-sense theories to exist side by side, because they may both account for the available data, although they may emphasize different aspects of everyday observations and they may draw quite different inferences from them. It is partly to make the propositions developed in this study explicit that we are comparing them here with what appear to be those of others, and partly to sharpen the contrast between two fundamentally different ways of looking at the aging phenomenon.

Below, we will sketch briefly the main features of our disengagement theory, and then spell out in some detail what we understand to be the theory implicit in some other writings on the subject of aging. In the ensuing chapters, we will describe evidence that led us to formulate the new theory, and finally, in Chapter XII, we will develop it in detail and examine some of its implications.

■ Disengagement Theory

Starting from the common-sense observation that the old person is less involved in the life around him than he was when he was younger, we can describe the process by which he becomes so, and we can do this without making assumptions about its desirability. In our theory, aging is an inevitable mutual withdrawal or disengagement, resulting in decreased interaction between the aging person and others in the social systems he belongs to. The process may be initiated by the individual or by others in the situation. The aging person may withdraw more markedly from some classes of people while remaining relatively close to others. His withdrawal may be accompanied from the outset by an increased preoccupation with himself; certain institutions in society may make this withdrawal easy for him. When the aging process is complete, the equilibrium which existed in middle life between the individual and his society has given way to a new equilibrium characterized by a greater distance and an altered type of relationship.

This theory is intended to apply to the aging process in all societies, although the initiation of the process may vary from culture to culture, as may the pattern of the process itself. For example, in those traditional cultures in which the old are valued for their wisdom, it may well be that the aging person openly initiates the process; in primitive, and especially in impoverished cultures, he may resist the process until it is forced upon him. In our own culture, the assumption implicit in writings about old age appears to be the latter rather than the former. Since our purpose here is not to make cross-cultural comparisons, we will confine ourselves to delineating as many characteristics of the aging process of healthy, economically stable Americans as we can.

In any process in which the individual becomes less bound to the social systems of which he is a member, it should be possible to distinguish changes of three orders. First, changes in the number of people with whom the individual habitually interacts and changes in the amount of interaction with them should be observable. At the same time, changes may occur in the purposes of the interaction, so that shifts in the goals of the systems to which the aging member belongs should be discernible.

Second, we should find qualitative changes in the style or patterns of interaction between the individual and the other members of the system, that are commensurate with the decreased involvement.

Third, we should see changes in the personality of the individual that both cause and result in decreased involvement with others and his increased preoccupation with himself. In addition, we should observe evidence, if this process is indeed the modal style of aging, of its institutionalization in society.

We will attempt to define the beginning and the end of the series of changes we will call the disengagement process, and will report evidence which bears upon the nature of the process. We will also comment on the way in which certain social institutions appear to be geared to this process. Our formulations were not thought out before the study reported here was undertaken, but were developed bit by bit as the study proceeded. Because the theory was built with the data of the study and then tested against other data from the same study,* we consider it a tentative theory or a set of hypotheses about aging.

Before we proceed to elaborate on our theory, however, we will discuss a theory that seems to be implicit in much of the current thinking about aging.

■ An Implicit Theory of Aging

When we read any "problem-oriented" publications about aging, it is possible to tease out of them a number of related themes which rest on a set of assumptions amounting to an implicit theory of the aging process. This does not mean that there is any complete expression of such a theory in the literature but, rather, widespread evidence of its various assumptions.

In the first place, investigators have often used the word "aging" misleadingly, as if it meant "old." It seems to be assumed that middle age lasts for a certain length of time and is followed abruptly by old age. Sometimes retirement is said to be the point at which this occurs, or, possibly, widowhood;

---

* This procedure is circular—we are influenced in our predictions by familiarity with the material. However, we are not so badly influenced that we can afford the luxury of new subjects every time we modify our concepts. Eventually we hope to see all of the conclusions here reported tested on other populations.

more often failing health seems to be the turning point. There is no discussion of the possibility that this change from middle to old age may be adumbrated in any important way.

Available literature has sometimes suggested that every man ages alone, in the sense of being cut off, by the fact of his age, from others. Thus, people have been advised, as they get older, to start cultivating friends of their own age so that they will have shared interests and problems. It seems to be assumed that the "one" who is the reference point is the only one doing any aging, and the tendency for people to think of themselves as remaining much the same has sometimes been overlooked. Most people seem to see their friends as "girls" and "boys" long after these terms have any literal meaning. There is little indication of people aging in ranks, echelons, or generations, but rather some feeling that growing old is a solitary experience, unique to each individual. This may reflect the intense individualism of middle-class intellectual scientists and their weak identity with ranks or echelons of people. These problems face all social researchers, and the reader will have to decide to what extent we have resolved them in the work reported here.

This reflection of individualism in the literature on aging is related to a projection of the standards of middle-aged behavior onto that of the old. Thus, many studies reach such doubtful conclusions as the following: the members of a group of aging people have low morale (8) if they answer certain questions with responses other than those appropriate for a middle-aged respondent. For example, an answer of "no" to the question, "Do you still feel useful to those around you?" was assumed to reflect lowered morale.

Britton and Mather (13) have been sensitive to this tendency, and in an interesting factor analysis of the content of good-adjustment norms among older people they showed that the one clearly evident factor was "general activity." This is the bench mark of the young and the middle-aged. As these authors point out, "It could be theorized that adults, still clear in mind, growing into the very late years could lose their capacity for overt activity, but that they could still be well adjusted *if our criteria allowed them to be so* [italics ours]."

In short, there appears to be a latent assumption that successful aging consists in being as much like a middle-aged person as possible.* "Feeling useful" has not been defined, however, and it has not been made clear why old people should be expected to feel that way.

An extension of this implicit theme of continuing usefulness is the feeling that the life span must, in order to be successful, undergo steady expansion (32, pp. 54-55). Much of what has been written advises the aging person to continue to develop new interests and to make new contacts. Although physical infirmity is acknowledged, ingenious ways have been offered of overcoming its confining effects. The individual is seen as unfolding and expanding in such a way that every time a role or a relationship is lost, a new one fills its place—perhaps even more than fills it. Studies based on such an assumption are unlikely to deal with the idea of death. As a matter of fact, death is excluded from most of the literature on aging, and it emerges only occasionally and as if by accident. This is probably a direct consequence of the belief in the desirability of an ever-expanding life. It is hard to reconcile this idea with death, because the death of old people is a slipping away. If it is believed to be a good thing to remain tightly bound to the fabric of life, death must be a tearing away, and this is not a matter to which much thought has so far been given. It is assumed, but seldom talked about, that death is not an important issue for normal people—that only the morbid or perhaps the gifted think of death. Yet death is a logical preoccupation for those who are

* We are aware that the class of the investigator is often an important factor in what he assumes about his respondents, but we will not complicate the issue with this problem at this point.

going to die, and it seems reasonable that those who are approaching death should give some thought to it, as well as to how their departure will affect the people with whom they have close ties.

Although it makes no room for death, the implicit theory does concede that while the individual is expected to continue to expand, he must overcome some resistance to doing so. This has been blamed on a society oriented to youth and to achievement, and tending to neglect the older person and to remove support from him. Much current writing (69) whether it says so explicitly or not recognizes that it is functional for a modern industrial society to pass on roles to the young, because it allows the young both to learn the roles *while* they are still young and to bring to them modern training and perspective. But here again is the assumption that when these roles are handed over at retirement, there is a loss of support for the older person which must be compensated for by other roles and other activities. It has seldom been suggested that people past sixty are glad to quit some of their activities. Handing over is usually described as a loss for which there must be compensation, and, indeed, studies have shown that people anticipate retirement with dread (44, pp. 20-37). However, evidence is accumulating that suggests this is not so. Streib (70; 71) and Tyhurst (75) have both reported that among a population of middle- and working-class people adjustment and satisfaction increase after retirement, and our findings, as we will report below, are in line with this.

In the implicit theory, the *quality* of interpersonal relationships among the aged is often assumed to remain unchanged. First, the old are apparently expected to maintain indefinitely a desire for instrumentality, or competence in managing the environment. Thus, "feeling wanted," a middle-aged feeling, is projected onto old people as an end in itself, because old people are believed to want to continue to be needed because of their usefulness to others. There is some doubt that this is so. Primitive people do not value feeling needed or wanted for its own sake but, rather, because such a feeling guarantees them survival. Consider Simmons' (65, p. 177) general statement about the old person in primitive society. He makes it plain that if old people strive to feel wanted, it is because they wish to be warmed, fed, and cared for in their old age:

Social relationships have provided the strongest securities to the individual, especially in old age. With vitality declining, the aged person has had to rely more and more upon personal relations with others, and upon the reciprocal rights and obligations involved. The strongest reinforcement of these has been through continued performance of useful tasks. . . . [Tb] withstand the strain of obligations, social ties have had to be continuously revitalized, and for the aged the surest move to this end has been continued execution of socially useful work.

It is difficult to say why we assume that everyone desires to continue instrumental activity in a society where the performance of useful services is not inevitably tied up with being adequately cared for. Why is it not suggested instead that old people may want recognition for having *been* useful, for a *history* of successful instrumentality?

When inner states are considered, the suggestion is that personality should, ideally, be immutable, that the valued "outgoingness" of middle-aged Americans should persist throughout life. Yet there is considerable evidence that increased introversion with age is ubiquitous, and this fact is at odds with a belief in an ever-expanding life. Indeed, a continuing expansion, as suggested above, does imply a persistent extroversion. Some workers have tentatively raised a question about this. Slater (66) asks, for example, if, in view of the increased introversion with age, it would not be reasonable to call young introverts and old extroverts deviant, which is absurd. But on the whole the subject is not raised; it seems to be assumed that if introversion starts to increase with age, something should be done to correct the tendency.

Much current writing assumes that while older people of high morale have outgoing, rich, and satisfying relationships, these relationships are entirely free of sexuality.* In spite of Plato's relief at being freed of the tyrant desire, there is clinical evidence that sexual relationships are often lifelong, and Kinsey's findings certainly support this view. On this point, Kinsey says:

The most important generalization to be drawn from the older groups is that they carry on directly the pattern of gradually diminishing activity which started with 16-year olds. Even in the most advanced ages, there is no sudden elimination of any large group of individuals from the picture. Each male may reach the point where he is, physically, no longer capable of sexual performance, and where he loses all interest in further activity; but the rate at which males slow up in these last decades does not exceed the rate at which they have been slowing up and dropping out in the previous age groups. This seems astounding, for it is quite contrary to general conceptions of aging processes in sex (40, p. 235).†

It is obvious that the oldest age groups contain an *accumula-*

---

* There is ambivalence in this asexual view of old people, as many jokes show. For example, there is the story of an old man in his seventies who married a girl of eighteen. He consulted his doctor about how he could be most sure of producing an heir. The doctor, embarrassed, suggested that, as she was just a girl and might find it lonely living with him, they should take a lodger. This would keep her cheerful and make her more likely to conceive. A short time later, the old man came to the doctor and said, "You were quite right, she's pregnant." The doctor offered congratulations and asked cautiously, "And how is the lodger?" "Fine," replied the old man. "She's pregnant, too." The laughter that follows this joke is caused not only by surprise but by the unexpected upward revision of our opinion of the old man, when we realize that we were wrong in assuming him impotent.

† Since this writing, there has been evidence of increasing scientific interest in sexuality among older people. Duke University has such a research under way.

tion of people with no further sexual desire, but age alone by no means guarantees this.

Finally, the usual writing about aging suggests that the whole process involves a digging in of the heels and a refusal to be moved. The implication is that aging means moving away from something—the "prime of life," or "usefulness"—but there is little suggestion that it means moving toward something qualitatively different and perhaps, in its own way, equally attractive. Some writings do suggest, with various metaphors such as "the dividend years," that there are compensations in being older, but only if the aging person first achieves resignation and is able to "accept reality." Sometimes it is assumed that old people have a constant temptation to be eccentric and impulsive, or childlike, but this is believed to be a sign of failure and should be controlled. Old people who are really admired do not act like that, but keep on performing and cause the remark, "You'd never guess he was that age!" Finally, nobody, it seems, really looks forward to being old.

To summarize, the over-all tone of what is written suggests that aging is an uphill affair. It seems to require much swimming against the stream for the old person to overcome the natural tendency for the world around him to withdraw its support, leaving him deserted. It is implied, however, that if the aging person is watchful and does not let his roles fall empty, and if his family and friends and community are properly oriented toward him and energetic in their convictions, he can be kept in a permanent equilibrium, differing only biologically from his middle-aged equilibrium. From this it is inferred that the middle-aged state is much preferable to the aged state, and that to remain in it indefinitely is to succeed, while to leave it and shift openly to a different stage of the life cycle is to fail.

In interesting contrast, the writings about the maturation of the child do not indicate whether adolescence is preferable to early childhood or less desirable. Usually a transition is just described. And yet surely the loss of childhood is in some ways more poignant than the loss of middle age. Writers certainly do not make it sound so.

In some ways, we have set up a straw man here. However, we think it useful to set forth the doubts which visited us as we examined the underlying assumptions of the work we reviewed. Furthermore, as we have said above, we are substituting one common-sense theory of aging for another, and it is useful to see what we are discarding when we examine what we are offering in its place. Having indicated some of the inconsistencies we have seen in the implicit theory of aging, we will try to be as critical of our own theory as we develop it.

CHAPTER III

The Study

T HE IDEAL WAY to study a process is to watch it happen and measure its extent. However, as we remarked above, even the biological sciences have only recently been able to observe such processes as growth, and then only with elaborate techniques. In the social and psychological sciences we are doubly hampered. First, we rarely have the necessary techniques, although Bales's technique for studying the interaction process in small groups is a notable exception (7) and, second, we lack the conceptual equipment to talk about process. For example, we talk freely about extroversion and introversion, and we have measures of these states. But these are essentially structural concepts; when we are confronted with the process of "introverting," we discuss it in impressionistic terms, and cannot observe or measure it.

Furthermore, although we are probably able to ask each other questions which gauge our relative state of introversion at any given time, we find it hard to ask one another about the experience of introverting, probably because we lack concepts of this kind of process.

Because of this, we usually resort to making consecutive observations of structure and from them inferring the process of change. This is a standard method in biological science, where, to use our earlier example, every student learns how embryos grow from looking at cross-sections made at given intervals of time.

Corresponding to this biological technique is the so-called panel method, which is used similarly for developing hypotheses about process. Whenever interviews are conducted at intervals and identical material is gathered each time, within the limitations of interviewing itself, it is possible to array a series of social or psychological structures and make inferences about processes that occurred in between them.

Unfortunately, we do not know much about how often we may reasonably expect to interview people without changing or alienating them, and we do not know how frequently we can reinterview them and still expect to see differences. Nevertheless, even with these drawbacks, the panel method is one of the best available to us. It combines three different approaches: The respondent can be subjected to the measurement techniques we have at hand, he can be observed while interacting with the interviewer, and he can be asked to describe his own subjective experience of the process of aging.

If we knew which years of the life cycle were most crucial for the aging process, we could focus on them; without this knowledge, there is some danger that the crucial aging experiences may occur outside the points of observation selected for study. Furthermore, there is no way of knowing how short a period will show results. Finally, discrepancies which may be hard to reconcile can occur between subjective reports of the aging experience and objective judgments of it. Fortunately, it is often through these latter discrepancies that new insights are gained.

There are several technical problems in carrying out a panel research (63). Unfortunately, a panel of people is hard to keep together, and a staff capable of administering intensive interviews is hard to keep in one place for any great length of time. To circumvent the difficulties of following a panel—especially in a mobile society such as ours—for a period of, say, two decades, it is possible to resort to reconstructions of the past. By asking respondents to recall certain periods of their lives, we may elicit from them descriptions of themselves when they were, in a sense, different people, and we may, perhaps, arouse in them consciousness of past change. This method obviously lacks an outside check upon the validity of the recalled material, but it should always be remembered that the so-called objective data we gather suffers from validity problems of its own. It is not by any means certain that asking a person about his life yesterday and today and his hopes for tomorrow yields material any more valid than what he recalls for us from twenty years back. On the face of it, one might imagine that we might tend to idealize the older material, but there is at least as strong a chance that we all tend to describe our current lives in terms compatible with our image of how people of our age and status should present themselves to the public. The past, which is perhaps freer from ego investment, may indeed be reported more dispassionately than the present; some respondents may feel that they earn the right to idealize their current mode of life if they are scrupulously honest about the past. Therefore, with necessary reservations, recalled material lends itself well to comparison among groups of people.

■ Selection of the Study Group

While keeping these problems in mind, our research group set up a study of the aging process in Kansas City in 1955. A stratified random sample of the "urbanized" area of Kansas City was used. This included the city and its satellites.

A sample was chosen from a population of physically healthy adults who had no major economic worries. It was studied in serial cross-section. Comparisons of the age groups within the panel were available for generating hypotheses, as well as respondents' memories of their earlier life. This panel is described in detail in Appendix 1; here we will merely sketch in outline its main characteristics.

The most important criterion for selection of the panel members was age. There was some reason to believe, from earlier work by Havighurst (33), that middle age is a rather long, stable period beginning somewhere between forty and fifty and lasting until about seventy. Thus, in order to follow a panel of people whose youngest members were entering middle age and whose oldest were entering old age, we decided upon a twenty-year range, from fifty to seventy. However, analysis of the first data collected indicated that there were "natural" cutting points very close to the seventy-year mark, and that we had to augment our group of respondents with some older people. However, random samples of very old people are expensive and difficult to secure, just because very old people are something of a rarity. Therefore, a separate quasi-sample was constituted. This auxiliary group was obtained by the so-called "bush-fire" method. Three interviewers were chosen who came from markedly different socioeconomic classes. They were asked to collect a group of people over seventy years of age who met, as nearly as they could discover, the criteria of health we had imposed on the panel. The respondents were located by inquiry in the neighborhoods where the interviewers themselves lived. Except that the upper-middle class seems a little underrepresented, these older people do not differ markedly from the panel.* Details of how they compare with the panel appear in Appendix 1.

We decided to minimize heterogeneity in the panel itself because we were concerned mainly with making new formulations about the aging process through intensive interviews with a relatively small group of people. Therefore, the panel was restricted to white respondents of the working and middle classes as determined by a modified Index of Status Characteristics (78). The sample deviates further from the general population by being equally divided among the upper-middle, lower-middle, and working classes. We attempted to get equal numbers of men and women, for while this does not reflect the population composition, it facilitates analysis. We ended with slightly more men than women, unlike the general population.

An important stricture upon both the panel and the quasi-sample was that its members should be free of such chronic illnesses as would render them incapable of acting in their customary roles at work or in the home. This would allow us to investigate the nature of the aging process without being distracted by problems arising out of illness.

We ended, after the losses caused by these circumscriptions and by 17 per cent refusals, with a panel of aging white respondents, and a quasi-sample of old white respondents whose basic characteristics are shown in Table III–1. There are approximately the same number of respondents in each of the ten-year age groups from fifty through seventy (84, 75, and 82, respectively). However, there are only 38 respondents who are over eighty.

---

* This difference may well be an age-related factor and caused by the generally lower incomes and inferior housing of widows.

At the time of this writing, the panel has been interviewed five times.* The quasi-sample of old people has been interviewed three times. The five interviews each averaged an hour and a half in length, although they were of different types of

TABLE III–1

COMPARISON OF PANEL AND QUASI-SAMPLE BY SOCIOECONOMIC CLASS AND SEX (WAVE I)

Respondents	Upper-Middle Class (ISC 24-54)		Lower-Middle Class (ISC 55-72)		Working Class (ISC 73-102)		Total
	Male	Female	Male	Female	Male	Female	
Total interviewed	37	34	52	58	49	49	279 a
Panel (50–70)	25	27	31	29	32	28	172
Quasi-sample (70–90)	12	7	21	29	17	21	107

a For a discussion of the totals used in the tables, see Appendix 1.

content. They are too long to reproduce in full, but wherever answers to specific questions are analyzed the question will be reproduced except where the nature of the answer makes the question evident. Many of the questions have yet to be analyzed, and some failed to elicit the type of material they were designed to get. A short summary of the main areas covered by each interview follows for the purpose of giving a general sense of the type of social situation set up between the interviewer and the respondent.

■ The Interviews: Purpose and Procedures

Interview 1 was designed to get a general and necessarily superficial picture of the respondent and to secure his co-operation for future interviewing. All interviews

* They have been interviewed once more since then.

begin with an inventory of the household members and a discussion of their general health. About one-sixth of the first schedule is focused on the respondent's attitudes about Kansas City, compared to where he has lived before and where he hopes eventually to live. About one-fifth elicits the respondent's daily round of activities, and his usual weekend round, and the division of labor in the household. This is followed (approximately one-fifth of the schedule) by questions about income and work. A few questions about religion and voluntary organizations are asked, an inventory of "closest friends" and "immediate family" is made, and identifying data are collected.

Following about six months after Interview 1, Interview 2 begins with a general query about the respondent's welfare and asks him to describe the best and the worst things that have happened since he was last seen. The interview proceeds with questions about increase or decrease in activity. Next, a long section is devoted to gains and losses in the number of household members, in the kinship circle, and in the friendship group. An inventory of the relatives to whom the respondent feels closest is made and a description of the kind and frequency of contacts with them elicited. This procedure is repeated for relatives to whom the respondent feels less close, and finally he is asked to list relatives with whom he has lost contact. The section following inquires in detail about interactions with neighbors. A fairly complete occupational history is then taken, and attitudes toward retirement are discussed. The respondent is asked to discuss his image of the future and then to describe in what way he would amend his life if he had it to live all over again. Finally, he is asked to respond to six Thematic Apperception Cards.*

Interview 3 followed six months after Interview 2 and is composed almost entirely of precoded short-answer questions.

---

* Cards 1, 2, 6BM, 7BM, 10, and 17BM of the Murray set were chosen as most suitable. See Murray, reference 47; Henry, reference 35.

Many were designed to discover the respondent's perception of his present interaction rate compared with the past, and some were designed to yield comparisons between the amount of different kinds of interactions. It contains items from the F-scale (1), the Kutner morale scale (41), and the Srole Anomia scale (67); questions regarding favored activities; and attitudes toward old age, illness, death, and immortality. From two questions in this interview and two in Interview 1, an index of morale was constructed.

Interview 4 was designed primarily to collect psychological material and secondarily to test some hypotheses developed from the first three interviews. It contains questions about loneliness, boredom, anger, irritation, and aggression. It inquires as to the respondent's "view of the world" and his "way of life," and estimates whether he tends to project or introject the causes of his difficulties. It makes inquiry about the respondent's role models and ego-ideal, his self-image, and his image of his past life and of his own aging crises. The respondent's "orientations to interaction" are elicited, and he is asked to describe in some detail his spouse, his children, and his grandchildren.

Interview 5 repeats questions from earlier interviews about the daily and weekend rounds of activity, the morale index is repeated, and material regarding various "crisis points" in the respondent's life is gathered. "Role conflict" situations are presented for solution, and some "preferences" are gathered.

In our analysis of these interviews we have used both comparisons of the panel members at different times and comparisons of groups of people of different ages although the latter raises problems. First, there is no doubt that one generation differs from another in many ways, especially in the flavor of its attitudes and values.* It is not easy to decide which of

---

* It has been suggested by Bennett M. Berger that in America there is an especially noticeable shift in mood from generation to generation. In his article

the differences between age groups arise from the generations the members have lived their lives in, and which are endogenous to the aging process. A very good example of this type of doubt is the matter of religious attendance among Roman Catholics. The norms about the number of Masses which people are obliged to attend changes through time. Therefore, different generations of people learn different patterns of church attendance. Hence there may be correlations between church attendance and age that really reflect a generational difference.

Allied to the problem of generation is the problem of attrition. In searching for age-related changes, it is sometimes necessary to analyze the attitudes of very old people. But very old people are not just chance survivors of a general population; they are people whose special qualifications have enabled them to outlive their peers. Therefore age-related findings derived from comparisons of different age groups may merely be reflecting the differences between the type of person who survives into old age and the type of person who does not.* As we will point out later, there seems to be a point, somewhere past seventy-five years, where the survivors form an elite. It is our *impression* that the panel members will resemble that part of the quasi-sample which is under seventy-five when they reach that age, but that very few of them will, at that age, resemble the octogenarians.

Our first examination of our population was in terms of its place of origin, occupation, income, marital status, religion, plans for the future, and household composition. If we look at

---

"How Long Is a Generation?" (reference 10), he points out that though Victorian Britain lasted for sixty years, there have been four distinct phases in the sixty years of this century in America—the age of tycoons, the jazz age, the proletarian decade, and the age of conformity. This is particularly pertinent to a study such as ours, which tries to discriminate between the effects of aging and the effects of generation.

* For this and other reasons, we have analyzed the respondents who are past eighty separately. A rather detailed and partly intuitive analysis of this group appears in Chapter XI.

the panel alone, we find that a third of the members were born on farms, one-third in small communities, and the remaining third in large cities. Most of them plan to remain in Kansas City. Seven of the men had retired when the panel was selected; the remainder were employed in jobs ranging from skilled and unskilled labor to the professions. Half of the women were working. Because of the bias in our sample, these people are wealthier than the general population; they had, in 1954, a median household income of six thousand dollars. Almost half of them have supplementary income from savings and investments. Fifteen per cent of the respondents in the panel lived alone when we first encountered them. Fifty-seven per cent lived with one other person, 17 per cent with two other persons, and the remaining 11 per cent in larger families. Only 8 per cent of the panel members have never been married, although nearly 20 per cent of them were without a spouse when we found them. Most of these were widows. On first contact, only nine people reported no immediate kin. Seventy-three per cent of the remainder had some immediate family member nearby, while 22 per cent had children or siblings only at some distance from Kansas City. Our respondents were almost all affiliated with churches, 80 per cent of them being Protestant, 16 per cent of them Catholic, and 4 per cent Jewish. Sixty per cent were regular church attendants, and the same percentage belonged to at least one organization.

In summary, the majority of our panel members belonged to stable working- and middle-class families; they were relatively affluent, had no chronic illnesses, and lived in small household units. They had a history of mobility, for almost all of them had come to Kansas City from somewhere else. On the whole they appeared to conform quite closely to the stereotype of Middle Westerner.

We have to enumerate at this point several important sources of error in this book. In the first place, as we have said, the panel does not represent the same universe as the people in their seventies and eighties. Apart from this, the over-eighties had an abridged questionnaire, mainly because it was difficult for them to undergo such a long interview session. The addition of the seventy-to-eighty decade to the analysis is justified on the grounds that shifts at around the age of seventy are obscured if this group is not included and that observing these shifts leads to useful hypotheses.

A serious problem in interpreting the results is raised by the drop-out rate. Each wave of interviewing suffered considerable attrition, as we can see in Appendix 1, which describes the population. As we point out there, our attempts to evaluate the 17 per cent that initially refused to be interviewed led us to believe that these people were either extremely busy and involved or else much too suspicious and isolated to consent to participate in the panel. Subsequent losses are divided among deaths, removals, and refusals, as Appendix 1 shows. It is our impression from interviewing some of the respondents ourselves that there is a survival principle involved and that it is connected with narcissism. In short, those people who like to talk about themselves to outsiders remain, while those who find this distasteful fall out, and this difference may be related to some of our findings. Some of the latter do, however, remain out of a sense of duty or because they gave us their word, but it cannot be overlooked that some personality factor is probably at work in selecting the continuing members of each wave.

Allied to this source of error is another, arising from the inability to keep the same interviewer with the same respondent throughout the study in most of the cases. Not only did the interviewer shift during the study period, but some respondents had three different interviewers and a few as many as four. The effect of this has not been studied.

When we look at the starting characteristics of the people

in the panel and those in the quasi-sample under eighty, combined, who are still with us by Interview 5, we see that 66 per cent of the men and 62 per cent of the women remain. The attrition by age unexpectedly left us with fewer men in the middle-age range and fewer women in the aged group. Of those who were between fifty and sixty at the beginning, 77 per cent of the men and 65 per cent of the women survived to Interview 5; 58 per cent of the men and 62 per cent of the women between sixty and seventy remained; and 63 per cent of the men and 59 per cent of the women over seventy also remained for the equivalent of five interviews. Of the married men 64 per cent, and of the married women 61 per cent, were still with us, and 78 per cent of the nonmarried men and 63 per cent of the nonmarried women remained, in spite of the generally higher death rate of widowed men. Of those with a high rate and wide variety of interaction at the beginning, 78 per cent of the men and 71 per cent of the women remained; 49 per cent of the men with a low rate and narrow variety of interaction and 57 per cent of the corresponding women were still in the group. It should be borne in mind that there is some bias caused by attrition.

Throughout this book, we will discuss people who are in their seventies as if they were identical with the people in their fifties, except older. This is a common fault of cross-sectional studies, and ours is no exception. We shall present some before-and-after data, but they are not yet available in large amounts because the panel is not old enough. In future reports we hope to give a good deal more information gathered at different intervals from the same people. There is always the possibility that we are getting generational effects where we say we are getting aging effects. Only the testing of the theory put forward here will determine this.

Any sample which is less than national in scope is certain to have regional biases. The population we used, although representative of the metropolitan area of Kansas City (within the limits described), is by no means representative of the United States. The ethnic composition of the area is markedly more Anglo-Saxon than that of many of the urban parts of the country. Nor do we have more than a sprinkling of second-generation Americans, let alone immigrants. Negroes were excluded and so was the very important lower class. All of these limitations lead to caution in generalizing too widely from our findings and reduce the generality of our theory.

The relative smallness of our numbers has meant that we were unable to hold many things constant while we analyzed what appeared to be crucial variables. For this reason some of our findings will have to be replicated on larger samples before they are taken as seriously as the theory demands they be. We had a self-sufficient and physically healthy population, and for this reason some of our findings may seem unduly sanguine. Our theory itself may need important modifications before it will predict the behavior of the sick or the impoverished.

Finally, the nature of our theory should be borne in mind. It is a system of related postulates which were developed from the data and then tested against those same data. Furthermore, although no data controverting the theory have been omitted, many data irrelevant to it are not reported, and from these, other observers might construct another theory entirely.

CHAPTER IV

Social-Structural Evidence for Disengagement

with David S. Newell

OUR FIRST STEP is to determine the validity of the basic postulate that the individual and his society become disengaged from each other. Although it is "common knowledge" that this is so, we must determine to what extent it is true. In Chapter II we said that disengagement would involve a thinning out of the number of members in the social structure surrounding the individual, a diminishing of interactions with these members, and a restructuring of the goals of the system. This is the social-structural aspect of disengagement; in this chapter we will array the evidence of its occurrence and comment on social mechanisms that appear to facilitate it. In Chapter V we will look at the attitudinal, or social-psychological, aspects of the disengagement process, and in Chapter VI we will examine the evidence for a concomitant psychological change.

37

In considering our respondents' disengagement from the social structures in which they were enmeshed, we looked for a decrease in the number of social roles being played, for a shrinkage in the size of the "social life space," for a lessening of the amount of daily interaction with others, and for a restructuring of social goals. Full details of the characteristics of the indexes we have used are given in Appendix 2. Briefly, they are as follows: the Role Count is an inventory of the number of relationships in which the respondent is currently *active*, and the Interaction Index is a subjective rating, assigned to each respondent, of the amount of each day spent in normatively governed interaction with others. Social Lifespace is a score derived from an estimate of the number of separate contacts he makes with others during the course of a month. Kinship contacts are dealt with separately, because they are such an important part of the respondent's life. Social Mechanisms that appear to be institutionalized around the disengagement process are discussed briefly, and the Restructuring of Goals is inferred from the respondents' descriptions of the best and worst things about their current age. We will deal separately with each of these aspects of the process of growing old.

■ **Role Count**

When the aging individual disengages himself, or becomes disengaged, he may do so by reducing the number of his interactions with others, by reducing the variety of others with whom he has interactions, or by doing both. If he reduces the number of roles he is actively engaged in, he has automatically reduced the variety of his contacts with others.

Role Count has been scored in this study by adding the number of *active* roles the respondent holds. He can get a score for each of the following: household member (if he does not live alone), kinsman (one score for each category of relative he interacts with regularly), friend, neighbor, worker, churchgoer, organization- and club-meeting attendant, and the role of "specific person" (shopper, customer). The scores ranged from one to nine and the median was five.

In Table IV–1 (Column I) we see the percentage of our respondents whose scores were six or more. The pattern for the whole population is quite stable between the ages of fifty and sixty-four; about 60 per cent of this younger group act in six or more roles, but by age sixty-five only 39 per cent do, and the proportion decreases steadily until at age seventy-five and over, only 8 per cent act in more than five roles. The decline with age is significant. When we examine the men and women separately, we see that the women undergo some expansion before discarding roles, and although this slight difference in pattern is not significant, it adumbrates a pervasive difference between the sexes in the manner of growing old. We will discuss the implications of these differences in Chapter VIII.

The shrinkage in the number of roles played by the older members of the panel squares with what we know about retirement, widowhood, and withdrawal from voluntary organizations.* Not all roles are shed at the same time, however, as Table IV–2 shows. There is a difference between men and women here, too, in the pattern of role loss. As we can see, the proportion of men in each category is remarkably stable throughout the age structure, except that the number of people who are working (Column VI) drops dramatically after age

* The loss of some roles may lead to further loss, whereas others may lead to the temporary adoption of compensating roles. Retirement, for example, can bring with it withdrawal from work-related associations. On the other hand, widowhood may bring with it, once the initial desolation is outlived, freedom for activities there has never been time for in the past, and new peer-group activities with other widows. The retired men in our panel sometimes miss the associations they had at work, whereas the widows sometimes tell us that this is the most active and involved time in their life. As one respondent says, "I'm always busy. . . . I don't bother the women with husbands. I go with widows and leave the married women."

TABLE IV–1

RATES OF INTERACTION BY AGE AND SEX
(PANEL AND SEVENTIES, WAVE III)

Sex and Age	Number Interviewed	Per Cent of Numbers Interviewed		
		Large Number of Roles [a]	High Daily Interaction [b]	Large Lifespace [c]
		(I)	(II)	(III)
Both sexes	*211*	*41.7*	*47.9*	*49.3*
50–54	36	61.1	72.2	86.1
55–59	34	61.8	58.8	70.6
60–64	34	58.8	58.8	67.6
65–69	31	38.7	45.2	32.3
70–74	50	22.0	34.0	18.0
75 and over	26	7.7	15.4	26.9
Males	*107*	*42.0*	*46.7*	*62.6*
50–54	19	68.4	78.9	94.7
55–59	18	61.1	50.0	100.0
60–64	19	47.4	52.6	84.2
65–69	12	50.0	50.0	33.3
70–74	25	20.0	32.0	24.0
75 and over	14	7.1	14.3	35.7
Females	*104*	*41.3*	*49.0*	*35.6*
50–54	17	52.9	64.7	76.4
55–59	16	62.5	68.8	37.5
60–64	15	73.3	66.7	46.7
65–69	19	31.6	42.1	31.6
70–74	25	24.0	36.0	12.0
75 and over	12	8.3	16.7	16.7

NOTE: Role Count: Chi Square between all over 65 and those under = 28.5, d.f. = 1, P< .001.

Interaction Index: Chi Square between all over 65 and those under = 18.8, d.f. = 1, P< .001.

Lifespace: Chi Square between all over 65 and those under = 52.2, d.f. = 1, P< .001.

[a] Six or more roles.
[b] Scores of 3, 4, or 5.
[c] Scores of 25 and larger.

TABLE IV-2 [a]

KINDS OF SOCIAL ROLE BY AGE AND SEX

(PANEL AND SEVENTIES, WAVE III)

Sex and Age	Number Interviewed	Per Cent of Number Interviewed Who Have These Active Roles								
		Spouse	House-hold	Relatives	Friends	Neighbors	Work	Spec. People	Church	Orgs., etc.
		(I)	(II)	(III)	(IV)	(V)	(VI)	(VII)	(VIII)	(IX)
Males	*107*									
50–54	19	89.5	100.0	68.4	73.7	68.4	94.7	100.0	42.1	36.8
55–59	18	88.9	94.4	61.1	50.0	66.7	100.0	94.4	50.0	55.6
60–64	19	84.2	84.2	63.2	73.7	47.4	78.9	94.7	52.6	21.1
65–69	12	91.7	100.0	83.3	83.3	66.7	33.3	91.7	41.7	33.3
70–74	25	64.0	76.0	76.0	72.0	48.0	24.0	92.0	56.0	20.0
75 and over	14	78.6	85.7	71.4	71.4	35.7	21.4	92.9	35.7	7.1
Females	*104*									
50–54	17	82.4	82.4	64.7	70.6	58.8	82.4	94.1	76.5	35.3
55–59	16	62.5	87.5	87.5	75.0	75.0	31.3	100.0	56.3	43.8
60–64	15	60.0	86.7	80.0	66.7	73.3	53.3	93.3	80.0	53.3
65–69	19	36.8	57.9	52.6	63.2	57.9	26.3	94.7	73.7	36.8
70–74	25	28.0	52.0	56.0	60.0	52.0	16.0	84.0	64.0	32.0
75 and over	12	16.7	50.0	50.0	83.3	50.0	16.7	91.7	50.0	25.0

[a] Table IV–1 (Column I) is not a summary of Table IV–2. Table IV–2 includes only those who have each *type* of role. For example, a man who had both a wife and a mother-in-law living with him would score 2 on Table IV–1 and if he had regular contact with other kin, the number of categories of relatives would be counted in Table IV–1 but not in Table IV–2. Thus, it is possible to achieve a higher role number on Table IV–1 than Table IV–2 suggests.

sixty-five. For women, however, this is not the only critical
shift, for they tend also to lose the roles of household member
(Column II), spouse (Column I), and kinswoman (Column
III). Very few of either the men or the women hold member-
ships in organizations even when they are in the youngest age
group, and both tend to give them up as they grow older.*
They also withdraw from neighbors, although neither of these
is a significant trend. The role of church member is quite stable
through the age structure, and we will discuss this in Chapter
V in more detail.

When we examine the role of household member (Column
II) more closely, we find in Table IV–3 (Column I) that only
18 per cent of the women in the youngest age group live alone,
while half of those in the oldest category do so, and this difference is highly significant. However, not nearly so many men
live alone. As we also see in this table (Column II), men are
more likely as they get older to be found in two-person households than are women. Both men and women (Column III)
live less frequently in larger households as they grow older.
These findings directly reflect the fact that women lose their
spouses much more frequently than men do. However, while
a larger number of women live alone, about the same *proportion* of widowed men as of widowed women live by themselves;
52 per cent of the widowed, single, divorced, and separated
men live alone, compared to 58 per cent of the women in the
same category. Of the 12 men living alone, two, or 17 per cent,
have kin close by. Among the 33 women living alone, four, or
12 per cent, live close by a relative.

In summary, though men are less likely to live alone, when
they do they are just as likely as women to be cut off from
intimate contact with kin, and to lose the role of kinsman.

* The figures here are consonant with the finding for the whole country
that one in three people is active in organizations, which is reported by Wright
and Hyman, reference 81.

TABLE IV–3

HOUSEHOLD COMPOSITION BY AGE AND SEX
(PANEL AND SEVENTIES, WAVE III)

Sex and Age	Number Interviewed	Per Cent of Numbers Interviewed		
		Living Alone	One Other in Household	Two Others in Household
		(I)	(II)	(III)
Both Sexes	*211*			
50–54	36	8.3	44.4	47.2
55–59	34	8.8	70.6	20.6
60–64	34	14.7	64.7	20.6
65–69	31	25.8	54.8	19.4
70–74	50	36.0	50.0	14.0
75 and over	26	30.8	53.8	15.4
Males	*107*			
50–54	19	0.0	42.1	57.9
55–59	18	5.6	72.2	22.2
60–64	19	15.8	57.9	26.3
65–69	12	0.0	83.3	16.7
70–74	25	24.0	64.0	12.0
75 and over	14	14.3	64.3	21.4
Females	*104*			
50–54	17	17.6	47.1	35.3
55–59	16	12.5	68.8	18.7
60–64	15	13.3	73.3	13.3
65–69	19	42.1	36.8	21.1
70–74	25	48.0	36.0	16.0
75 and over	12	50.0	41.7	8.3

Table IV–4 shows a stable pattern of co-residence at each of the five waves of interviewing,* but we have not reported here the changes in residential status between interviews. Many of our respondents spend varying times in the households of their children, parents, and siblings without defining themselves as living there. These "visits," however, can be protracted for

* This is very different from the situation in London. The American group has many more isolated members within this age group. See Townsend, reference 74. Firth, reference 25.

TABLE IV-4
LIVING ALONE BY AGE AND WAVE NUMBER

Starting Age	Wave I		Wave II		Wave III		Wave IV		Wave V	
	Number Interviewed	Per Cent Living Alone	Number Interviewed	Per Cent Living Alone	Number Interviewed	Per Cent Living Alone	Number Interviewed	Per Cent Living Alone	Number Interviewed	Per Cent Living Alone
Total	*174*		*158*		*211*		*181*		*156*	
Males										
50–59	44	4.5	40	5.0	37	2.7	34	5.9	34	2.9
60–69	36	8.3	33	6.1	29	10.3	26	11.5	21	9.5
70–79	8	25.0	7	28.5	7	28.5	7	42.8	7	28.5
Quasi-sample	0	a	0	a	34	17.6	26	19.2	19	21.1
Females										
50–59	40	12.5	35	14.3	33	15.2	31	12.9	26	15.4
60–69	40	25.0	37	24.3	32	28.1	27	33.3	24	20.8
70–79	6	16.7	6	16.7	4	0.0	3	0.0	3	0.0
Quasi-sample	0	a	0	a	35	54.3	27	51.9	22	54.5

a Not applicable.

months. Because of the value placed on independence, such people report themselves as living alone. People living alone and people living with others are equally likely to get lost from the study group in successive waves.

The implications of these findings will be discussed below when we deal in more detail with the meaning of kinship contacts for this population. In the meantime, we observe that, as we predicted from the disengagement theory, roles become fewer with age for both men and women, although the loss of work and kinsmen, respectively, accounts for most of this diminution.

■ **Interaction Index**

Role Count was concerned with the variety of interactions, and the Interaction Index is concerned with the density of interaction. This, too, we expect to lessen with age. A respondent might have a high role count because he attended meetings of a number of clubs and organizations, but these might not involve him in any considerable interaction. In contrast, the Interaction Index is a subjective rating based on the amount of each day spent in normatively governed interaction with others. Judges based their rating on the first two interviews, and they studied especially the respondent's account of his daily round of activities. Reliability between judges was .8. By normatively governed interaction, we mean contact with others of such a nature that their expectations of the interaction have an impact upon behavior. It is sometimes possible for people to spend long periods in close physical proximity without influencing one another's behavior. Some factory work is of this order; people are close together but owing to noise or other interfering conditions they are not in interaction. It is in interaction that hints and cues and guides that govern and control behavior are exchanged, and a lowering of interaction results in a loosening of the web of normative control which interaction generates. A low interaction rate, therefore, implies a disengagement which has consequences for behavior. For example, Tec and Granick (72), studying admissions to an old people's home, found that the behavior of isolates was more likely to be non-normative and therefore disruptive than that of non-isolates of the same degree of impairment. It is interesting that they did *not* find that isolation *necessarily* led to admission to the home, but that when the other conditions for admission were present, the isolates differed in being less normatively governed. Of course, non-normative behavior can lead to avoidance by others, and hence to isolation. This isolation then reinforces the cycle. In a later study, Granick (26) found that women who had been isolated before admission to the home were not only less normative but they took longer to learn the norms of the institution than women who had not been isolated.

It has long been known that norms are developed and changed in interaction.* Granick's work has demonstrated that in the absence of interaction there is an impaired ability among her population to learn new norms. The disengagement theory would lead us to believe that in general the loosening of social ties will result in a greater freedom from the norms that control everyday interaction, and that therefore there will be more idiosyncratic behavior with age. One respondent appears to be recognizing this process when she says, "I'm seventy-six and I don't have to worry about what people think of me any more."

As we can see in Table IV–1 (Column II), there is a steady decrease in the percentage of people with a high daily interaction as we proceed up the age range. There is a slight difference between the women and the men paralleling the one we saw in the numbers of roles played; that is, in the middle of the age range there is an increase in the number of women with

* We are using here the sociological axiom that "interaction creates sentiments." For a clear exposition of this principle, see Homans, reference 36.

high daily interaction, but again it is not a significant difference. However, the ultimate decrease in interaction is highly significant, and this measure provides evidence of an age-related disengagement of the individual from his social system. In Chapter V we will discuss the evidence for a resulting freedom from normative control.

■ **Social Lifespace Measure**

The number of social roles played reflects variety of interaction; the amount of each day spent in contact with others reflects density of interaction, and our third measure, Social Lifespace, is a composite. It is derived from an actual count of the number of interactions the individual engages in during a given period; the details of its construction are given in Appendix 2. Social life space is related to, but not the same as, psychological life space, a concept developed by Lewin (43). The concept of a changing social life space during the aging process was developed by Williams and Loeb (80). They conceived of the individual as standing at the center of a network of mensurable social interactions; in their own words, "One starts with the individual and works out to his broader social relations rather than starting with society and working toward the individual." We have departed somewhat from the meaning these authors assigned to this term, and have restricted it, for our purposes, to a quantitative estimate of the numbers of discrete contacts with others which the respondent has in a month.* The score is based on the answers to pre-coded questions about the number of contacts with all categories of people shown in Table IV–2 excluding church and organizations. This measure does not take account of the length of time that any interaction lasts, and therefore it is complementary to the index

* Excluding attendance at church and voluntary organizations where interaction need not occur. These are included in the Role Count, however, and in the Interaction Index when the description of the events connected with such attendance warranted it in the opinion of the scorers.

described above. The Social Lifespace Measure, like the Role Count, by disregarding the length of each interaction, tends to give high scores to those whose lives have variety. The Interaction Index and the Social Lifespace Measure have a correlation of 0.6, but it is quite possible for a person to have a high score for one index while a low score for the other. For example, an elderly married woman who is her husband's constant companion but who sees few other people would have a high score on the Interaction Index and a low Social Lifespace. On the other hand, a man who lived alone and had very little sustained social interaction but who had, during the course of a day, a large number of brief encounters with different people might have quite a high Social Lifespace and a relatively low Interaction Index.

All three measures are estimates of the degree of the respondent's engagement with society, and all should decrease with age, according to our theory. However, as they estimate somewhat different aspects of engagement, we would not expect them necessarily to decrease at the same rate.

Table IV–1 (Column III) shows that Social Lifespace, like the other two measures, varies very markedly with age. The whole group shows a steady decrease in the proportion with high scores as we go up the age range. When we look at the men and women separately, we see that there are almost no men with low Lifespace scores until the age of sixty-five. This is because the heaviest weight in the score is contributed by work. As the description in Appendix 2 points out, this reflects, so far as we were able to verify it, the situation for men in America today. For women, there is always a substantial minority with small scores, and after the age of fifty-five the majority are in this class.

When we look at Table IV–5, we see that the proportion which the various elements contribute to the total Lifespace varies somewhat with age and with work status. Among the

TABLE IV-5

PER CENTS ABOVE THE MEDIAN [a] BY ITEMS IN PERCENTAGE CONTRIBUTION TO TOTAL LIFESPACE SCORE
(PANEL ONLY, WAVE III)

Age	Number Interviewed	Items					
		Household Member	Relatives	Friends	Neighbors	Specific People	Fellow Workers
Total workers	91						
50–64	76	48.7	46.1	53.9	47.4	50.0	51.3
65+	15	60.0	73.3	33.3	66.7	53.3	46.7
Total nonworkers	51						
50–64	28	57.1	57.1	57.1	53.6	42.9	0.0
65+	23	43.5	43.5	43.5	47.8	60.9	0.0

[a] Medians computed separately for workers and nonworkers.

workers there appears to be a drawing-in process. Relatives, household members, and neighbors all contribute proportionately more to the total score of those over sixty-five. These increases are made at the expense of friends, and suggest that relationships which are neither "given," as with kinsmen, nor immediately accessible, as with neighbors, are cut back.

Among the nonworkers, there is a small but consistent decrease with age in all of the categories except "specific people." When it is recalled that these are people whom the respondent sees in the course of shopping, traveling, and so on, it appears that the disengaging older person who does not have the more or less neutral atmosphere of work filling a large part of his day tends to substitute neutral contacts of a more discrete sort. In contrast, the person past sixty-five who is still working turns more to the intimate contacts of home and neighborhood, even though, as we saw in Table IV–2, there are fewer of the kinship circle remaining. This shift in balance suggests a shifting allocation of available energy with age.

When the distribution of each respondent's Lifespace is examined in terms of patterning, we find that only about 5 per cent of the respondents have life space scores composed of an array of components that are all, or all but one, below the median, and another 5 per cent of them have components that are all, or all but one, above the median. There appears to be some principle of equilibration which sets a maximum and minimum beyond which the number of interactions cannot rise or sink. It is easy to imagine that time is the limiting factor on the high end, and that some inherent need for human contact may be operating at the low end.

It is interesting that for all three measures of social involvement—Role Count, Interaction Index, and Social Lifespace—decrease in involvement is abrupt, but it occurs five years earlier among women than among men. Although with these small numbers we cannot be sure that this is not accidental, it tallies with other evidence that the aging process is somewhat different for men than for women, although the end result is strikingly similar. At first glance it may seem that men work and women do not, and that this may account for the differences between them, but as we shall see later, it does not entirely do so. A third of the women in our group were working when we first encountered them, and this brings them closer to the men in their pattern of aging, but it by no means bridges the gap. Nevertheless, the difference in pattern between the men and the women is not so striking as the similarity: as age advances, the involvement with society, by any of the measures we have employed, becomes less. The aging person sees fewer kinds of people, less often, and for decreasing periods of time as he grows older.

■ **The Kinship System**

So far we have not dealt with the importance of the interactions to the individual who is relinquishing them. Our next task is to examine in fuller detail the relationship of the aging respondent to his kindred. The importance of the family is universally recognized, and has been taken for granted in all of the literature on aging. It is reasonable to imagine that this basic social unit will be not only an important support to the aging individual but a point of continuing engagement when other contacts are abandoned. We are used to thinking, however, of the isolated nuclear family—the man, his wife, and their children—and of the changing relationships among these people during the latter part of the life span. Indeed, there is good reason to believe that the aged person is very dependent on kin, especially upon his children.* We will return to this in our discussion of the very old respondents,

---

* Seymour Bellin, reference 9, has demonstrated that when old people can no longer live alone, they turn first to their children, and *the children expect them to do so.*

but in the meantime we would like to draw attention to some other aspects of the family that we have found important to our aging respondents.

To begin with, we have examined the categories of kindred each respondent considers himself to be on intimate terms with, and the percentage of these people who have at least one person in such a category available to him. By "intimate" we mean those kindred who are named in response to the question, "Which relatives other than those who live here with you, do you feel closest to?" By availability we mean living near enough so that a visit can be made comfortably during the course of a day and an overnight trip is unnecessary. As Table IV–6 shows, of the 75 women remaining in Wave V, 49 have intimate children, and 77.6 per cent of these have at least one available, while of the 81 men, 57 have intimate children and 87.7 per cent of these have at least one available. Fifty-one men and 54 women have intimate siblings, and 60.8 per cent of the men and 50.0 per cent of the women have at least one available. Forty-two women mention intimate kindred other than children or siblings, and of these 47.6 per cent have at least one available. Forty-six men mention other intimates, and 65.2 per cent of them have at least one available. Very significantly, more children than other categories of intimates are available to the total group.

Table IV–7 shows the visiting patterns among these intimate kindred. Both the men and the women visit their children or are visited by them significantly more often than they visit their siblings or their other intimates (many of the latter are parents). The women keep in closer touch with both siblings and children than the men do, but this difference does not reach significance. Furthermore, women maintain their level of contact with their siblings and children as they get older somewhat more than men. (This is a demonstration of the

TABLE IV-6

NUMBER OF RESPONDENTS WITH INTIMATE KIN BY AGE AND SEX OF RESPONDENT AND AVAILABILITY OF KIN

(PANEL AND SEVENTIES, WAVE V)

Age and Sex	Total Interviewed Number	Respondents with Intimate Children		Respondents with Intimate Siblings		Respondents with Intimate Other Kin	
		Number	Per Cent Who Have at Least One Available [a]	Number	Per Cent Who Have at Least One Available	Number	Per Cent Who Have at Least One Available
Total women	75	49	77.6	54	50.0	42	47.6
50-54	12	9	66.7	9	44.4	10	60.0
55-59	14	9	66.7	12	66.7	7	42.9
60-64	13	10	70.0	11	54.5	7	42.9
65-69	13	8	100.0	8	12.5	8	50.0
70-74	17	9	77.7	11	54.5	7	57.1
75-79	6	4	100.0	3	66.7	3	0.0
Total men	81	57	87.7	51	60.8	46	65.2
50-54	17	11	90.9	12	50.0	14	57.1
55-59	17	11	100.0	11	63.6	8	37.5
60-64	13	8	75.0	8	75.0	9	77.8
65-69	9	8	75.0	4	25.0	3	100.0
70-74	17	14	85.7	11	54.5	8	75.0
75-79	8	5	100.0	5	80.0	4	75.0

NOTE: Very significantly more children are available than are siblings for men and women, $\chi^2 = 18.95$, d.f. $= 1$, P $<$ .001; or than others, $\chi^2 = 14.82$, d.f. $= 1$, P $<$ .001.

[a] Within a distance which can be reached and returned from in one day, allowing time for a visit.

TABLE IV-7
Frequency [a] of Visiting of Available Intimate Kin by Age and Sex
(Panel and Seventies, Wave V)

Age and Sex	Total Interviewed Number	Respondents with Intimate Available Children		Respondents with Intimate Available Siblings		Respondents with Intimate Available Other Kin	
		Number	Per Cent Visiting at Least One Frequently	Number	Per Cent Visiting at Least One Frequently	Number	Per Cent Visiting at Least One Frequently
Total women	75	38	89.5	27	66.7	20	65.0
50–64	39	19	94.7	18	66.7	12	66.7
65–79	36	19	84.2	9	66.7	8	62.5
Total men	81	50	86.0	30	56.7	30	56.7
50–64	47	27	92.6	19	68.4	18	55.6
65–79	34	23	78.3	11	36.4	12	58.3

NOTE: Intimate children are visited more often than intimate siblings (men and women combined). $\chi^2 = 11.96$, d.f. = 1, $P < .001$.

[a] Once a week or oftener.

common-sense knowledge that women maintain sociability ties.)

As we can see from these two tables, there is a lot of inter-action between kinsmen in this age group, and we will now describe, in more detail, our inquiry into the particular struc-ture and meaning of kinship activity among these respondents as they grow older.

For the purpose of examining the family and kinship struc-ture in added detail,* fifteen respondents were chosen as being reasonably representative of the panel with regard to age, sex, and socioeconomic status, and reasonably certain to co-operate. They were interviewed in considerable detail. A genealogy was constructed, and in addition six general areas of kinship be-havior were inquired into. They were (1) patterns of sociabil-ity with kindred, (2) patterns of mutual aid in crisis, (3) power, authority, and influence in the kinship system, (4) solidary groupings within the kinship system, (5) co-residential patterns, and (6) the history of the marriage and nuclear family. From the general impressions derived from this small group, we developed ideas of how relationships with kindred change during the life cycle. We later checked these ideas against the total group.

The salient pattern emerging from our fifteen families was, not surprisingly, the importance of the nuclear family, and there was a good deal of well-formed opinion about its bound-aries. All fifteen respondents agreed that to include non-nuclear kin in the household is an error, and especially so if adding extra members means that there will be three genera-tions present under the same roof. This belief is reflected in the number of widowed respondents we found living alone, and the small size of the domestic units in which our panel members live. However, fourteen of these fifteen people *had*

---

* For a more detailed account, see Cumming and Schneider, reference 16.

lived in extended families at some time during their lives, and for an average of five years. Thus, they had all experienced the situation they condemned. They all expressed the hope never to have to live with their children, although some thought it might happen if luck deserted them. Very probably many of them recognized that they would eventually do so.*

Although within the nuclear family the parent-child bond was manifestly strong, the sibling bond appeared to run it a close second. We were not impressed with the importance of the spouse bond, which we had expected to find very strong among this post-children group. It seemed surprisingly little emphasized among our respondents compared to the parent-child and sibling bonds, and in particular the sister-sister bond seemed to override it among the women. We will return to this in Chapter VIII, when we talk about differences between men and women in aging.

When we look at the responses to the question, "Which of your relatives other than those who live here with you do you feel closest to?" we find that 84 per cent of the respondents with a living parent mention that parent; 96 per cent of those with children list children; and 79 per cent of those with siblings mention siblings. When we add up the answers to the question, "Whom do you feel close, but not quite as close, to?" the totals rise to 98 per cent of those with children who choose children, and 97 per cent of those with siblings who choose siblings, but there are no more parents chosen. These choices show the persistent closeness not only with the family of procreation but also with the family of orientation. Of course, the question did not give the respondent an opportunity to affirm his solidarity with his spouse, so our comments upon the spouse bond remain impressionistic.

* For a detailed discussion of how the norms *against* the extended family are reconciled with the fact that most people experience it at some time, see Bellin, reference 9.

When we turn to visiting patterns, we see from Table IV–7 that there is a significant preference for visiting children over visiting siblings, and this is true for both men and women and for all age groups. Nearly 90 per cent of those whose children are chosen as intimates and are within available visiting distance visit them once a week or oftener. Among the oldest respondents, this often means the children are "keeping an eye on" their parents. Only 67 per cent of women and 57 per cent of men with available intimate siblings visit them this often.

When we look at the "substitutes" for intimate kin, however, we see a different picture. A substitute for any kinsman is one of the same generation who is chosen as an intimate. Thus, if a respondent includes a niece in the list of people she feels closest to, that is counted as a substitute for a child. A cousin or a brother-in-law substitutes for a sibling, and an aunt or uncle for a parent. In Tables IV–8 and IV–9 there is a consistent trend toward substituting collateral rather than ascending or

TABLE IV–8 [a]

SUBSTITUTES FOR AND ADDITIONS TO INTIMATE KIN BY AVAILABILITY
OF SIBLINGS AND CHILDREN
(PANEL, WAVE II, AND SEVENTIES)

Class of Kin Alive	Number Interviewed	Per Cents Choosing			
		Collaterals	Descendants	Both	Neither
Totals	*225*	*29.3*	*20.4*	*20.4*	*29.8*
Siblings and children	133	27.1	16.5	20.3	36.1
Siblings only	53	24.5	34.0	24.5	17.0
Children only	27	40.7	18.5	11.1	29.6
Neither	12	50.0	8.3	25.0	16.7

[a] Adapted from Cumming and Schneider (16).

TABLE IV–9 [a]

SUBSTITUTES FOR AND ADDITIONS TO PRIMARY KIN BY AGE OF RESPONDENT
AND AVAILABILITY OF KIN

(PANEL, WAVE II, AND SEVENTIES)

Availability of Kin	Number Interviewed	Per Cent Choosing Substitutes and Additions Whether or Not These are Available
Age 50–69		
Class of kin lacking entirely		
Parents	114	26.3
Siblings	19	63.2
Children	40	50.0
Class of kin alive but unavailable		
Parents	20	90.0
Siblings	84	59.5
Children	22	36.4
Class of kin available		
Parents	17	83.2
Siblings	48	43.7
Children	89	30.3
Age 70 +		
Class of kin lacking entirely		
Parents	74	10.8
Siblings	20	55.0
Children	25	64.0
Class of kin alive but unavailable		
Parents	0	0.0
Siblings	42	31.0
Children	8	37.5
Class of kin available		
Parents	0	0.0
Siblings	12	25.0
Children	41	36.6

[a] Adapted from Cumming and Schneider (16).

descending kin. Thus, we see that though children are more often chosen as intimates, and are visited more frequently, siblings are more often substituted for. The parent-child bond may be closer than the sibling bond, but as we see in Table IV–8 and IV–9, the sibling bond is more widespread.

There is probably an important difference between these two types of relationship. The parent-child bond is interdependent and mutually obligatory although at first the flow of obligation is from parent to child and reverses only quite late in life. In contrast, the sibling bond tends toward independence and sociability—a relationship between equals. One respondent says, "When we have a funeral in the family, we all (brothers and sisters) get together and anyone wouldn't think it was a funeral. We get in another room and eat and have a picnic."

When we look at this tendency by age, we find that there is a shift at about the seventieth year. Looking at siblings alone, we find that 43.7 per cent of those under seventy tend to add to their collateral kindred when they already have siblings available, while only 25 per cent of those over seventy do so. Among those with children, however, the situation is different. A slightly larger number of those over seventy add a descendant even if they have a child available.

When we look at the group who lack a category, we see the same trend. Sixty-three per cent of those under seventy who have no sibs at all substitute a collateral, and 50 per cent of those without children substitute a descendant. However, only 55 per cent of those over seventy who have no sibs substitute collateral kin, while 64 per cent of those over seventy who have no children substitute descendants. The same pattern holds for those whose sibs and children are unavailable. We see then that the disengaged group are either more content than the engaged with the number of siblings they have, or lack substitutes for them. The disengaged are more likely, however, to substitute for children if they lack them. We can infer from the fact that the younger engaged group have larger life spaces and more interaction, that they find other forms of relationship and do not so much require substitute kinsmen. There are no differences between men and women in this respect.

It seems clear that although siblings or other collaterals are the choice for sociability, when the seventy-year mark is past, children become more important. The pattern of substitutions then reverses, and children become more essential. It may well be that when the respondent is over seventy, his siblings are in need of help and succor and are no longer available to him, and he turns to the younger, more competent generation, as he has probably anticipated he would do. At any rate, the children or substitutes for them—nephews, nieces, children-in-law—are the group with whom these people feel most engaged at the end of life.

Although, as we have seen, people maintain a feeling of closeness to their primary relatives (parents, children, and siblings), this is not so for grandchildren. Only 5 per cent of our respondents declared that they felt closest or even close to their grandchildren. Although many respondents describe buying gifts for grandchildren, the tone in which they speak of interacting with them is best caught by a man in his sixties who says, "I'm always glad to see them come and equally glad to see them go." The role of grandparent does not seem focal for them in their spontaneous remarks about their children's families. As we shall see later, they do not consider grandparent-hood a good aspect of being their present age. Granick * has observed in a very different population—foreign-born Jews— a similar failure of interest in grandchildren. In view of the traditionally held belief that grandparents "spoil" grandchildren, and in view of the fact that there is a close grandparent-grandchild relationship in many non-literate societies, we feel that our finding merits some explanation.

We suggest that the grandparent-grandchild alliance is

* Ruth Granick, personal communication.

most pronounced when there is an authoritarian relationship between parents and children. This means that in the course of socialization, the child, when he comes under parental sanction, has an ally. The grandparent, on the other hand, who has no real remaining control over his adult child, may find it easier to establish a close relationship with his grandchild than to try to transmute his relationship with his child. The child then is a mediator between his parent and his grandparent. In America, however, where the bonds between children and parents are defined as friendly rather than hierarchical, and where the generational difference is minimized, not only does the child not need a friendly ally but the grandparent presumably has maintained an unbroken friendly relationship with his own child, and thus does not need a mediating relationship. As a result, there is no need for the "alternation of generation" type of behavior shown in the old-fashioned authoritarian family and in some non-literate societies.

Apple (3) has reported that closeness between grandparent and grandchild occurs only when the grandparent is dissociated from family and authority. In another place (4) she has developed the hypothesis that the close, indulgent grandparent role can be assumed by women only after they have given up the mother role. We would extend this idea by suggesting that in a culture where the parent-child relationship is defined as egalitarian and friendly, there is very little pressure to terminate the mother role, or to change its quality.

We see, on the whole, persistent close bonds between our respondents and their most intimate kinsmen, and these bonds remain intact until the end of life. There is, however, a strong possibility that they shift in quality with age, and we will discuss this in a later chapter.

We have not examined in great detail the role of friendship, but we have assumed that in some respects it also acts as a substitute for kinship, especially as the respondents referred to their relationships with their kinsmen in terms of sociability and friendliness. Among our fifteen special respondents, we discovered that this friendliness covered a potentially helping relationship. Their stand appeared to be that kinship should, ideally, be identical with friendship but that when it is necessary to seek help, kin are the ones to turn to.

The panel members were asked to define friendship, and by far the largest number could produce only a very vague statement. However, when they were asked to describe their own best friends, they gave descriptions differing sharply from respondent to respondent and couched in relational terms. These descriptions were coded as to whether they were predominantly diffuse, such as "she's my old friend and would do anything for me," or predominantly specific, such as "she's my bridge-playing friend." When these are analyzed, as we see in Table IV–10, there is a significant tendency for those without siblings to use the diffuse descriptions and those with siblings to describe their friends in terms of specific activities undertaken together. The impression that friendship in itself is poorly defined and may be quasi-kinship for many respondents is

TABLE IV–10 [a]
DIFFUSE DESCRIPTIONS OF FRIENDS
BY PRESENCE OF SIBLINGS
(PANEL, WAVE II, AND SEVENTIES)

		Per Cent Giving		
		The Most	Less	
	Number	Diffuse	Diffuse	No
Respondents	Interviewed	Descriptions	Descriptions	Answer
Totals	225	51.6	41.8	6.7
With siblings	186	47.3	45.7	7.0
Without siblings	39	71.8	23.1	5.1

NOTE: Of those who answered, those without siblings give the most diffuse responses more often than those who have siblings. $\chi^2 = 6.8$, d.f. $= 1$, P$<$ .01.

[a] Adapted from Cumming and Schneider (16).

strengthened by the fact that 13 per cent of the group mentioned their siblings among their best friends. Of the fifteen panel members who claimed they had no friends, only one was without siblings. Perhaps for some people friendship outside the sibling group is redundant. In a later chapter, when we discuss the oldest respondents, we will suggest that friends are used as substitutes for intimate kin at the end of life, when there is a great need for help and support. There is evidence that friendship for its own sake is not sought out by older respondents. One respondent says, "My friends have died or moved away and I haven't made the effort to make new ones." Another says, "As you grow older, you don't make friends as readily."

Summarizing our findings so far, we see that there is a steady diminution in interaction with age as the individual disengages himself from society, but this is not equally so for all types of relationship; contacts with intimate kin do not diminish except when these kin are no longer available. It is probable that disengagement from kin is a shift in the quality of the relationship rather than in the amount of interaction.

■ Social Mechanisms

If disengagement is the modal pattern of aging, we should see, in the way society organizes itself, evidence of "permission" for the process to take place. Although this book is concerned primarily with the social-psychological aspects of growing old, we can understand the process better if we project it against a sketch of the society in which it takes place and of which it is a part.

A useful point of departure in discussing social permission for disengagement is age-grading. This is a facet of social life we are sometimes blind to, because we live with it and take part in it every day, and it seems the "natural" way to organize life. We think it "natural" that people prefer the company of their age mates, for example. However, compared to other societies, we show marked age-grading. We make a distinction between a nursery-school child and a kindergarten child, and both differ from a school-age child. We have pre-teens and teens, and subdebs and debutantes, and young married couples. At this point, we seem to relax our efforts, only to begin again with middle age, late middle age, older people, the elderly, and, finally, old age.

This rather fine age-grading probably has two important sources: first, it is generated by the egalitarian ideology, which renders us less comfortable with vertical relationships than with horizontal ones, and, second, by an industrialized society of refined technology in which it is important to keep the young out of many key roles until they know enough to fill them, and to remove the old before what they know becomes obsolete. Age-grading is one of the ways of defining who is ready for certain roles and who has grown too old, and thus it is structurally compatible with a sitiuation where older people tend to disengage themselves from the working world. Retirement policies in most industries reflect age-grading; they are based by and large upon the principle of retiring echelons of people, rather than upon criteria related to their function.*

There is familiar evidence for age-grading besides retirement policies. We know about adolescent gangs and cliques, and women's clubs; men's groupings are familiar features of American life. Furthermore, as we have reported, we have found a persistent sociability between siblings and other collateral kin, which appears to be a reflection in the kinship system of the age-grading of the larger society. This age-grading, in turn, is associated with shifts from vertical to horizontal solidarities during the life span, and is associated with changes

---

* Retirement policies also reflect the economic organization of the Western world, with its difficulties in consuming its production, but this is another question.

in the nature of relationships during the disengagement process.

The difference between vertical and horizontal solidarity is important for us to understand when we discuss the aging process. Durkheim (20), the classical French sociologist, has described the difference between what he calls organic and mechanical solidarity, and this difference characterizes vertical and horizontal relationships. In organic, or vertical, solidarity, there is a division of labor, mutual dependency and mutual obligation, a dissimilarity of the individuals either in competence or in type of function, and a restricted degree of choice of people with whom such solidarity is appropriate. The parent-child bond exemplifies this type of relationship. The child depends on the parent for care, and the parent depends on the child for the gratification that providing this care gives him. In mechanical, or horizontal, solidarity, the individuals are tied to one another by bonds of similarity rather than dependency. There is social permission to consider a wider choice of individuals available for such solidarity; the bonds are more flexible, more easily broken, and the individuals more interchangeable. The sibling and friendship bonds are of this sort.

The spouse bond is a special kind of solidary tie. There are division of labor and mutual dependency, but at the same time there are equality and interchangeability in a society that recognizes women as the equal of men. Thus the divorce rate is highest when there are no children and after the children are grown—times in the marriage when horizontal or mechanical aspects of the tie outweigh the organic aspects, which in turn are strongest during the time of child-raising.

In general, the individual seems to be permitted and encouraged to pass through five phases of solidarity during his lifetime. He has a dependent, vertical solidary relationship with his parents during his childhood, and assumes strong horizontal relationships in adolescence. In adulthood he maintains both kinds of ties, but emphasis in the modal case is probably upon the vertical tie with children. During aging there is a shift back to peer-group ties, especially among women, and finally, at the end of life, there is a reversal of the childhood role and the parent is dependent upon the child. We will describe the details of this shift in relationship in much more detail as we proceed to discuss the attitudes and orientations of our respondents in later chapters.

A second useful point of departure for talking about permission to disengage is the division of labor itself. Generally speaking, men perform what are called the "instrumental" tasks and women the "socio-emotional" ones.* This means that by and large, when men and women interact together, they divide the labor so that men take on the job of "defending the system" from the outside, and women see that there is a minimum of tension among the members. In practical terms, this means that, on the whole, men work for a living and women attend to the family and household, and each feels comfortable doing it, because it is socially prescribed and socially rewarded.

The implications of this division for the aging and disengagement processes are important because they are asymmetrical. It is easy to see that women, although disengaging from the main task of child-raising, do not have to learn a new skill. Their task becomes not so much different in kind as different in quantity. Inasmuch as it is qualitatively different, it is only in the direction of more freedom and less obligation. Men, on the other hand, must disengage themselves from their main life occupation, and then face the probability that they will have to develop a new set of skills more suitable for pure sociability and less practical and instrumental. That this division of labor leads to important differences between men and women during the disengaging process is the subject of Chapter VIII. At present we would like to draw attention once more

---

* For a clear and detailed account of this division of labor, see Parsons and Bales, reference 52.

to the fact that the men in our study do not retire abruptly in many cases, but slip in and out of the labor market as if trying to get used to the change in role they are experiencing. Furthermore, there is evidence of practical compromises with the retirement status. As we shall point out later, there is evidence that men soon grow comfortable with retirement, but basically the division of labor that we Americans practice makes the permission to disengage a different thing for men than it is for women.

■ Shifts in Goal Structure

An examination of shifts in the goals of the individual respondent as he gets older leads us away from the social-structural features of disengagement and toward the attitudinal and perceptual characteristics of the process. Nevertheless, we report these along with the social variables because life goals are linked, on the one hand, with the society in which they appear and, on the other, with the state of mind of the individual. Thus this discussion of the restructuring of goals stands as a kind of bridge between this chapter and Chapter V, which concerns itself with attitudes, orientations, ideologies, sentiments, and perceptions.

We did not make a direct inquiry into the restructuring of goals among these respondents, but we have analyzed the answers to the question "What are the best things about the age you are now?" and "What are the worst things about the age you are now?" with the hope of inferring whether or not the respondents appear to have restructured their goals so as to maintain a greater distance from society than they had in their younger years. Table IV–11 shows their responses.

By far the most popular response was concerned with health. Almost two-thirds of the women and more than half of the men said that poor health, or failing health, was the worst thing about their age, even though this is a healthy population.

TABLE IV-11

ANSWERS TO THE QUESTION, "WHAT ARE THE BEST AND WORST THINGS ABOUT THE AGE YOU ARE?"

(PANEL AND SEVENTIES, WAVE V)

	Men	N=81	Women	N=75
Item	Per Cent Choosing Best [a]	Per Cent Choosing Worst	Per Cent Choosing Best	Per Cent Choosing Worst
Better physical health vs. worse physical health	9.9	56.8	14.7	61.3
Opinions are respected vs. nobody listens	29.6	1.2	17.3	0.0
Loss of instrumental roles vs. freedom from them	22.2	16.0	29.3	5.3
Satisfaction with status vs. dissatisfaction with it	25.9	4.9	20.0	4.0
Increased freedom to move vs. inability to move	6.2	13.6	8.0	24.0
Idiosyncratic and general answers	9.9	3.7	16.0	4.0
Loss of socio-emotional roles vs. freedom from them	1.2	0.0	10.7	2.7
Contemplation of the past vs. contemplation of death	3.7	9.9	4.0	8.0
Nothing different now	9.9	7.4	9.3	9.3
Evasions	8.6	6.2	6.7	6.7
Grandparenthood	4.9	0.0	4.0	0.0

[a] A few people chose the same item as both best and worst. When the data are reanalyzed to take this into account, there is no difference in the pattern of response, nor in any of the significances reported here. Significant differences are discussed in the text.

This difference between the men and the women is not significant, but there is a significant difference between those over and those under sixty-five years in the tendency to complain. Of the 58 people under sixty-five who mentioned health, 93 per cent felt that failing health was a disadvantage. Of the 44 over sixty-five, only 86 per cent complained, and 32 per cent, some of them the same people, regarded their continuing good health, or improved health, as one of the advantages of aging. This may be a survival factor, inasmuch as those over sixty-five may indeed be healthier, but it may well reflect a frustration of the younger, engaged respondents with the impairment of poor health compared to a disengaged disregard and acceptance of less robust health among the old. A respondent in her fifties says, "I've just had an operation. I'm off work trying to regain my strength. I went to the doctor for something else and when he took X-rays he found I had gallstones. I wish I had never gone to him. It is taking me a long time to get over it. I'm awfully bored staying at home and not being able to do much." The older people show more patience with this kind of interruption, which may reflect a restructuring of goals in line with abilities, leading to a release from the amount of concern felt by the younger group with their state of health.*

The next most popular category has to do with being listened to. Thirty per cent of the men feel that their opinions are important, and that this is a real advantage gained with years. Seventeen per cent of the women report the same satisfaction. Only one man complained that nobody listened to his opinions because he was old, and no women did so. However, this advantage seems to be much more pronounced in the younger group. Of the 38 people who gave this response, 27

---

* Streib has shown that immediately after retirement men feel the pinch of lowered incomes, and this depresses their morale. However, they shortly become acclimated to reduced income, and this may be the process which we see in the reduced tendency to complain of health. See Streib, references 70 and 71.

were under, and only 11 over, sixty-five. This proportion is significantly different from that of the population, and suggests that late middle age is the time when people feel they have a maximum influence. On the other hand, loss of this influence is not accompanied by complaints. Again, goals have perhaps been reconstituted to dispense with power and influence.

Nearly a quarter of the men and nearly a third of the women feel that freedom from their instrumental roles is a great advantage. Not having to work so hard or not having to work at all is a great relief to this group. On the other hand, 16 per cent of the men feel the loss of an instrumental role as a disadvantage, and so do 5 per cent of the women. Abrogation of the socio-emotional roles are not nearly so commonly talked of, and only one man mentioned this as a feature of aging. Women feel satisfied with giving up the parent-wife role three times as often as they feel frustrated by it, although only 13 per cent of the women mention it in either context. When we combine the two categories of role loss, we find that although there is no difference by age, there is a very significant difference between men and women in their response. Of the 32 men who mention role loss (and 31 discuss only instrumental roles), 19, or 59 per cent, feel that freedom from the role is an advantage, while of the 36 women, 30, or 83 per cent, feel that freedom from role responsibility is a relief. Of these women, about half are referring to freedom from working either in jobs or in the household, and the other half are referring to the emotional responsibilities of a family. Apparently restructuring is easier for women than for men. However, it may be that men, on the average, have retired more recently than women have given up child-raising, and are therefore less acclimated.

A quarter of the men and a fifth of the women feel that success, the status they have achieved, and the security they have earned are satisfactions, while 5 per cent of the men and 4 per cent of the women look upon failure to achieve security and status as one of the disadvantages of age. There is no difference by age or sex in this tendency.

When the responses concerned with looking back at the past in general are compared with those about looking ahead toward death, we find that 10 per cent of the men and 8 per cent of the women find the prospect of death coming closer to be one of the least satisfactory aspects of aging. On the other hand, reflection about the past is given as one of the pleasures of age by only 4 per cent of the men and of the women. In view of the number offering their achievements as one of the gratifications of age, it appears that remembered accomplishments, which have outward and visible signs, are more important than memories for their own sake.

Those who find the thought of death most alarming are the men under sixty-five. The others have apparently come to terms with it. Of the eight men who complained of thoughts of death, only one is over sixty-five. There are about equal numbers of men over and under sixty-five, and the preponderance of those under sixty-five fearing death is significantly high. These are small numbers; when we asked the panel directly what their ideas and thoughts of death were like, almost all of them denied ever thinking of it, although there is some intimation of norms that operate against admitting that death is a preoccupation. One woman says of her husband, "Now you take the mister. He's always going on about dying and all. Gives you a pain." We do not know what makes the eight men give a non-normative response and admit to their worries about death, but it may be evidence that the period around sixty is a crisis point. Other works have made this observation, and later on we will discuss this more fully.

Almost a quarter of the women and 14 per cent of the men find that a decrease in mobility, competence, and the ability to get around is a frustration associated with their age. A typical comment is, "Just can't do things I'd like to do like I did when I was younger. Can't do my work as well as I'd like to, and keep it done." On the other hand a minority, 8 per cent of the women and 6 per cent of the men, have the satisfaction of being able to get around more than they were able to before, because now they are not tied down. Of the 15 people under sixty-five who mentioned mobility, seven felt it was an advantage and eight a frustration, but of the 24 over sixty-five, 20 felt that the decreased ability to get around was one of the worst things about growing old. While this difference is not statistically significant, it probably reflects very directly a concrete disadvantage. It will be recalled that Britton and Mather (13) found that scales of "adjustment" used with aging and old people depended upon a general factor of activity for their greatest weight. Here we see that the aging people themselves are frustrated by decreased mobility and apparently subscribe to the activity value that the scale-makers impose upon them.

Sixteen per cent of the women and 10 per cent of the men gave idiosyncratic answers that the interviewers unfortunately accepted without challenge. These included such things as "I've just been remarried," "my daughter has been ill but is better," and "our house is very comfortable." Although the men and women do not differ, there is a very significant difference by age. Of the eight people under sixty-five who gave idiosyncratic answers to the questions on the best and the worst things about their age, three gave this type of specific answer to the query on best things; while of the 18 over sixty-five, 17 gave such answers. This difference is highly significant statistically, and suggests that the pleasanter preoccupations of the older people are self-referred and specific. It also suggests that their interest in answering this type of evaluative question is less marked than that of the younger respondents. We might tentatively say that they are disengaged from the norm that requires them to answer the question very precisely, and we will return to this point later.

A uniform number of men and women find there is no difference between things as they are at their present age and things as they were before. About 7 per cent of the men find this stability a disadvantage and 10 per cent find it a virtue of growing old. Nine per cent of the women make this response, and there is no difference with age.

A slightly smaller group of men and women give what we called evasions. Typical of these answers were, "I can't say because I don't feel any particular age" or "I can't say because I feel as young as ever." Again, this tendency is markedly more common under sixty-five. Twenty-one per cent of those under sixty-five (18 cases) gave these evasions; only 6 per cent (4 cases) of those over sixty-five did so. We see what may well be another sign of anxiety about a turning point in life and a need to confront the task of restructuring goals.

Generally speaking, these answers suggest a restructuring of life goals—calling for less responsibility and allowing more focus on the self. At the same time we see problems of health and approaching death becoming less bothersome as age increases. Although there is persistent frustration with decreased mobility and with role loss among men, the move is away from tight enmeshment with the social system where health and competence in the instrumental role are the important features. One respondent, a middle-aged bachelor, had devoted much time and enthusiasm to collecting Georgian and Regency silver and furniture. He says reflectively, "One of the best things is that you *want* fewer things. You've satisfied a great many of your half-baked earlier wants. You realize some things you wanted were more trouble than they're worth. Like the old silver we had—I started giving it away. I've started divesting myself of things. You live more simply. Those things were nice to have had, but you don't really need them. They fulfilled a worn-out pattern."

We have seen that the basic postulate of the disengagement

theory—that there is a diminution of the interaction between the individual and his social system—is upheld by the data. Furthermore, it is apparent that there are some classes of people from whom the disengaging person does not withdraw, namely, intimate kin. On the other hand, there is reason to believe that in the society where this process is occurring, there will be a change in the nature and quality of the individual's relationship to the people he remains engaged with, and that this will be part of a general shift in orientation, related to the decline in interaction. In the following chapter, we will discuss the shifts in the individual's stance toward society as he disengages from it.

CHAPTER V

The Evidence for Disengagement in Attitude and Orientation Changes

with Lois R. Dean
and David S. Newell

In THE LAST chapter, we saw evidence of a separation between individual and society that accompanies aging, and discussed some of the ways in which the expectation of this separation is built into the social structure. In this chapter we will analyze the way the individual shifts his orientation and modifies his attitudes so as to "ready" himself for the disengagement process. We will examine a number of variables, all roughly attitudinal, in a manner parallel to our examination of the social-structural variables. These include Orientation to Interaction, Authoritarianism, Religious Piety, Conformity-Alienation, and Perception of Constriction of Social Lifespace.

75

■ Orientation to Interaction and Relational Rewards

In Chapter IV we saw that the kinds of roles discarded during the aging process are, in one sense, more central than those which are kept. Thus, men and women both discard the work role, and women, because they live longer than men, eventually discard the roles of kinswoman and household member. This means that they can discard the more task-oriented, more goal-directed roles of middle age, and retain the more peripheral, less involved ones. Here, we will inquire whether there is an accompanying shift in the *style* of interaction as the balance of roles changes. In order to do this, we will examine the changes in preference for "relational rewards" that come with age, and infer the changes in orientation that led to them.

Relational rewards are part of everyday interaction. People seek them in all situations, although the rewards differ with the varying situations in which we find ourselves. We are symbol-exchanging animals, and we look for symbolic interpersonal response and encouragement all the time. Telling a joke, we expect laughter; in return for a good dinner, we expect groans of satisfaction; and when we go to see a tragic play, we expect to exchange with each other a little of the pity and terror we feel. It is probably no exaggeration to say that when we interact with others, we prefer a frown or even a curse to no reaction at all. Almost as disturbing as no feedback is an inappropriate one.* We recognize that there are different emotional states appropriate to different occasions. Our orientation is such that the interpersonal cues we feed back to one another are suitable to the context of the interaction. Thus, we kiss children, congratulate bridegrooms, and nod at a familiar bank teller.

* For a detailed discussion of man's symbolizing behavior, see Langer, reference 42. For a discussion of the consequences of inappropriate feedback, see Cumming, reference 17.

Here, we are investigating whether there are types of relational reward or feedback appropriate to the disengaged state that are less appropriate to the fully engaged state. To do this, we have inquired into shifts in "orientation to interaction."

Parsons has developed an ideal typology of relational rewards by combining two pairs of his pattern variables that describe "set toward interaction (50, p. 130)." The variables are "diffuse versus specific" and "affective versus affectively neutral." When they are combined, they produce, as we see in Table V–1, a two-by-two table of relational rewards: love, esteem, approval, and responsiveness or receptiveness. Reasoning that there should be a shift in attitude toward interaction during the disengaging process, we have used this reward typology to determine whether this is empirically true. We give below a detailed description of the qualities of these variables and their corresponding reward types, and present our findings.

TABLE V–1

A TYPOLOGY OF RELATIONAL REWARDS [a]

	Specificity	*Diffuseness*
Affectivity	Receptiveness or Responsiveness	Love
Neutrality	Approval	Esteem

[a] From Parsons (50).

We are probably safe in saying that everybody seeks all kinds of rewards and can summon up all the sets toward interaction. However, individuals are characterized by a preference for one rather than another, and at different times in the life span there should be differences in the balance among them. As well as searching for such differences, we must look more closely at the meaning of these rewards and the interactions in which they are characteristically produced if we are to use them in interpreting age changes and readiness for disengagement.

In the functionally diffuse set toward interaction, even a suggested addition to the range of interactions is in itself sufficient to demand justification from the participant who resists it. When, for example, a child clamors for his mother to play with him, she may refuse, but she lets him know in some way that it was all right to ask. Similarly, if a colleague invites us to dinner, we feel obliged to justify our refusal even though we may both know we are only making excuses. In such diffuse relationships, the set toward interaction of the participants includes expectations of mutual obligation and interpersonal responsibility.

Some functionally diffuse relationships—with family and close friends, for example—are primarily affective; that is, on balance, the interactions comprising them are intrinsically gratifying. Love is the relational reward generated in interactions we enter into with a diffuse-affective set. In contrast, some diffuse relationships are neutral rather than affective, and we participate in them primarily for the sake of some valued end. Fraternal relationships among members of some churches, and some extended kinship relationships, especially among families strongly devoted to tradition, emphasize not only mutual obligations but a moral engagement with shared goals. Esteem is the reward for interacting in these relationships.

In contrast to the inclusiveness of these total-person relationships, the functionally specific set toward interaction implies a segmental relationship. If improvisations are suggested, they must be justified by the initiator. Although we may deal with the same bank teller for years, he would be shocked if we invited him to dinner, and he would certainly expect a convincing reason for such an astonishing gesture. In a small town, the bank teller may reappear in our lives as the Boy Scout leader, but this does not change his functional specificity.

Sometimes we might interact with him in his separate roles as if he were two people.

Our approach to the bank teller, with its specific and neutral set toward interaction, is the model for the whole world of contractual arrangements. The primary involvement is with the *content* of the interaction, not with the bank teller himself. Approval for the specific task, appropriately performed, is the reward we expect from and give to such interactions.

Those specific relationships—affective rather than neutral—are gratifying for their own sake; they involve little mutual obligation, and demand minimal involvement. Their gamut spans quasi-relationships * with entertainers, friendly interchanges with strangers, and repeated interactions with "drinking buddies" or "bridge friends." Again, the continuity of the relationship comes from the *content,* and that is where the meaning resides. The characteristic reward of such interaction is response to the specific act gratifyingly performed.

Of the four types of set toward interaction, the diffuse-affective, in some ways, requires the firmest engagement, and the specific-affective the weakest. The diffuse-neutral and the specific-neutral are probably intermediate. In fact, it may be possible to classify these orientations still further in terms of their psychological implications. The diffuse-affective set involves the individual in systems that include people he thinks of as close to him, and toward whom he admits responsibilities. This admission of diffuseness, together with the reward of love, involves the person in both mutual obligation and the handling of ambivalence. For this reason the diffuse-affective set may belong to one of the most highly "engaged" kinds of relationship, invoking the most binding kind of reward, although, as we shall point out later, when the people in this relationship are of unequal power or competence—such as a mother and a

* For a detailed discussion of this type of relationship, see Horton and Wohl, reference 37.

child—it is more "difficult" for the more competent member. By the same token, the love aged people feel for their adult child is not so demanding as the love the child returns to them.

The diametrically opposite, and therefore complementary, specific-neutral set toward interaction should involve only a minimum kind of engagement, since it requires no handling of ambivalence and implies no reciprocal obligation, but it does require control of the desire for relational gratification. Furthermore, such interactions are often carried out in a business context, and the content itself, rather than the quality of the interaction, may bind the actors in a different kind of obligatory network, a contractual one. Thus, business interactions that are part of a total instrumental scheme demand much more engagement than the transaction with the bank teller, which requires very little. Interactions whose set is neutral and diffuse occur at an equal or somewhat greater level of engagement. Here we have obligatory bonds but no emotional investment. Unless these relationships move over into close friendship, generating affection and acceptance, and therefore requiring a different set, we have no ambivalence to cope with. However, all neutral interactions, specific or diffuse, by definition (53, pp. 1-12) involve evaluation, either moral or aesthetic, and this in turn involves control over the initial impulse to act.

The specific-affective set almost certainly commits us least. Its functional specificity spares us continuous bonds, and its affective tone does not generate ambivalence, because the responsiveness is tied to the act and not to the person. Furthermore, it allows immediate gratification and does not commit us to evaluate before we act. People with whom we characteristically play cards or bowl or drink ask nothing of us but the receptiveness or responsiveness appropriate to the moment. If they call the next day to invite us to dinner, they have changed the nature of the relationship, and we must acquire a different set toward them.

The rewards of love and approval should characterize middle life, and for two reasons. First, they are associated with family life and the working world, and, second, by their very nature they are orientations implying commitment to others and, therefore, engagement. The diffuse-neutral set, however, with its reward of esteem, is also a relatively "engaged" set; thus the only disengaged set is specific affectivity, and the most sought-after reward of old age should be responsiveness.

Our method for determining the relational rewards our respondents were seeking is described in detail in Appendix 2. Briefly, they were asked to choose which two of the four rewards they considered themselves likeliest to elicit in others. Intensive interviewing of ten respondents of different socio-economic status satisfied us that the words were well comprehended and their meaning uniform from respondent to respondent.*

Table V–2 shows the distribution of rewards that the respondents chose as most characteristic of the reaction they were getting. As we expected, those who were working declared that approval is the commonest response they receive from others. Nevertheless, *within* the group of workers there is a change with age. The predicted drop in approval-seeking can be seen in the contrast between the percentage of the youngest group choosing this reward, and that of the oldest (62 *vs.* 18 per cent). This seems to imply that the role does not entirely determine the choice of reward, and that the orientation to interaction with others changes independently of it. The rewards of love, esteem, and responsiveness all increase

---

* Dr. Lois R. Dean has reported her careful attempt to assign reward types to the panel members on the basis of their responses to other questions. Her results differed in some ways from those reported here. For the time being, we are using the respondents' self-statements, because we believe that the attempt to judge orientation through information about the daily life is confounded by the fact that certain roles *demand* certain orientations and the judgments are therefore determined to some extent by the roles the respondent holds. See Dean, reference 18.

TABLE V-2

Type of Primary Rewards Sought in Interaction
According to Work Status and Age
(Panel and Seventies, Wave III)

Work Status and Age	Number Interviewed	Per Cent of Number Interviewed Seeking			
		Approval	Esteem	Love	Responsiveness
Total	*164*[a]	*38.4*	*21.3*	*23.2*	*17.1*
Working					
50–69	71	60.6	19.7	15.5	4.2
(50–59)	45	62.2	15.6	17.8	4.4
(60–69)	26	57.7	26.9	11.5	3.8
70 and over	11	18.2	27.3	27.3	27.3
Nonworking					
50–69	37	16.2	18.9	43.2	21.6
(50–59)	13	23.1	15.4	46.2	15.4
(60–69)	24	12.5	20.8	41.7	25.0
70 and over	45	26.7	24.4	17.8	31.1

[a] Exclusive of 47, or 22 per cent of those who completed the third interview, but failed to answer this question.

automatically in the over-seventy age group, but only responsiveness, as we predicted, increases significantly.

Among the nonworkers, love-seeking decreases significantly with age, which parallels the shift away from approval-seeking among the workers, and the increase in all other categories. It is not the increase in the three other categories but, rather, the over-all *decrease* in love-seeking that is significant, and we see no significantly increased choice of responsiveness, as we do among the workers. Furthermore, the differences we observe are the same for men and women. Although the workers are mostly men and the nonworkers women, nevertheless it is work and not sex that affects the choice of relational reward—an exception to this population's general tendency to show differences by sex.

Although our hypothesis—that approval and love, the typical rewards of work and kinship, would tend to disappear with middle age—is corroborated, the increase in responsiveness that we expected was confined to the workers. Furthermore, a good deal of caution is needed in interpreting these data because they were collected in the third interview, and 22 per cent of those interviewed failed to answer this question. It is quite reasonable to assume that those who refused favored one or another of the reward types. But on the basis of this table, we can conclude that approval and love-seeking, the appropriate rewards of the instrumental world of work and the socio-emotional world of family, fall off during disengagement, and that a new freedom to choose among relational rewards emerges. This finding tends to support our hypothesis that the greater the freedom from normative control, the more idiosyncratic does behavior become.

In Table V–3 we see the shift by age in the type of reward sought when both the first and second choices are taken into account. This table identifies the chosen reward in terms of the element *missing* from the full selection. In the nature of the task, one element at most can be omitted if two rewards are chosen, so that the choices can be labeled either redundant or complementary. Thus, if approval and love are chosen, or esteem and responsiveness, no element is omitted and the choice is complementary. But if, for example, approval and responsiveness are chosen and diffuseness is omitted, specificity is chosen twice and the choice is redundant.

We note in the table a strong tendency toward the specific-neutral orientation showing up among younger men in the high percentage that omits either the diffuse or the affective element. There is a significant tendency for the respondents to choose complementary reward types more often as they grow older. This means that they choose the combinations of love and approval or esteem and response rather than redundant pairs. Hence, the tendency to choose a variety of rewards increases

TABLE V-3
REWARDS SOUGHT BY AGE
(PANEL AND SEVENTIES, WAVE III)

Element Lacking from Both First and Second Choices	Total		Age 50–59		60–69		70–79	
	Number	Per Cent	Number	Per Cent	Number	Per Cent	Number	Per Cent
Total males	107		37		31		39	
Total known	86	100.0	31	100.0	24	100.0	31	100.0
None	18	20.9		6.5		37.5		22.6
Diffuse	33	38.4		48.4		37.5		29.0
Specific	5	5.8		3.2		12.5		3.2
Affective	18	20.9		35.5		4.2		19.4
Neutral	12	14.0		6.5		8.3		25.8
Total females	104		33		34		37	
Total known	76	100.0	26	100.0	25	100.0	25	100.0
None	19	25.0		19.2		32.0		24.0
Diffuse	12	15.8		23.1		20.0		4.0
Specific	12	15.8		15.4		12.0		20.0
Affective	14	18.4		15.4		20.0		20.0
Neutral	19	25.0		26.9		16.0		32.0

NOTE: Those over sixty choose all four elements more often than those under sixty. $\chi^2 = 4.68$, d.f. = 1, .05> P> .02.

TABLE V-4

Rewards Sought by Age and Socioeconomic Class
(Men Only)
(Panel and Seventies, Wave III)

Elements Lacking from Both First and Second Choices	Total	Age					
		50–59		60–69		70–79	
		Number	Per Cent	Number	Per Cent	Number	Per Cent
Higher socioeconomic status	43	13	100.0	10	100.0	20	100.0
None	5		7.7		10.0		15.0
Diffuse	14		30.8		60.0		20.0
Specific	4		7.7		20.0		5.0
Affective	13		46.2		10.0		30.0
Neutral	7		7.7		0.0		30.0
Lower socioeconomic status	43	18	100.0	14	100.0	11	100.0
None	13		5.6		57.1		36.4
Diffuse	19		61.1		21.4		45.5
Specific	1		0.0		7.1		0.0
Affective	5		27.8		0.0		0.0
Neutral	5		5.6		14.3		18.2
Total	86	31	100.0	24	100.0	31	100.0
None	18		6.5		37.5		22.6
Diffuse	33		48.4		37.5		29.0
Specific	5		3.2		12.5		3.2
Affective	18		35.5		4.2		19.4
Neutral	12		6.5		8.3		25.8

Note: The chance of as great a difference between those fifty to fifty-nine and those sixty to seventy-nine in the lower socioeconomic status occurring by chance alone is .006 by Fisher's exact test.

at the same time that the individual disengages from the social structure.

To sum up, we observe three changes in orientation with age. First, approval- and love-seeking become less common; second, the reward sought seems more open to choice among the older group than among the younger—that is, for the whole *group* there is a wider distribution among the reward types— and, third, those over sixty, as individuals, choose more complementary rewards; in other words, a pair that omits none of the elements. The accomplishment of one or all of these three changes may be a sign of the readiness to disengage.

When we examine the sexes separately, we find that, although the primary choices are the same, when the second choice is also taken into account there is a tendency toward a wider variety of relational rewards among the men. When we look at the distribution by class (Table V–4), the men in the lower half of the class structure make up the entire difference, and there is no difference by class among the women. We did not expect this difference, and we are hesitant to interpret it. However, it is perhaps related to the retirement shock that has been assumed to be so hazardous for middle-class men. It may reflect a reluctance to prepare for disengagement. Perhaps working-class men are more able to diversify the rewards they seek, and to get satisfaction from more reward types, just because they have less invested in their work than middle-class men. Furthermore, society probably finds working-class men more dispensable. In this case, we should find certain segments of the working class resembling the middle class. For example, working-class men who have a deep investment in skilled work, or who are attached to traditional occupations, should have more difficulty disengaging from their work, and should thus resemble middle-class men in this respect. We would expect, for instance, to find railroaders, a group known for their diffuse attachment to their occupation, exhibiting more signs of investment in their work. We cannot examine our population in this way because we have so few people in each occupational category, but when we divide them into a lower and upper half on the basis of their Index of Social Class scores, we find no differences in their morale, nor do we find significant differences in any other variables excepting only alienation or conformity to the major cultural values, itself a class phenomenon. For this reason, we suggest that it is the occupational aspect of the class position of the men which is showing a relationship with orientation and rewards.

Orientation to interaction and the sought-after reward are not in themselves associated with morale, and we must conclude that, although love and approval are modal among the middle-aged, the wider freedom characteristic of the older people probably reflects emerging styles of interacting that are associated more with personality than with situation.

We have spent a good deal of time analyzing the types of reward and the orientation to interaction because these are very general variables. By the same token, it is difficult to apply them to concrete data. Our hope is that this preliminary attempt will lead to more refined techniques for evaluating this important aspect of interaction. More particularly, we anticipate more specific ways of relating each of the orientations and each of the relational rewards to the process of disengagement.

Another way to think about orientation toward interaction is in terms of the respondent's ideology. We have had access to several aspects of our panel members' ideologies, and three of them will be discussed here.

■ **Authoritarianism**

One of the best-known ideological measures is the authoritarian-personality or F-scale (1). In our third interview, we included six F-scale items that had shown high correlation with the total score in other studies. (The items are reproduced in Appendix 2.) The original authors used this measure to distinguish between those who, owing to childhood experiences, are anti-democratic, ethnocentric, compulsively conventional, punitive to inferiors, and submissive to authority. The democratic personality, less clearly delineated, was defined more or less as the opposite of these qualities. The disengagement theory would suggest that people who are relatively free from the norms are *less* authoritarian. Recently, however, Stewart and Hoult (68) have recast the concept of the authoritarian personality in terms of role theory. They postulate that rigidity of outlook arises in situations where the individual is not given the opportunity to practice taking the role of others, and therefore is out of sympathy with or afraid of those who differ from him. We might expect, then, that disengagement between the individual and society, accompanied by a decreasing life space, would result in higher F-scores. However, all respondents with small life spaces, at whatever age, should have high scores. We have postulated that people who come from farms or villages should have higher F-scores than those who come from cities, because they had less opportunity in youth to sympathize with a variety of roles. Generally speaking, men who have greater access to more kinds and types of interaction might be expected to have lower F-scores than women. The highest scores can be expected from older women with rural backgrounds, and the lowest from younger men with urban backgrounds, if both disengagement and childhood learning are important.

Analyzing our respondents' scores in terms of these variables, we found, as Table V–5 shows, that our predictions were entirely correct for the women. In fact, taken as a group, women with large life spaces have significantly lower F-scores than those with small life spaces; younger women have significantly lower F-scores than older women, and women who

TABLE V-5
AUTHORITARIAN PERSONALITY (F-SCORE) BY SEX, AGE, LIFESPACE, AND PLACE OF ORIGIN
(PANEL ONLY, WAVE III)

Respondents	Age 50–59			Age 60+	
	Total	Number Interviewed	Per Cent Low [a] F	Number Interviewed	Per Cent Low [a] F
Total women	69	33	66.7	36	36.1
High Lifespace	32	19	68.4	13	61.5
Rural	18	10	70.0	8	62.5
Urban	14	9	66.7	5	60.0
Low Lifespace	37	14	64.3	23	21.7
Rural	21	6	33.3	15	20.0
Urban	16	8	87.5	8	25.0
Total men	73	37	62.2	36	52.8
High Lifespace	61	36	61.1	25	56.0
Rural	33	21	61.9	12	41.7
Urban	28	15	60.0	13	69.2
Low Lifespace	12	1	0.0	11	45.5
Rural	5	0	[b]	5	20.0
Urban	7	1	100.0	6	66.7

NOTE: A greater number of the younger women had low F-scores than of the older women; and also a greater number of women with a high lifespace had low F-scores than of those with a low lifespace. Both are statistically significant between the .05 and the .02 level. There were no statistically significant differences among the men.

[a] At or below the median.
[b] Not applicable since no men in this group were interviewed.

come from cities have significantly lower F-scores than those who come from farms and villages (although this is true only for those who now live in small life spaces). In short, and very dramatically, aging in women, with its accompanying disengagement, tends to lead to an authoritarian outlook. Only 20 per cent of the women from rural areas who are over sixty and live in small life spaces have scores at or below the median. The least authoritarian are young urban women with small life spaces (88 per cent low F), although they do not differ significantly from the young women, rural and urban, with large life spaces (70.0 and 66.7 per cent, respectively).

When we turn to the men, we find that there are no significant differences at all, and the men as a group do not differ from the women as a group. In fact, the men *over sixty* who have large life spaces and come from urban areas are the least authoritarian of the whole group; 69.2 per cent of them have low F-scores. The men, of course, vary less in their scores than the women do.

There are two difficulties in interpreting this unpredicted finding.* First, the respondents who were over seventy are not represented, because they were not measured on this variable. This means that the oldest group of men is inadequately represented. In view of the trend in the older group, we cannot rule out the possibility that the men become significantly more authoritarian with age, but do so more slowly than the women. This would, of course, be in line with the findings of other investigators. Furthermore, the lower variance among the men may reflect their more uniform opportunities for role-taking. This may also give them "momentum," so that they remain non-authoritarian for longer.

When we look at the group of older women with the par-

---

* It is sometimes suggested that the F-score increase with age reflects a generational difference—the older people are said to have been brought up by methods more likely to produce this trait. The difference between men and women in this sample indicates that this is very probably not the case.

ticularly high concentration of high F-scores, we find that they are fully disengaged; mainly, they are widows living in a restricted life space. We will go into the significance of this finding later, but we should point out here that widowhood narrows the variety of interactions available to women, and this is consonant with the suggestions of Stewart and Hoult (68) that the lack of opportunity for assuming other people's roles leads to an authoritarian outlook.

We conclude, then, that for women, and perhaps for men, disengagement is accompanied by changes in the individual's orientation in the direction of a personal narrowness and rigidity of outlook on *general* issues, and a decreased ability to take the role of others.* This trait, like orientation to interaction, is not related to morale.

■ **Religious Piety**

It is the common belief that religious piety and practice increase with age, and that the old are the backbone of the churches. This is part of a general assumption that the old are more conservative than the middle-aged. On the other hand, disengagement theory would predict a decreasing interest in religion as normative control is lessened. From a battery of questions about religious beliefs and religious practices, we have developed a Religious Piety score. (The details are given in Appendix 2.) This score rates the respondent according to the secularism of his orientation toward religion. Thus, those who feel that religion offers social interaction, group experience, a meeting place, an integrative experience, or a philosophy of life have low religious-piety scores. Those who see religion as fundamentally concerned with the brotherhood of man are also scored low. In the same way, disbelief in

---

* Our panel members show the same educational and occupational variation in F-score that other workers have found, but we are not immediately concerned with these variables, since they are not closely related to changes connected with age.

life after death cuts down the score. Those scoring high are concerned in their religious beliefs with man's relationship to God, with sin, redemption, and the possibility of life after death. Most practicing Roman Catholics and most fundamentalists rate high scores, and many Protestants of non-liturgical and non-evangelical denominations get low religious-piety scores. As we see in Table V–6, religious piety, although some-

TABLE V–6

RELIGIOUS PIETY, AGE, AND SEX

(PANEL AND SEVENTIES, WAVE III)

Age and Sex	Number Interviewed	Per Cent High [a] Religious Piety	Per Cent Seldom Attending Church
Males	*107*	*36.4*	*54.2*
50–54	19	36.8	57.9
55–59	18	33.3	50.0
60–64	19	57.9	42.1
65–69	12	33.3	50.0
70–74	25	28.0	60.0
75 and over	14	28.6	64.3
Females	*104*	*61.5*	*34.6*
50–54	17	58.8	35.3
55–59	16	81.3	25.0
60–64	15	80.0	20.0
65–69	19	73.7	42.1
70–74	25	56.0	24.0
75 and over	12	8.3	75.0

NOTE: Women are more often high in Religious Piety than men. $\chi^2 = 12.3$, d.f. $= 1$, $P < .001$.

[a] Above the median.

thing like the religious conservatism related to the authoritarian scale, does not increase directly with age but, rather, first increases and then decreases again. Among the women, those under fifty-five and those over seventy are significantly less pious, in our sense, than those in the intermediate years.* The

* This is comparable to a finding of the Detroit Area Studies Series reported by Harold L. Orbach. See reference 49.

same trend occurs among the men, but is not of statistical significance. This is not likely to be a generational matter, but may represent a turning toward a more orthodox religious position at the age when crises such as retirement and widowhood occur. In fact, the majority of our respondents declare that religion has been of the greatest value to them in time of trouble. However, they appear to become less pious after this time, and this seems inconsistent with their response to the F-scale. We conclude that our religious-piety score may be picking up the difference between a normative concern with appearing religious and a personal commitment to the unique aspect of religion; that is, a concern with the transcendental. This is not necessarily related to authoritarianism, since it is not inherently a more conservative stance. In terms of disengagement, however, it seems logical for a concern with the transcendental to decrease with age, as does the concern with death and dying.* We will return to this question again in Chapter XI, when we consider the very old respondents, but in the meantime it seems clear that the hypothesis about piety decreasing with age was poorly formulated, because although the high-scoring people are a good deal more committed to religion and involved with it, they are also more *idiosyncratic*, and less *social*, in their orientation to it. According to the disengagement theory, they should become more idiosyncratic and less committed, and these two effects should cancel each other. We cannot tell whether the low scores among the people over seventy are due to an increased secular orientation or to a decreased involvement, but since these findings, a brief inquiry among some respondents has suggested that deep religious commitment, including belief in personal immortality, is connected with a sense of immanent justice. The middle-aged person feels that death would be "unfair." The old person

---

* One question—whether the respondent often thought of dying—was a failure because only a tiny fraction admits ever thinking of death or dying.

feels that he has lived his allotted span and begins to lose interest in a life after death. Middle-aged people think of death as an abrupt departure (in our terms, a ripping away from the network of social interaction) while old people think of it as a logical termination (in our terms, a slipping away from a situation to which they are weakly bonded).

When we examine church attendance, we see (Table V–6) that the percentage attending church frequently decreases in extreme old age.* Among the women, the highest attendance coincides with the age at which religious piety is highest. This is not true of the men, and perhaps religion, traditionally a feminine preoccupation, is a more sensitive area for women. This cannot be taken for granted, however, for many traditional suppositions about the old turn out, when scrutinized, not to be so.

In summary, religious piety and religious attendance show some decrease with age and are in this respect consonant with the disengagement theory.

■ **Conformity to Versus Alienation from the Dominant World View**

Our final ideological variable is what we call the World View, and we interpret it as a distinction between conformity and alienation. This measure has been built up from two different kinds of items that prove, nevertheless, to be related. The one group of items asks whether the respondent sees his own life as generally satisfactory or not, and the other asks him whether he agrees with some of the major values of the culture—that people can be trusted, that things will get better rather than worse, and so on. (The items are listed in Appendix 3.) Inasmuch as the dominant American values tend

---

* It is hard to decide whether this difference would disappear if all of our oldest respondents were equally competent physically. On the other hand, our group of octogenarians contains two clergymen, and this may bias the results so as to obscure a significant difference. We await a thorough inquiry into religious beliefs and practices among the very old.

to stress the ultimate meaningfulness and beneficent purpose of events,* this score can be looked upon as conformity to versus alienation from a dominant value of our culture, with a personal overtone of optimism or pessimism. Since the items can be scaled by Guttman's technique, this can be thought of as a unidimensional ideology.

Disengagement theory would anticipate less conformity among the aged because of their small life spaces. Table V–7 shows alienation by age and sex. The striking aspect of this

TABLE V–7

WORLD VIEW BY AGE AND SEX

(PANEL AND SEVENTIES, WAVE III)

Age and Sex	Number Interviewed	Per Cent Relatively Conforming [a]
Both sexes	*211*	*46.0*
50–54	36	58.3
55–59	34	41.2
60–64	34	44.1
65–69	30	50.0
70–74	51	52.9
75 and over	26	19.2
Males only	*107*	*42.1*
50–54	19	63.2
55–59	18	44.4
60–64	19	36.8
65–69	12	25.0
70–74	25	48.0
75 and over	14	21.4
Females only	*104*	*50.0*
50–54	17	52.9
55–59	16	37.5
60–64	15	53.3
65–69	19	63.2
70–74	25	60.0
75 and over	12	16.7

NOTE: Significantly fewer men and women over seventy-five are conforming. $\chi^2 = 7.35$, d.f. $= 1$, P$<$ .01.

[a] Scores of 7-11 were considered to be conforming; 13-21 as alienated.

* The dominant American outlook might be termed "Panglossian."

distribution is the lack of shift with age until we get to the very oldest group. One finds considerably fewer men and women over seventy-five who subscribe to the dominant optimistic world view that one does in the younger age group. This difference in alienation between those over seventy-five (both men and women) and those under that age is significant. For the moment, alienation-conformity is one of a constellation of variables that all have one thing in common. At the very end of life, there is a tendency for people to take a less normative stand. They are more alienated, less pious, and less active as churchgoers, even though they are ambulatory. It is possible that increased alienation reflects merely the loosening of the normative web surrounding these old people. It is sometimes said that old age is an "unveiling," that the old become "more like themselves," more intensely individual. When they cease having frequent intensive interactions with their peers, and their eccentricities are allowed to emerge, they may care less about giving the "right" answer to the interviewer, and we may be getting responses from them which reflect their very personal view of the world, uncolored by residual feelings of what is a "proper" answer. Furthermore, all these issues may merely be less meaningful for the very old, less relevant to the vital part of their lives—that is, themselves, their own past.

■ Perceived Lifespace

We have used one final variable that represents the individual's point of contact with his social system. This we call Perceived Lifespace, and it was developed to gauge whether the respondent's view of his life was consonant with the constriction we had discerned in role number, interaction rate, and social life space. In order to determine this, the respondent was asked, with respect to five important categories of relationship* (see Appendix 2), to compare his present rate

* Relatives, friends, church, clubs, "people seen every day."

of interaction with the one he remembered from the age of forty-five. In Table V-8 we see that here, too, there is a shift with age; the percentage of both men and women seeing themselves acting in relatively constricted life spaces is greater in the older age groups.

TABLE V–8

RATES OF PERCEIVED INTERACTION BY AGE AND SEX
(PANEL AND SEVENTIES, WAVE III)

Sex and Age	Number Interviewed	Per Cent with Perceived Constricted Lifespace
Both sexes	*211*	*65.4*
50–54	36	38.9
55–59	34	55.9
60–64	34	47.1
65–69	31	71.0
70–74	50	84.0
75 and over	26	96.2
Males	*107*	*64.5*
50–54	19	36.8
55–59	18	44.4
60–64	19	42.1
65–69	12	83.3
70–74	25	88.0
75 and over	14	100.0
Females	*104*	*66.3*
50–54	17	41.2
55–59	16	68.8
60–64	15	53.3
65–69	19	63.2
70–74	25	80.0
75 and over	12	91.7

NOTE: Fewer men and women under, than those over, sixty-five, perceive their Lifespaces as constricted. $\chi^2 = 28.74$, d.f. $= 1$, $P < .001$.

It is, however, logical to inquire about reasons other than age for this variation in perceiving constriction. People who have recently been bereaved or retired may well see themselves as acting in a constricted sphere. Accordingly, we examined the relationship of work status to this perception, and although this is difficult, since there are relatively few nonworking men under sixty-five or working men over sixty-five, the findings are presented in Table V–9. It is interesting that more than a third

TABLE V–9

PERCEPTION OF CONSTRICTION IN LIFESPACE
ACCORDING TO WORK STATUS, SEX, AND AGE
(PANEL AND SEVENTIES, WAVE III)

Sex and Age	Number Interviewed		Per Cent with Perception of Constriction	
	Working	Nonworking	Working	Nonworking
Total males	64	43	48.4	88.4
50–54	18	1	38.9	0.0
55–59	18	0	44.4	a
60–64	15	4	33.3	75.0
65–69	4	8	75.0	87.5
70–74	6	19	83.3	89.5
75 and over	3	11	100.0	100.0
Total females	36	68	55.6	72.1
50–54	12	5	50.0	20.0
55–59	5	11	60.0	72.7
60–64	8	7	50.0	57.1
65–69	5	14	60.0	64.3
70–74	4	21	75.0	81.0
75 and over	2	10	50.0	100.0

a Not applicable.

of the men between fifty and sixty-four saw themselves as acting in constricted life spaces, although they were still working full time.* There is an abrupt and significant increase in this proportion at the age of sixty-five—about 80 or 90 per cent, *regardless of work status.*

When we look at the comparable data for the women, we see that the proportion of working women who see themselves operating in a narrow arena hovers at about 50 to 60 per cent

* It is unfortunate that the Perceived Lifespace categories do not exactly replicate the life space categories.

throughout the age span, whereas the nonworking women seem to perceive a gradual increase in constriction with age. If we assume that the majority of these women are housewives who had never engaged in outside work, this finding supports the fact that perception of constriction occurs among men even when they are working, suggesting that retirement does not account for all of the increased perception of constriction associated with age, even though work itself dominates the actual life space.

We turn now to marital status. Because we have such small numbers, we combined the widowed with the divorced, separated and single, as shown in Table V–10. We find, however, that the difference in the proportion of married and non-married with a perception of constriction in life space is not statistically significant.

TABLE V–10

PERCEPTION OF CONSTRICTION IN LIFESPACE ACCORDING
TO MARITAL STATUS, SEX, WORK STATUS, AND AGE
(PANEL AND SEVENTIES, WAVE III)

Sex, Age, and Work Status	Number Interviewed		Per Cent with Perception of Constriction	
	Married	Other	Married	Other
Total males	86	21	61.6	76.2
Working	53	11	47.2	54.5
50–69	48	7	41.7	42.8
70 and over	5	4	100.0	75.0
Nonworking	33	10	84.8	100.0
50–69	12	1	75.0	100.0
70 and over	21	9	90.5	100.0
Total females	49	55	61.2	70.9
Working	16	20	56.3	55.0
50–69	14	16	50.0	56.3
70 and over	2	4	100.0	50.0
Nonworking	33	35	63.6	80.0
50–69	26	11	57.7	63.6
70 and over	7	24	85.7	87.5

We felt it possible that some perceptions of constricted life space could be associated with reductions in family size. In looking at household size, we assumed, first, that married persons living in two-person households were sometimes families reduced in size by the departure of children and, second, that one-person households might include people whose families had been reduced by the death of a spouse, and unmarried persons whose families had been reduced by the death or separation of parents or siblings. One could expect the effects of such losses to show up in differences in the rates of perceived constriction within these groups. But the married people in our panel live mostly in two-person households; married people living in larger households, presumably more like the general run of intact families, are generally too few to allow comparisons by age and sex. In fact, there are only two married women over the age of fifty-five who live in households of more than two persons. Similarly, one-person households, the result of widowhood, are concentrated in the older age groups, where perceived constriction appears to be almost universal. However, five of the eight married women in their early fifties in two-person households do perceive their lives as narrower, while none of the six women of comparable ages in larger households do so. The probability of a difference as large as this with such small numbers is .04, and this suggests that a perception of constriction is likely to occur among women, although not among men, when children leave the home. It is interesting that loss of children is said to affect women in the same way retirement is said to affect men. However, in this case the women seem more sensitive to this role loss than the men do. Later we shall note that morale is somewhat higher among women whose children have left home, as indeed it is among older men who have retired. In the meantime, our interest is focused primarily on the persistent shift with age in perception of constricted social life space, which characterizes *all* the sub-groupings we have examined, regardless of status.

If we consider perceived life space in combination with actual life space, an interesting process is suggested, one we might expect to find if we studied a group of people over the years from the age of fifty through the rest of their lives. It is suggested in Table V–11 that the perception of constriction seems to occur *before* extensive constriction actually takes place. A gradual shift with age through three stages is suggested: (1) working, with a large life space, and no perception of constriction, to (2) an intermediate category, in which there is perception of constriction while still working, with a large life space, to (3) a final stage of not working, a small life space, and a perception of constriction. As shown in Table V–11, almost all of the men in the fifty to fifty-nine age group are in the first and intermediate stages in the proportions of 57 and 41 per cent, respectively; those in the sixty to sixty-nine age group are almost evenly distributed with approximately one third in each of the three stages; a total of 82 per cent of those in the seventy and over age group are in the intermediate or final stages with the largest proportion (64 per cent) in the final stage.

A similar process is observed among the 104 women included in the study, except that there appears to be an alternative beginning group including nonworking women who have small life spaces without perceived constriction. There are relatively few men in this category.

To summarize our analysis of this variable, it is suggested that the modal middle-aged, or engaged, state is that of acting in a large life space and perceiving it as stable, while the aged, or disengaged, state is that of acting in a small space and perceiving it as constricted. Logically, there could be three pathways toward the aged state; either the person could experience the sensation of constriction before extensive constriction actually occurs; or he could act in a small life space before he

TABLE V-11

WORK STATUS, LIFESPACE, AND PERCEPTION OF CONSTRICTION IN LIFESPACE, ACCORDING TO SEX AND AGE
(PANEL AND SEVENTIES, WAVE III)

Sex and Age	Number Interviewed	Per Cent of Number Interviewed				
		Working With Large Lifespace		Not Working With Small Lifespace		
		Perceived Unconstricted	Perceived Constricted	Perceived Unconstricted	Perceived Constricted	Other[a]
Total males	*107*	30.8	28.0	3.7	32.7	4.7
50–59	37	56.8	40.5	2.7	0.0	0.0
60–69	31	35.5	25.8	3.2	32.3	3.2
70 and over	39	2.6	17.9	5.1	64.1	10.3
Total females	*104*	15.4	17.3	16.3	46.2	4.8
50–59	33	24.2	27.3	18.2	24.2	6.1
60–69	34	17.6	17.6	20.6	38.2	5.9
70 and over	37	5.4	8.1	10.8	73.0	2.7

[a] Working with small Lifespace or not working with large Lifespace.

perceives the constriction; or both could occur at approximately the same time. These data seem to suggest that the first pathway is the most common, although it is possible that they reflect a sensitivity to relatively small constrictions in life space which are insufficient to result in changes in classification from large to small life spaces.* This, however, is not inconsistent with the suggestion that perception appears before actual constriction since the degree of sensitivity reflected in a response indicating a perception of constriction is perhaps out of proportion to the relatively small amount of the actual change in life space taking place. It is also possible that the second pathway does exist more frequently than suggested in these data but that the duration of the first stage is so short that we did not pick it up owing to the nature of our study.

If it is assumed, as seems reasonable from these findings, that the commonest pathway to the aged state is that of first experiencing a shrinking of the life space, then we raise the question of the nature of this change in perception. It is possible that the responses exactly reflect reality, because, although the Perceived Lifespace score does not inquire directly about work, the most important category, it does ask about the number of people seen every day, and it is probably safe to assume that work is accounted for in the response. On the other hand, it seems possible that some anticipatory socialization is occurring among these people and that they are, as it were, looking ahead to a time when they will be less involved than they are now—that they are familiarizing themselves with old age. As one respondent said, "I'll be old enough to want to get away from the hustle and bustle of the city. I'll want to be where it's peaceful and quiet."

It is also possible that there is a process, more purely psychological in nature, which we can call "withdrawal of object

---

* It will be recalled that a high Social Lifespace score without working is unlikely.

cathexis," and which we shall later discuss at greater length. Thus, if interactions are experienced less intensely and seem less important, they may be reported as fewer. A respondent says, "The things that seemed so important are not so important."

This is thought of as a circular process and is not incompatible with the fact that the reported constriction may be partly accounted for by retirement and the loss of household members. It is, on the other hand, compatible with the finding that the perception of constriction occurs persistently with age, regardless of the other variables. In a later chapter we will suggest that this withdrawal of object cathexis is related to important changes in the perception of time. Certainly, it is possible that some inner shift such as reduction of involvement in the outer world is an important jumping-off point for the disengaging process; it may be the most important sign of the individual's readiness for the process of growing old.

In the next chapter we will discuss the concept of "ego energy," and object cathexis.* For the moment we suggest that there may be some intrinsic change with age—the analogue of maturation in children—which results in a removal of psychological involvement from the environment and which leads the individual to *initiate* the disengagement process. This process may be hastened by a withdrawal of the environment but, as we shall elaborate in the following chapters, we believe certain important inner changes may be autonomous.

Some studies of very old people have adumbrated our own research. Cosin (14) expresses the opinion that "deterioration of 'communications' through declining mental and physical abilities is not the main source of senile failure, but that more basic personality functions described in terms like 'drive' or

* Fifty-five members of the panel had Ego Energy scores. These were compared with their Perceived Lifespace scores and the relationship, though not strong, was significant at the .05 level. For the remainder of this book we will *assume* that low Perceived Lifespace scores reflect some form of lowered object cathexis.

'self-motivation' have become defective." At any rate, as we can see from our table, the disengaged state, as we have defined it for the moment, seems to be an almost universal end point, whether it is a responsive rather than an intrinsic phenomenon.

In this chapter we have seen that we can combine several shifts in orientation with age, and call them "readiness for disengagement." First, in the orientation to interaction as we have estimated it, the older people show an increase in variety of relational rewards sought; presumably this reflects an increased freedom of choice when the constraints of the general norms, and the particular bonds to the occupational world and the obligations of child-raising, are removed. At the same time we see a decrease in religious orthodoxy. On the other hand, we get an increasing ideological conservatism, as this is measured by the F-score. Conformity to the dominant world view of optimism and orientation toward the future, as measured by our alienation score, does not start to disappear until after the seventy-fifth year. In the younger ages, there is a remarkable evenness of score, suggesting a general commitment to the major values of the culture. Though it is generally claimed that old people are conservative, our respondents seem to shift in their old age toward a freer and more expressive interpersonal style. Nevertheless they do become more rigid about those larger issues which are concerned not with the immediate, and presumably known and trusted, circle but with the outside world, and this may make for a public image of conservatism that is only half true. As we have said before, there is undoubtedly a tendency toward greater individuation, and less compulsion to give normative responses and do the expected thing.

In the next chapter, we will examine the personality changes that accompany these changes in orientation and perception, and subsequently we will go into the inner aspects of the disengagement process.

CHAPTER VI

Personality Variations With Age

DISENGAGEMENT THEORY is anchored at one end in social-structural theory and at the other in psychological theory. Here we intend to use a psychological frame of reference in which personality events are part of the person-person interactions that constitute the main axis of disengagement theory. In examining personality, we have been guided by our anticipations of the likely and logical personality correlates that might result from the severing of normatively governed social bonds. This has two implications: (1) we view personality, on the one hand, and social interaction on the other, as two facets of a single, if heterogeneous, system; and (2) in examining the interface of these two facets, we have relied primarily on hypotheses already developed from the differences in social interaction we have observed. In assuming a gradual lessening of the bonds between self and others, we have been led to look for two things: those elements of personality which may give evidence of reduced cathexis to persons and social events, and those elements suggesting an altered basis in the person for the reception and initiation of social events.*

Most theories about the interrelation of personality and social events do not provide logical extensions that could serve as a base for hypotheses on the later phases of the life cycle. In his review of personality theory and aging, Riegel (59) notes that there is no single theory that fully accounts for the aging personality. In fact, the majority of theories he reviews have only the slightest reference to aging, and many have none. But this is not to say that our own basic psychological stance does not have its roots in some psychological theories. While we are not in a position to test elements of these theories, the ideas included in the general category of ego psychology have influenced our thinking. Rapaport (57), Hartmann (29), and Hartmann, Kris, and Loewenstein (31) have reformulated Freud's concept of the origin and structure of the ego so as to suggest that it has greater autonomy from "instinct" than Freud thought. Their formulation, which posits a "conflict-free" portion of the ego rooted in innate talents and growing in interaction with the environment, makes possible the investigation of *normal* persons within a theory of social processes. Also important in our thinking, as we pointed out earlier, has been Erikson's view of ego identity as essentially a psychosocial process, since it "connotes both a persistent sameness with oneself . . . and a persistent sharing of some kind of essential character with others (24)."

In analyzing the personality of our respondents, our central

* As with other spheres of disengagement theory, our personality findings are, by their nature, hypotheses. They were developed in a process of interchange of theory and data and have not been independently tested outside the population in which they were developed.

concern has been to consider variables that could be related to disengagement theory. We anticipated that correlations would appear in two broad areas. First, we expected alterations of the ego structure, especially in terms of the balance between inner-world and outer-world events, that would correspond to the severing of social bonds. This would suggest that in the face of new tasks, there would be an altered ego orientation, including changes in perception, in the management of inner emotional resources, and in the rate at which action is initiated.

Working with our sample, David Gutmann * developed a system of personality types that included the concept of balance between control mechanisms and the amount of inner affect. From this conception Gutmann developed an *affect-control typology*. This typology was not initiated to test disengagement theory, since analysis of the personality variables began independently at about the same time as the work on the social variables that led to the formulation of disengagement. Since it is a conception relating inner affect to reality controls, however, it seems appropriate to regard these types as constituting some of the personality correlates of the severing of social bonds.

Second, we anticipated changes in the nature of involvement with outer-world events and in the energy available for engagement with others. The work of Jacqueline Rosen † began with the effort to test some notions of ego energy changes

* The work briefly described here is contained in the publications of Gutmann listed in Appendix 6 and in two unpublished working papers by him: "Personality Change with Age in Males (March, 1959)," and "Personality Change with Age in Females (June, 1960)." Selections and adaptations have been made here of only those aspects of these works which seem to the present authors to have relevance for disengagement theory.

† The work of Jacqueline Rosen briefly reviewed here is fully presented in her doctoral dissertation: "Ego Functions in the Middle and Later Years: A Thematic Apperception Study," Committee on Human Development, University of Chicago, and in the report by Rosen and Neugarten, reference 62. Selections and adaptations have been made of only those aspects of these works which the present authors feel bear directly on disengagement theory.

in older persons, again independently of the developing frame-work of disengagement. Rosen used four measures from the TAT for her purposes. In this presentation, however, we have arranged her divisions into two groups: measures of the *extent of ego involvement* in the outer world and, by implication, the extent of ego-centeredness, and measures of the *quality of ego-energy* portrayed in interaction with others. Each appears to us to have relevance for disengagement theory, because each reflects, in part, energy available for involvement with others and the nature of cathexes to outer events.

Psychologically as well as sociologically, men age differently from women, especially in the ways in which they control affect and emotion. Accordingly, Gutmann has analyzed his variable separately for men and women. On the other hand, the ego-energy measures appear to be independent of sex, and therefore Rosen was able to use identical categories for both sexes, combining men and women in her analyses. We will report here the measures developed and the differences found.

■ **Affect-Control Typology—Men**

The data are the TAT (47) stories of the 70 men in the panel who gave usable responses. They were aged fifty-two to seventy-two at the time the material was collected. To develop the typology, a sub-sample of men aged forty to seventy-one was drawn from a population of the same milieu as our panel.* By adding these additional cases to our population, we ended with usable stories from 145 men, aged forty through seventy-one, providing not only a larger population but an extension of the age range into the forties.

Earlier work by various members of our research group provided clues to the nature of personality changes we could expect among the men. First, from the work of Schaw and Henry (64) one could logically anticipate an age-related shift

* The Carnegie Study which preceded this research.

away from a firm commitment to socially normative interaction toward a more quiescent inner preoccupation. This appears to be an ego change that permits movement from an active, combative, concrete outer-world orientation to an adaptive, conforming, and abstract inner-world orientation.

Secondly, Neugarten and Gutmann (48) had reported an analysis of the *expectations* of people of different ages, based on data from the Carnegie Study. In a four-figure TAT card, subjects aged forty through seventy were asked to tell a story and to characterize each of the figures—a young man, an old man, a young woman, and an old woman. Neugarten and Gutmann assumed that while the respondents were not necessarily portraying their own personalities, they were probably reflecting their own experiences with, and expectations of, young and old people. In the respondents' stories, the modal expectations differ between the men and the women described, and they differ with the age of the portrayed figure. The differences between the expectations of the younger man and the older one consist in describing the younger man as instrumental and active, and the older man as inactive, submissive, and introspective. For the females portrayed in the card, the shift is from expecting the younger woman to be subordinate to the goals and directives of the younger man, to assuming a markedly increased dominance and assertion in the older woman.

These two analyses of aging seem to anticipate the concept of readiness for disengagement. The first study, of a somewhat younger group of men, describes a weakening of attachment to social bonds which coincides with disengagement theory. The second study, an analysis of role expectations, suggests an important distinction between men and women and, at least in the case of the men, a similar gradual reduction in effective instrumental exchange with society—a movement from assertive involvement to submissive inner preoccupation.

For Gutmann's analysis, the stories of each respondent were blinded for age and then analyzed in terms of the major concerns displayed, especially with reference to inner impulse life, the major means of coping with problems, and relative success or failure. In each instance, the balance between control and impulse was described, taking into account the nature and intensity of affect expressed, its level of containment, and the degree of the respondent's reality orientation. Gutmann felt that five types satisfactorily accounted for all the TAT responses. These types were then arranged in terms of their adaptive potential, using two clinical assumptions. First, it was assumed that the most adaptive human state is an optimum balance between socially integrated ego defenses, the utilization of freely available energy, and an accurate perception of reality. Second, it was assumed that the most adaptive balance of control will be accompanied by indications that the ego mobilizes affect in the interest of constructive, assertive solutions to problems. Less adaptive balances of control would be either where control becomes constriction and obsession, dampening all responsiveness and inner feeling, or where ego control fails and erratic emotion predominates.

The most adaptive type is labeled I, the least adaptive is labeled V. Assigning each case to its proper category, and arraying the types by age, Gutmann finds, as Table VI–1 shows, in the full combined sample of 145 cases, a significantly greater number of the younger men showing the more adaptive responses. The older men are concentrated in the less adaptive categories. The majority of the men in the age group forty to forty-nine fall into the two most adaptive categories. Of the 29 men of this age, 17, or 59 per cent, are found in Types I and II. These describe an active engagement with others and an essentially assertive and achievement-orientated affect. We will, therefore, consider Types I and II as subtypes of the

TABLE VI-1
Affect Control Types of Men Only, by Age
(Wave II and the Carnegie Study)

Age	Number Interviewed	Per Cents Showing Each Personality Type				
		(I) Focused Active Mastery	(II) Achievement Doubt	(III) Adaptive Retreat	(IV) Fixed Conformity	(V) Ego Defect
Total men	145	13.1	25.5	26.9	11.7	22.8
40–44	12	16.7	50.0	25.0	0.0	8.3
45–49	17	29.4	23.5	29.4	0.0	17.6
50–54	33	18.2	33.3	30.3	3.0	15.2
55–59	34	8.8	20.6	26.5	14.7	29.4
60–64	25	12.0	20.0	36.0	20.0	12.0
65–71	24	0.0	16.7	12.5	25.0	45.8

NOTE: Types (I) and (II) are more common before age fifty-four. Types (III), (IV), and (V) are more common after age fifty-five. $\chi^2 = 10.9$, d.f. $= 1$, P $< .001$.

category Active Mastery, even though they differ in their adaptive success. They can be described in detail as follows:

Type I: Focused Active Mastery. The younger men of this type tell stories in which the hero moves directly and resourcefully toward valued goals. Energy is ascribed mainly to the hero, and the opposition of others does not materially interfere with his interest. Sympathy with others or reflections on his own condition are secondary to goal-directed action. A story typical for this group is given by a man of fifty-six in response to the card depicting a man climbing a rope:

This thing here . . . . Once there was a boy who wanted to go to sea and sail the sea more than anything else. But his parents wanted him to be a lawyer like his father. When he was missing they would go to the dock and inquire and take him back home. As he became older and bigger it became harder to take him back home. In his late teens he decided to go whether his parents wanted him to go or not. They put him in the attic and locked the door. While searching the attic he found a coil of rope. He tied the rope to a trunk and started down. As a sailor he knew how to climb a rope. This time the ship sailed before they had time to search it. That's how a captain of one of our largest ships got his sea legs.

As a group, these men tend to be self-propelled. Their stories reveal them to be clearly cognizant of the outer world. Their heroes dissipate conflict or frustration through goal-directed action, in an accurately perceived environment.

Some of the stories, however, anticipate those of the older men. Sometimes, active mastery seems to suggest a defense of a masculine stance. In these cases, the typical story is one in which some authority figure tries to force the hero into a conforming or submissive action, and the hero vigorously resists. Thus, in the picture of a boy with a violin, the boy angrily rejects the violin practice his mother tries to force upon him, and runs off to some more "manly" activity. It is possible that we are seeing here conflict between an emergent desire for passivity and a compensating attack upon the figures who draw attention to the loss of autonomy.

Type II: Achievement Doubt. In this group, the men tell stories in which the heroes act in the outer world, but in the face of inner doubt. As compared with Type I heroes, they show increasing concern over the consequences of bold action, and alternate between action and constraint. A typical story for the card showing the boy with a violin is given by a man of fifty-seven:

Poor guy's asleep. He's dreaming for the future more than anything. He can't figure out what's going to happen. He just can't make up his mind whether he wants to go on with it or just . . . [left up in air]. Finally made up his mind, he's going to get down to business and become a good violinist.

It is inferred from their stories that these men are becoming preoccupied with passive-dependent wishes; they perceive these wishes as a threat to continued achievement autonomy, but do not yet see them as part of freedom from the need to achieve. However, where Type I men place the dependency struggle in the environment, the Type II men place it within the individual. They rarely propose that their heroes surrender to dependent wishes, but they frankly admit the temptation. Though competitive motivations still appear to direct these men, they are less able to commit themselves wholeheartedly to a vigorous engagement with society. Doubt and increasing fantasies modify their mastery, and suggest a readiness to give up the intense engagement of middle life.

The younger group, as a whole, depicts heroes engaged in mastering the outer world, even though some of them doubt the meaning of their striving and begin to question the moral justification for self-assertion. Their increased concern with themselves does not have enough intensity or conflict to bind ego energy and prohibit active transactions with others. They respond to the pull from the environment, and see it as the focus of their endeavors. The solutions they propose to the problems they see are fully engaged and normatively approved.

The older men, between sixty and seventy-one, fall primarily into Types III and IV which describe, respectively, passive coping devices and inner retreat, and Type V, a category including various forms of defective reality-testing and ego control. Of our 49 older men, 37, or 76 per cent, fall into these last three types, and of these, 14, or 29 per cent, fall into the Ego Defect category. A detailed description of these types follows:

Type III: Adaptive Retreat. The men in Type III describe heroes who are humble in the presence of authority figures. They are friendly, adaptive, and sensitive to any transgression they might make against the rights of others. The ego appears to be tackling the problem of affiliation rather than achievement.* They are more likely to assert themselves for the benefit of others than for themselves. Aggression may be turned against the self as punishment. They see overt aggression as a quality of criminals; such behavior, they seem to say, is neither amenable to social control nor available to the socialized ego. The outer world is dominated by social mandates, and authority must be obeyed. A typical story of this type is given in response to the picture of an older and a younger man.

Two members of a law firm. Senior and Junior. The young man

---

* This shift of orientation among aging men is a well-known culture theme; movies like *You Can't Take It With You* are built around the transition from aggressive achievement to affiliation with others.

thinks he hasn't handled the case as well as it should have been handled and the old man is giving him a few words of advice.

The competitive motivations inferred from the stories of the younger men may no longer be useful to these Type III men. They have partially resolved the assertive-dependence conflict by disavowing their own anger and stressing their humility. These men may have replaced their interest in mastering their environment with an interest in control of themselves. They conscientiously reshape themselves in accord with outer demands, thus emphasizing integration rather than competition with others. They do not distort the outer world, but they remain in touch with their own inner lives. The chief difference between the first two types and those of Type III is the loss of interest in shaping the world to suit their needs, and the substitution of an interest in re-ordering their lives in harmony with the world, which they appear to believe has become fixed and unchangeable. Alternatively, they may feel they haven't enough time left to re-order it.

Type IV: Fixed Conformity. The older men in Type IV give sparse responses lacking in elaboration. The stimulus is described correctly, but the story is rarely developed beyond a bare outline. An example is, "That's a boy looking at a violin. I guess he's thinking about playing the violin."

Heroes blandly follow the directions of authority or conform automatically to available role stereotypes. The emphasis is upon acts rather than motivation, and the initiative is ascribed to an impersonal environment, not to human agents. As one man says, telling a story about a farmer, "If they have good weather, the crops will be O.K."

This group of older men relies on isolation and intellectualization for control. That is, they withdraw attention from disturbing stimuli, and if they cannot, they deal with them in an impersonal manner. They also appear uninterested in their own inner states and focus their attention neutrally upon the impersonal aspects of the environment. Things seem to happen to and around the heroes of these men without their personal intervention or initiative. They wait for outer stimulation, react minimally in reasonable accord with it, and presumably return readily to inner preoccupations when the external pressures are removed.

Type V: Ego Defect. Type V represents a generalized weakening of ego control and suggests that primitive motivations may be directing the perception of events. Here the stories contain occasional improbable interpretations of the stimuli, perceptual distortions stemming from ordinarily repressed feelings as well as from a weakened response to social sanctions. The following responses are characteristic of this group:

[To the man on the rope] That guy is getting ready to steal something. Swinging over a building or something. He don't want a job. He wants to get into some orneriness.

Is he in the nude? It looks to me he is. I don't know what I think he's doing. He might be spying on a neighbor. He looks to me like he would be that kind of person. I can't figure out, if he is in the nude why would he be climbing on a post? Unless there is water under there and he would be swimming.

[To the card with two faces close together] Looks like a statue or something. Don't know whether that's water or not. Looks like it could be a woman drowned and floating in the water.

Also included in this group are persons whose stories suggest that ego controls, though tenuous, still hold. Such responses as the following are included:

[To the two faces close together] I don't know what this means. Can't tell. Maybe they are sad. Can't tell. Don't know.

[To the man on the rope] I don't think—got a dirty look on his face. Silly look—no clothes on. Don't want to say any more about him. Could be he's escaping. Not all there. Look at that silly expression.

The term "Ego Defect" is used throughout this analysis because in a clinical evaluation these respondents would be judged as having inadequate ego control. However, it is by no means clear to the present authors that this is a suitable term for describing a nonclinical population. Ego organization may change with age in such a way that the Type A (I and II) men represent a psychological state in which active achievement motives are paramount, more passive affiliative impulses secondary, and distortions and misperceptions are absent. Type B (III and IV) men may have reached a stage where active mastery is less important, or less possible, for them, and passive mastery a paramount concern. It is possible, however, that these men have certain distorted perceptions of the TAT cards that they fail to report because they are under the social controls prohibiting certain types of answers. For example, both Types A and B men might see a voyeur in the rope-climbing card and think it an unacceptable response in the interactional context of the testing situation. The Type A man may then substitute an assertive achievement story, and the Type B man an affiliative one. The Type C (V) man *may* be the only one sufficiently free of normative control to describe this card in terms of a prohibited and deviant sexual activity.

If this were the case, the types would be a series in which Active Mastery is a starting point and Ego Defect an end-point that everyone could be expected to reach if he lived long enough. A number of studies have suggested, however, that there is a certain biological elite who live to be very old and do not become infirm or senile; there may also be certain people who are also relatively immune from the psychological process of change described above. If this is so, the Ego Defect group may be quasi-pathological men whose deterioration of ego control may have occurred at any time in the life span. The larger number in the older age group may represent not age-relatedness but an accumulation of men of this type who have survived. A population less healthy and less secure than this one might show a different proportion in this category.

This distribution of personality types suggests a falling off among our older men of active outer-world involvement and a concomitant shift toward intrapsychic preoccupations. In other words, they are ready for disengagement. Where the younger men ignore the inner realm and strive to remain engaged, the older men deploy their energies inward to the psychic world. The older men look to society not for stimulation and challenge but rather for cues to conformity to social expectations. The men over sixty seem to have resolved the conflicts of autonomy-dependence and assertion-passivity and to have done so by moving in a de-energized deferent direction. Whereas the younger men stress assertion, disavow passivity, and demand respect, the older men stress mildness, disavow competitiveness, and ask for support and guidance.

These trends were observed in our combined sample of 145 men between forty and seventy-one. Since relationships with other facets of disengagement will be used later, however, we present in Table VI-2 the way in which the men in our panel alone are distributed by type.

To recapitulate, Type A (I and II)—Active Mastery—includes men whose handling of the TAT suggests a vigorous and alloplastic, rather than autoplastic, approach to the world. That is, modification and control of the environment has greater value for them than a modification of the self to suit external pressures. Some maintain this stance with conviction, but others seem to do so in the face of doubt and conflict. Their well-organized stories refer to striving and autonomous heroes, characteristically fully engaged with the environment. They perceive the stimuli accurately, and they introduce good imaginative elaborations. They are not overly concerned with affiliation with others or with examining the meaning of their actions.

TABLE VI–2

AFFECT CONTROL TYPES OF PANEL MEN ONLY, BY AGE
(WAVE II)

		Per Cents Showing Each Personality Type				
		(I)	(II)	(III)	(IV)	(V)
	Number	Focused	Achieve-		Fixed	
	Inter-	Active	ment	Adaptive	Conform-	Ego
Age	viewed	Mastery	Doubt	Retreat	ity	Defect
Total men	70	*21.4*	*24.3*	*20.0*	*17.1*	*17.1*
50–56	23	39.1	21.7	0.0	8.7	30.4
57–63	30	16.7	33.3	33.3	10.0	6.7
64–70	17	5.9	11.8	23.5	41.2	17.6

Type B (III and IV)—Passive Mastery—includes men whose approach is essentially autoplastic. They alter and control themselves rather than the external world. They are sometimes defensively humble or overconstrained. They perceive the cards accurately, as do Type A men, but they respond minimally, seldom going beyond the bare essentials of the stimulus. Apparently disengaged from the social world, they react stringently but appropriately, and wait passively for the next demand.

Type C, identical with Type V (defined above), shows Ego Defect. It includes all men whose stories contain serious enough misperceptions of the stimuli to indicate that a weakening of the ego has resulted in perceptions and judgments that serve unconscious needs more than adaptive purposes; misperceptions seem to have autoplastic, rather than alloplastic, implications. Such misperceptions imply loss of normative control. Seeing a distortion but not reporting it may be an intermediate state. In fact, Ego Defect is related to reduced life space. Lack of normative control from the environment may aggravate decreasing inner control in these cases.

Complex judgments were involved in formulating these types and are difficult to repeat. In order to estimate the reliability of the inferences drawn from the stories, Gutmann made two special validating studies, reported in Appendix 5. Both studies suggest that the personality types are valid.

■ **Affect-Control Types—Women**

The life problems and circumstances of men and women differ, and this leads logically to differences in the way they age. Disengagement from characteristically different roles may require different techniques and different balances between impulse and coping mechanisms. (Chapter X will deal more thoroughly with these differences.)

The TAT records of the women were analyzed blind for age and within the over-all framework described for the men. After examining all the cases, Gutmann derived a set of personality types looking for the woman's characteristic concerns and preoccupations, especially with reference to inner-impulse life, the major mechanisms of coping with problems, and their relative success or failure. Five broad types appear to cover the variety of personalities involved. They are ordered along a continuum ranging from good ego control and reality orientation to ego defect, and simultaneously along a parallel continuum from social orientation to egocentric orientation. The five types are:

Type I: Externalized Personal Mastery. In this type are grouped the women whose stories are expressive, who are accurate in their perceptions and focus on personally stimulating outer events and interactions. It is inferred that these women maintain their emotional balance by managing the environment. They justify their actions not by their usefulness, as do the men of the Active Mastery Type, but rather with a more narrowly personal rationale. They tend to find moral justification in identifying with their children's rebellion against restrictive authority. Thus, they maintain a brisk but vicarious engagement with the outer world. This is expressed in altruistic terms, and intrusive motives are disavowed. They are able to act assertively with minimal doubt or self-recrimination by describing highly personal issues as socially useful. A typical story of this type describes the card depicting two men, "You have an amused father or pastor trying to help an unhappy young man. He has a twinkle in his eye and the young man has a very upset jaw. It's a weighty problem to him but the old man sees it's not such a serious problem."

Type II: Internalized Passive Mastery. This group includes the women whose stories suggest autoplastic mechanisms of control. They, like Type I women, identify with children, but where Type I women seek to order and arrange their environment to their own personal, if altruistic, ends, these women stress stable, affiliative, predictable qualities. Their stories suggest that they are in the habit of adjusting quietly to inevitable problems. They deny assertive control, though some of them appear to domineer through excessive self-sacrifice. Both types of women are actively engaged with the socio-emotional tasks of the family. A typical story says, in describing a picture of an older woman and a young man:

"Evidently the man is talking to his mother about some decision. (What?) I wouldn't have any idea—some problem—or it could be somebody outside the family telling her bad news. He has a worried expression. (Think?) Well, I— she looks like she was trying to absorb some bad news or whatever trouble he's talking about but I don't know what trouble it is—he has his hat in his hand, so he might be someone other than the family. (Outcome?) Well, she's the type of person, whatever it is, that she'll make the most of it—and he'll do all right. He's feeling more concerned about the way she's feeling. He will get over it and she'll have to live with it."

Type III: Externalized Domination. In this group, the women are more strongly externalizing than Types I and II. They seem to be grappling in the outer environment with various projections of increasingly personal concerns. Rather than sympathizing with the problems of their children, these women appear more interested in retaining and domineering them. Where Type I women appeared realistic in their efforts to master their outer world, Type III women are prone to ignore reality if it interferes with personal justification and ego-centered gain. We may see here a "clinging on" phenomenon, such as we saw in some of the Type I men. It may be a last attempt to hold on to the maternal role. A typical story is: "The man is trying to tell his mother something that isn't getting across. She doesn't approve and he's unhappy. He'll go on and do whatever he must do. She'll understand but not approve—there's a difference."

Type IV: Internalized Rigidity. The stories suggest constricted women, victims rather than aggressors. While they share, with the more vigorous Types I and III women, the thrust toward moral justification, their stories suggest that they cannot unlock their aggressive energies. Rather, they tend to feel discouraged, aggrieved. While they resent the departure of children, they can neither implement their retentive wishes nor resign themselves. Their techniques are autoplastic. They overconform to external control, but with limited personal investment and low satisfaction. They appear unable to use the opportunities for freedom and self-indulgence that disengagement offers. A story from this type of women says, "This is a mother and a son. It surely must be her son. The son has a problem on his mind. She has turned her back as though—as if—she don't want to listen. It could be about his family, sweetheart, or business. At his age it could be his family."

Type V: Externalized Ego Defect. These women, like Type III, attempt to justify their highly personal motivations by externalizing them. Like Type III, they frankly express aggressive and retentive motivations, although with less logic, but unlike Type III, they misperceive the environment in arbitrary, uncritical, and highly personal ways. Like the ego-defective men, these women show reality distortion, probably from primitive motivation. And as with all three of the externalizing groups—Types I, III, and V—there is little guilt or doubt regarding their efforts to control their surroundings. A typical story about the man on the rope reads, "Think activity compensates him for a low mentality. Performing in gymnasium to spectators. Maybe trying to get out of prison. So long as has physical endurance to gratify needs. They won't have to put him in a loony house."

When we examine the women in our basic panel, we see in Table VI–3 that the fifty-to-fifty-nine-year-old women cluster in the first three types, and the sixty-to-seventy-one-year-old women are concentrated in Types IV and V.

The crucial difference between these two age groups of women is the extent to which personal motivations are externalized; that is, projected onto others and then used as functional guides to action. There is a shift with age toward dominance of personal motives over the dictates of reality. That is to say, expressivity is paramount in older women. There is less attachment to outer reality, less motive toward engagement, and an increasing tendency—whether compulsively or assertively maintained—to proceed on the basis of personal whimsy and egocentric demand. Thus, we see in the older women more self-centered eccentricity and less of the inturned self-preoccupation of the men.*

TABLE VI–3

AFFECT CONTROL TYPES OF PANEL WOMEN, BY AGE

(WAVE II)

| | | Per Cents Showing Each Personality Type | | | | |
| | | (I) | (II) | (III) | (IV) | (V) |
Age	Number Inter- viewed	Exter- nalized Personal Mastery	Inter- nalized Passive Mastery	Exter- nalized Domina- tion	Inter- nalized Rigidity	Exter- nalized Ego Defect
Total women	68	*23.5*	*11.8*	*16.2*	*22.1*	*26.5*
50–59	33	30.3	21.2	18.2	15.2	15.2
60–71	35	17.1	2.9	14.3	28.6	37.1

NOTE: Types (I), (II), and (III) are more common before age sixty. Types (IV) and (V) are more common after age sixty. $\chi^2 = 7.17$, d.f. = 1, P< .01.

We have discussed the qualitative shifts of men and women, with age, in psychological organization, and turn now to a more specific estimate of age-related ego changes.

■ **Ego Energy**

For the purpose of measuring ego energy changes, Rosen drew a sample from the combined group of cases, including men and women from both the Carnegie Study and the present study. The criterion for being included was usable TAT stories. This included 144 cases divided equally, on the basis of age, sex, and social class, into 18 groups of eight subjects each. Four measures of ego energy were developed, grouped by the present authors into two reflecting ego-

* As with the men, the possibility exists that Type V among the women represents not a true age trend but an accumulation of a type present throughout the younger ages.

involvement in outer-world events and two reflecting available ego energy.

The *ego-involvement* scores were (1) the number of human figures used in the stories beyond those actually portrayed in the stimulus (on the assumption that it requires more involvement to embellish a story with figures not actually given than to compose a story dealing only with the pictured figures) and (2) a score based on the presence in the stories of any conflict, controversy, or issue requiring decision, further plot development, or a choice between alternatives. It is easy to tell an adequate story about the card without introducing points of controversy or choice. The introduction of issues requiring resolution demands considerable ego involvement in the task. For both measures, the theory of disengagement would suggest a decline with age. A reduction in the number of people in the stories and in the complexity of situations should indicate weaker bonds with persons and events in the external world. Furthermore, the reduction in the Perceived Lifespace score (q.v. Chapter V) had been interpreted as a sign of reduced cathexis or ego energy, and is, as we saw, related to this measure.

The two measures of *ego energy* were (1) a count of the number of assertive rather than passive activities described, and (2) a rating of the emotional intensity of stories, based on the extent to which any emotional state described actually played a role in influencing the action and outcome of the story. Again, both measures, according to disengagement theory, should decline with age, and such a decline should be an indicator of reduced energy for engaging in sustained forward-moving interactions.

The TAT stories of all the subjects were scored without prior knowledge of the sex, age, or socioeconomic status of the subject. A three-way analysis of variance, using these three variables, showed that only age could account for a significant proportion of the variance. When arrayed against age, the predicted decline appears for all four measures, as Table VI–4 shows. These differences between the youngest and the oldest group are all statistically significant, and suggest that with in-

TABLE VI–4

Ego Energy and Involvement Scores of Men and Women (N=144)

| | | TAT Mean Scores for | | | |
Age [a]	Number Inter- viewed	Intro- duced Figures	Intro- duced Conflict	Assertive Energy	Emo- tional Intensity
40–49	48	2.23	3.02	13.19	5.75
50–59	48	1.67	2.38	12.27	5.17
64–71	48	.94	2.35	11.54	4.08

[a] This population was constituted from two different samples. For this reason there was a five-year gap in the age distribution.

creased age there is less ego energy available for responding to the environment or maintaining former levels of social involvement. The older person tends to respond to inner rather than to outer stimuli, to withdraw emotional investment, to give up self-assertiveness, and to avoid rather than embrace challenge. Men and women differ in the personality re-organization which accompanies ego-energy decline, probably in response to the different normatively governed roles they play. Ego energy, being more general, does not differ for men and women, and its loss, as we suggested in Chapter V, may well be an intrinsic feature of aging.

In summary, the psychological variables developed to describe the changes of ego structure with age yield differences which are harmonious with disengagement theory, especially in the reflection of increased self-preoccupation and decreased response to normative control.

CHAPTER VII

The Issue of Successful Aging

with LOIS R. DEAN,
ISABEL McCAFFREY,
and RHONDDA CASSETTA

AMERICANS SEEM concerned with growing old gracefully. Newspaper columns addressed to the aging are increasing. Some of them are frankly concerned with the economic problems of old age, but many concern themselves with less tangible matters. In the women's pages of some newspapers, columnists give advice to readers over forty about how to acquire charm, poise, good looks, and nice clothing, while not forgetting the spiritual side of life. Almost everyone who addresses himself to the aging reader emphasizes the need to stay active and involved, thus concurring, as we have pointed out in Chapter II, with many professional gerontologists.

In this chapter, we will discuss the difficulty of concretely defining the terms "graceful" or "successful" aging, and describe the technique we developed for separating those with relatively low from those with relatively high morale.

■ The Measurement Problem

It is possible for the reseacher to decide the nature of successful aging on the basis of some criterion, and it is equally possible to ask the aging person whether he considers himself to be aging successfully. Both are basic ways of evaluating such success, but both create such serious problems that we decided to use neither. However, we will discuss briefly our reasons for rejecting them, since they are acceptable evaluative practices.

We found it difficult to find criteria of success in aging and impossible to decide who fit them. Speaking generally, the more specific the criterion, the easier it is to assign people to it. For example, if we decide that everyone who stays out of a hospital or a home for the aged is successful, the definition fits all of our panel members. However, it is hard to believe that this is necessarily an index of success in other ways. Remaining out of an institution may be more important to some people than to others, depending upon such differences as temperament and cultural background. Furthermore, some old people living at home may be unhappy and apathetic, while some in institutions may be cheerful and of good morale.* A more general and hence more flexible criterion might be remaining healthy and independent, but this makes it difficult to assign people to the categories. For example, should a healthy seventy-five-year-old widow living with her married daughter be called dependent or independent?

---

* The word "morale" is inappropriate for describing individuals. It describes the *esprit* of bodies of people. However, an idiomatic use of the word is entering the language. Because people know what is meant when they hear one another say, "My morale is low," and because a number of works have used this term, we use it throughout this chapter. It is meant to have its ordinary connotation.

We might say that if people are able to act in the roles which are expected of them they can be called successful, and if they are not, they must be downgraded. Havighurst (33) has employed this technique, arguing that there is a recognizable set of role expectations applicable to performance that can be specified. He realizes that role-performance criteria are inevitably class-bound, but argues that since the middle class is the reference group for most Americans, it is therefore legitimate to use middle-class role expectations. These he derives from his own and his colleagues' general knowledge.

For our purposes, a serious problem of all such evaluations is the value structure of the researchers themselves (46). Nor does distortion arise so much from the researcher's values acting upon his interpretations as from the way they determine the questions to be asked, in the first place, and the categories that follow. For example, the role of street-corner-gang member is believed to be the cornerstone in the social life of the lower-class male (79; 45) but a middle-class investigator of his role performance might miss this altogether.

A similar problem arises in using criteria like "personal adjustment" or "mental health." Havighurst (34) and many others have used the former, but here again the inference is made by the investigator, usually from the answers to specific questions, and the biases of the evaluating group are hard to avoid. And, as Jahoda (38) has shown, there is no agreement about what "mental health" means, let alone how it can be measured. Furthermore, if we could evaluate mental health accurately, could we call a disturbed, maladjusted person who managed to cope with daily life less successful than a well-adjusted, balanced person who did the same?

When we abandon the attempt to develop criteria, and resort to asking the respondents themselves whether they consider themselves successful, we cannot be sure that they are not telling us what they think we want to hear and what it is right and proper to reveal. There are ways of circumventing the tendency to give such "normative" responses; one is to use "projective techniques (35)." However, the data collected in these basically clinical ways are difficult to translate into terms of success. We have no way of ranking in the same success series people with "weak" personalities who are carrying on satisfactorily in optimal circumstances and people of "strong" personalities who collapse under intolerable circumstances.

Because of these difficulties in making direct evaluations of success, we tried to use a logical correlate that could be estimated. Several people have used the concept of morale, and measures of it are available. One can reasonably expect those who are aging successfully to have good morale. After experimenting with available measures, we developed a Morale Index for estimating successful aging. A brief account of the instrument is given here; the full details are in Appendix 3.

■ Measurement of Morale

We began with two instruments: Kutner's (41) unidimensional "morale" scale which asks the respondent how the world impinges on his welfare, and Srole's (67) "anomia" or "normlessness" scale, which inquires directly about the nature of the world. In other words, Srole's items ask the respondent whether the social world is reliably and predictably controlled by the moral and ethical norms, while Kutner's asks him his response to the condition of the world. We assumed these instruments to be related when we were able to form a reproducible Guttman scale with four of Kutner's items and three of Srole's. However, some of the respondents who made low scores appeared, in a validating interview, to have good morale, and some who scored high seemed despondent and demoralized.

We resorted finally to a direct and intuitive judgment of the level of the respondent's morale. Ten respondents, who had been interviewed for an average of ten hours each, were ranked by the interviewer according to their morale. This process was based on the premise that the myriad complicated symbolic communications in the interview gave the most valid available indication of morale. The resulting ranking was found to be unrelated to the scores made on the Kutner-Srole instrument.

Four items which correlated with the interviewer's ranking were selected from the interviews already available, and these are paraphrased * here:

1. What age would you most like to be? (Credit of 1 given for a statement of satisfaction with the present age.)

2. Where in Kansas City would you most like to live? (Credit of 1 given for satisfaction with present location or plans for removal in the case of dissatisfaction.)

3. Of all the things you do on the weekend, which are the least interesting to you? (Credit of 1 given for statement that uninteresting things are avoided or that all weekend activities are enjoyed.)

4. Do you wish you could see more of your relatives, of your neighbors, of your friends? (Credit of 1 given for satisfaction as is.)

These items, chosen for their concordance with the interviewer's rankings, were carefully cross-validated. This process is described in detail in Appendix 3.

It is important to remember that the face value of these items is not the primary reason for their selection. It can be argued that these items ask only for expressions of placidity or contentment, which might actually be apathy. However, their correlation with the interviewer's ranking seems to us more likely to occur because when morale is high, life tends to have

* A literal reproduction of these questions out of the context of the interview would distort their sense.

a "halo" around it. The respondent may either be in such control of the situation as to arrange his life in a very satisfactory pattern, or he may experience it in a way that removes the likelihood of complaint. Just as a person accustomed to good health may fail to report passing indispositions, so a person accustomed to good spirits may fail to report passing discontents. Life is probably experienced more holistically than our questions sometimes assume.*

The highest possible morale score is 4; the lowest is 0. The most common scores are 1 and 2, each comprising about one third of the total number of scores. Fifteen per cent are found at the lower end of the scale with a score of 0; 21 per cent are at the upper end with scores of 3 or 4. Scores of 4 are relatively rare.

For the reasons stated above, however, our primary concern is not with individual scores per se but with relative levels of morale that may be associated with the disengagement process. Stages of disengagement are broadly defined for this purpose according to three simple measures: age, occupation with a characteristic central task (marriage for women, work for men), and reduction in ego investment or object cathexis, as indicated by the Perceived Lifespace Measure.†

The men and women in the study are sorted into four groups. In the first are those considered to be fully engaged,

---

* Since this writing, a second team of researchers, using a somewhat different set of assumptions and different techniques, has developed a "Life Satisfaction Rating" which has been validated in interviews with a sample of our respondents. This measure relates only weakly to our Morale Index. From this we infer that we are on our safest ground when relying upon the face value of our items, and we further infer that the tendency to find what is being sought is very hard to overcome. In the future R. J. Havighurst and B. L. Neugarten will report the details of their new measure.

† We have not used the variables outlined in Chapters IV and V because there are too many of them to control separately with our small population. The three variables we have used, age, marital status for women and work for men, and Perceived Lifespace, are related with various degrees of closeness to the total array of "engagement variables." For details, see Chapters IV and V and Appendix 5.

i.e., married women and working men under sixty-five years of age who have high perceived life spaces. Since the respondents in this group are in their fifties and early sixties, it is reasonable to think that many of them are approaching the end of a long plateau of full engagement, and might, in fact, show some early signs of disengagement if more refined indices were used. At the other end of the disengagement process are those women and men who are over sixty-five years of age and in nonmarried and nonworking states, respectively, who have low perceived life spaces. While this disengagement state seems to represent an "end point" in our study, conceivably another level or plateau might be found in a still older population, and logically, death is the only complete state of disengagement.

Between the beginning and end points, there are two intermediate states of disengagement, based on the respondents' characteristics of disengagement. These four states, the beginning, end, and two intermediate points, are thought of as four stages or steps in the process of disengagement. Those at the beginning or first stage have none of the three characteristics of disengagement; namely, over sixty-five years of age, withdrawn object cathexis, or lack of a central task. The respondents in this category are considered fully engaged. Those at the second and third stages are considered partially disengaged and have one and two characteristics, respectively. Those at the fourth level have all three characteristics and are considered fully disengaged. The acquisition of two or three characteristics may occur simultaneously or it may be spread out over different periods of time. The order in which they are acquired also may vary according to individual circumstances. Data of these kinds, however, are not available in this study.

Of the 104 women in the study, 16 are classified as fully engaged, whereas 31, or almost twice as many men are so classified (Table VII–1). This is because some women reach

TABLE VII-1

AVERAGE MORALE SCORES ACCORDING TO TYPE OF KIN LIVING IN SAME GEOGRAPHIC AREA AND STAGE OF DISENGAGEMENT

Type of Kin Living in Same Geographic Area	Number of Respondents					Average Morale Score				
	Total	Stage of Disengagement [a]				Total	Stage of Disengagement [a]			
		1	2	3	4		1	2	3	4
Male respondents	107	31	24	17	35	1.7	2.0	1.6	1.1	1.8
Siblings and children	35	9	9	5	12	1.9	2.4	1.7	1.2	1.9
Children only	31	6	6	5	14	1.4	1.5	1.3	0.8	1.6
Siblings only	19	8	5	3	3	2.2	2.3	2.0	1.7	2.7
Neither	22	8	4	4	6	1.5	1.4	1.5	1.8	1.5
Female respondents	104	16	26	32	30	1.5	1.6	1.4	1.3	1.5
Siblings and children	27	10	6	6	5	1.8	1.5	1.7	2.0	2.2
Children only	29	1	8	9	11	1.7	2.0	1.8	1.1	2.3
Siblings only	27	2	7	10	8	1.6	2.5	1.7	1.3	1.6
Neither	21	3	5	7	6	0.9	1.0	0.4	1.0	1.2

[a] Stage 1 is a stage of full engagement; Stages 2 and 3 are intermediate states of partial disengagement; Stage 4 is a stage of total disengagement.

a state of partial disengagement through widowhood at a younger age than the customary retirement age for men.

The levels of morale for both men and women in each of the four stages of disengagement are shown in Table VII-1. The total possible range of scores is 0 to 4. Because of the importance of kinship relationships in the disengagement process and since satisfaction with the frequency of social contacts is a component of the morale index, the data are presented according to types of close kin living in the same geographic area.

In spite of the small numbers in each category, there is a remarkably consistent pattern for both men and women. The highest levels of morale are found among those at the beginning and end stages of the disengagement process. The lowest morale, on the average, is among those at the intermediate or transition stages. In the total group of 107 men, the average morale score of those at the first stage of disengagement was 2.0. Those at the second and third stages had average scores of 1.6 and 1.1, respectively. In the fourth stage, the state of full disengagement, the average morale score increased to 1.8. The corresponding figures for the 104 women in the study are 1.6, 1.4, 1.3, and 1.5, respectively.

The exceptions to the pattern of decreasing morale in the second and third stages and increasing morale in the fourth stage of disengagement are those men and women who have no siblings or children living in the same geographic area and those women who have both types of kin easily accessible.

The different pattern for women who have both siblings and children living nearby is largely accounted for by the relatively low average morale of the group of ten women who are fully engaged, i.e., married women under sixty-five years of age who have not yet experienced a reduction in object cathexis. The average morale score of this group of ten women is only 1.5 as compared with 2.5 for those with siblings only and 2.0 for those with children only. Another distinguishing characteristic of this group is that most of them still have children living in their homes. Their low morale is somewhat surprising since their situation might be assumed to provide a "rich, full life." However, satisfactions with place of residence and/or age, were the biggest contributions to the morale scores in this group of women. All but two reported that they would like to see more of their relatives, neighbors, or friends. These findings may indicate that these women would like more freedom from their home responsibilities and the opportunity for different types of social interactions, such as might be found in the later stages of disengagement.

The other group of 22 men and 21 women, who do not have children or siblings easily accessible and do not show the changes in morale associated with stages in the disengagement process, comprise approximately one fifth of the total group in the study. The level of morale of this group is lower than that of any other group, particularly at the beginning and end stages of disengagement. The average morale score of the 22 men, as a whole, is 1.5. The comparable figure for women is only 0.9, partially because none of the 21 women in this category expresses complete satisfaction with the frequency of social contacts, compared to approximately one third of the men in the same category and approximately one third of the men and women in all other categories. Both men and women in this group, however, express more satisfaction in the other three areas of the morale index (age, place of residence, and weekend activities) than the other men and women in the study who have children or siblings living nearby.

While the individual morale scores and their components are thought to have little significance except as indices of the relative levels of morale, it is of some interest to note the general factors contributing to the changes in morale levels mentioned in Table VII–1. Of the four morale components (residence, age, weekend activities, and frequency of social contacts), place of residence and weekend activities contribute most to the total morale scores of the 85 men and 83 women who have children and siblings living in the Kansas City area. As shown in Table VII–2, 53 men (62.4 per cent) and 47 women (56.6 per cent) say that there is no other place in the

TABLE VII–2

RESPONDENTS [a] INDICATING SATISFACTION WITH INDIVIDUAL ITEMS USED AS BASES OF TOTAL MORALE SCORES

		Per Cent of Total Respondents			
Stage of Disengagement	Total Respondents	Residen-tial Area	Age	Weekend Activities	Social Contacts
Men	85	62.4	29.4	52.9	32.9
Stage 1	23	73.9	30.4	60.9	47.8
Stage 2	20	45.0	27.3	63.6	27.3
Stage 3	13	46.2	23.1	38.5	7.7
Stage 4	29	72.4	27.6	48.3	37.9
Women	83	56.6	38.6	48.2	27.7
Stage 1	13	46.2	53.8	38.5	30.8
Stage 2	21	47.6	42.9	42.9	38.1
Stage 3	25	40.0	36.0	48.0	16.0
Stage 4	24	87.5	29.2	58.3	29.2

[a] Includes only those who have siblings and/or children living in the Kansas City area.

city they wish to live. There are 45 men (52.9 per cent) and 40 women (48.2 per cent) who are satisfied with their weekend activities. There are, however, only 25 men and 32 women who say that they like their ages, and 28 men and 23 women are completely satisfied with the amount of contact with their relatives, neighbors, and friends. The difference between men and women in this respect is not surprising. It should be noted, however, that the odds against scoring 1 on this question are perhaps higher than on any of the other three questions used for the morale scale because of the three-part structure of the question. A response of dissatisfaction to any one part of the question precludes scoring on the total question.

It is still possible, however, to compare the frequency of responses indicating satisfaction (or lack of dissatisfaction) with each of the items at different stages of disengagement.

Differences between men and women are apparent when separate stages of the disengagement process are considered in the following way. As shown in Table VII–2, residence and social contacts are the only areas of satisfaction that, to a statistically significant degree, follow the pattern of the total morale scores, namely, decreasing satisfaction in the transition stages followed by an increase in the final or fourth stage of disengagement. This is particularly true for men and probably would be more pronounced in the women except for those women who are fully engaged with a central task which happens to include children still living in their homes. The low level of morale in this group, as compared with fully engaged men, is evident in three of the four areas of the total morale index: residence, weekend activities, and social contacts. Satisfaction with their ages, however, is reported more often (53.8 per cent) by this group of women than by any other group of women or men. Among men, the proportions reporting satisfaction with age remain fairly constant, ranging from 23.1 to 30.4 per cent throughout the disengagement process. Among women, however, reports of satisfaction with age decrease consistently from 53.8 per cent at Stage 1 to 29.2 per cent at Stage 4 and reports of satisfaction with weekend activities increase from 38.5 per cent at Stage 1 to 58.3 per cent at Stage 4. The proportions of men who are satisfied with their weekend activities decrease from 60.9 and 63.6 at Stages 1 and 2 respectively, to 38.5 and 48.3 at Stages 3 and 4. This change in Stages 3 and 4, although not statistically significant, may reflect changes in attitudes toward weekend activities after retirement.

Summing up, we have found that it is not uncommon to find general improvement in total morale and increasing satisfaction in most of the areas of the morale index in the later stages of the disengagement process among this group of healthy, economically independent men and women.

The notable exceptions are age for both men and women and weekend activities for men. This is still apparent in an analysis of morale scores taken on the same people after a lapse of two years, based on responses to the same question at the third and fifth interviews. The fifth interview took place two years after the third interview with a total of 81 men and 75 women available for the comparison. Those not scored at the fifth interview were lost from the panel because they no longer wished to participate in the study, or had moved, or died. Deaths account for heavy losses among those fully disengaged (Stage 4). The numbers are somewhat small for comparisons of males and females according to the types of kin living in the Kansas City area. Our chief concern, however, is a comparison of the changes associated with stages in the disengagement process.

There are no changes in the total morale scores of 61, or 39.1 per cent, of the 156 respondents who had measures of morale again after a lapse of two years. A total of 41, or 26.3 per cent, decreased and 54, or 34.6 per cent, increased. Comparable data are presented in Table VII–3 for men and women who have no children or siblings living in the same area and for men and women who have one or the other or both living in the same area. In each category, there are relatively more improvements in morale at the later stages of disengagement than at the earlier stages. Among men who have children and/or siblings available in the same area, there are 15 decreases and 9 increases at Stages 1-2, as compared to 6 decreases and 8 increases at Stages 3-4. Among women with similar types of kin available, there were 9 decreases and 3 increases in Stages 1 and 2. In the later stages of disengagement, however, the situation is reversed, with 5 decreases and 15 increases. This seems to confirm the earlier finding of a general improvement in morale as disengagement increases. These improvements in morale in the later stages of disengagement seem to represent changes in attitude toward the environment rather than actual changing of environment, since it is known that not many environmental changes actually took place in the two-year interval between Interviews 3 and 5.

TABLE VII–3

COMPARISON OF MORALE SCORES BASED ON THIRD AND FIFTH INTERVIEWS

Status of Respondents	Total [a] Respondents	Per Cent of Total Respondents		
		Lower at 5th	No Change	Higher at 5th
No siblings or children				
Male	17	11.8	23.5	64.7
Stages 1–2	10	10.0	30.0	60.0
Stages 3–4	7	14.2	14.2	71.4
Female	18	22.2	33.3	44.4
Stages 1–2	6	33.3	33.3	33.3
Stages 3–4	12	16.7	33.3	50.0
Siblings and/or children				
Male	64	32.8	40.6	26.6
Stages 1–2	38	39.5	36.8	23.7
Stages 3–4	26	23.1	46.2	30.8
Female	57	24.6	43.9	31.6
Stages 1–2	25	36.0	52.0	12.0
Stages 3–4	32	15.6	37.5	46.9

[a] Includes only those available for the fifth interview.

While it might be argued that the relatively higher levels of morale among the totally disengaged, as compared to the partially disengaged, could be associated with the different methods for selecting the older and younger respondents, a comparison of the morale scores of those selected by the two methods at the same stages in the disengagement process gives no indication that this is so.

In conclusion, we should point out that numerous studies have reported demoralization among older people. Our results seem to indicate that demoralization is only temporary among older people. This finding agrees with a suggestion made by Blenckner (12) regarding the satisfactions of an aging group which she was studying. However, we cannot preclude the possibility that our results are partly a function of our morale-measuring instrument, or that other studies do not discriminate among the various stages of disengagement. Future studies might usefully improve on the instrument used for measurement, and discriminate more finely among the various stages of disengagement.

CHAPTER VIII

Retirement and Widowhood

THIS BOOK has been concerned with theory rather than problems, and we have therefore not made any special study of retirement. However, it has been obvious throughout our analysis that the disengagement process is consistently different in detail for men and women, and this, we shall argue, has three basic causes. The first is the difference in the roles men and women play in modern industrial society; the second is the higher value placed on skill than on wisdom which has special implications for men and their working roles; the third is the difference in the death rates of men and of women. Retirement and widowhood represent the points at which the central tasks of men and women are terminated, and they can usefully be considered markers of the disengagement process. Therefore, we shall here draw together

143

some of our findings and discuss these two crisis points in terms of the causes for the differences in response to them. However, the data to support new formulations about retirement and widowhood are sketchy, and this chapter is therefore composed, for the most part, of new hypotheses related to the theory of disengagement.

■ Retirement

Retirement is not an important problem for women because, as we pointed out in Chapters IV and V, working seems to make little difference to them.* It is as though they add work to their lives, the way they would add a club membership. However, we do not have in our study group professional and intellectual women who may have different attitudes because they have more investment in their work. We do have thirty-six women who are working, sixteen of whom are married. To these women, working seems an activity to augment the income and fill up time; it does not express the whole woman in the way that work, no matter how uncongenial, tends to express the whole man. Neither is it connected, for these women, with morale score. The basic division of labor between men and women assigns to the woman the task of sociability, of keeping the social systems she belongs to free of tension, of maintaining the system's integrity against disruptive inner disturbances.

We have seen in Chapters IV and V that more women than men keep in close touch with all kinds of kinsmen, and that they more often have close solidary relationships with children and siblings. Men do not respond with reduced cathexis to children's leaving home, as women do. Generally speaking, too, role loss follows a different pattern for women, being more

---

* Among the women, working affected only one variable, although we examined all of them. This was orientation-to-interaction. In regard to the reward sought, the working women resembled the working men.

variable than for men and more subject to fluctuation. As we saw in Table 1 of Chapter IV, younger men have fewer roles than younger women, but they do not lose their roles as spouse and kinsman as they get older; only work and voluntary organizations show a marked decline. This seems to reflect a kind of buffering action performed by the socio-emotional role —as if women stood between men and the world of sociability, religion, and general culture in much the same way that men stand between women and the economic world. In other words, women mediate socio-emotional relationships for men, as men mediate instrumental ones for women. In Chapter IV, we saw that women do not feel the loss of responsibility about domestic tasks the way men do about work. Because their central function is socio-emotional, they apparently do not regret the passing of the attendant instrumental tasks.

The difference between men and women in authoritarianism, discussed in Chapter V, is probably related to this role difference. Women, charged with the job of tension management within their membership groups, may be more sensitive to the actions of others, more able to sympathize with their acts, more able to take their roles, and hence, during the periods of their lives when they are most tightly engaged, more in sympathy with others and therefore less authoritarian (68). The authoritarian scores of the men show the same tendency as the women's, but the differences are not nearly so marked, suggesting that a narrow experience has the same effect upon the men as upon the women, but that the women, because of their roles, are more sensitively responsive to it. For men, on the other hand, work is the central task, the index of prestige in the community, the measure of success, and, in a very real sense, an expression of the whole man. Retirement, for these reasons, is a man's problem. It is a problem which has been commented on extensively.* However, some authors

* See, for example, Chapter 11 of Tibbits, reference 73.

such as Tyhurst (75) and Streib (70, 71) have found that most men find satisfactory solutions to the problems of retirement. In this chapter, we will consider retirement and widowhood as transition states, and discuss the problems they raise and the resolutions that are possible.

In the first place, retirement is society's permission to men to disengage. Furthermore, retirement policies, which are geared to retiring echelons of men, on the whole disregard the issue of function. A few men with particularly valuable skills may have difficulty obtaining permission to disengage, but for most men it is automatic. Secondly, as we saw in Chapter V, most men appear to be ready to disengage—that is, to have withdrawn cathexis from the environment—by the time they retire. As one respondent says, "When we got back from my vacation last year, I found all that work piled up—nobody had done it—I got disgusted and retired a year earlier than I needed to." There is some reason to think that most men anticipate retirement—some even eagerly. Yet, because retirement signals the end of the central task and leaves men with a set of skills for which there is no further need and, indeed, requires of them in many cases a new set of skills, it causes an important, if temporary, discontinuity.

Nevertheless, there are important exceptions even to this generalization. Some occupations have by their very nature a style more compatible with the disengaged condition. We know from other studies that retirement for university professors means "freedom to get some work done (58)," and that most people with intellectual occupations look upon retirement as simply a rather favorable shift to a different type of work. Furthermore, men in expressive occupations apparently continue into old age without feeling the demoralization which can attend working for too long. Thus, preachers, artists, some teachers, and many entertainers either do not retire at all or move easily into the expressive orientation of the old. Sometimes men misjudge their capacity to shift their type of activity. One man who is newly retired says, when he is asked if he has missed his work, "Not a bit. Hasn't worried me a bit, and I don't think it will. I'll just substitute other activities for my work." But this is the same man whose wife complained bitterly to the interviewer that he was demanding and dependent and that her life had been very difficult since his retirement, because she had had to give up many of her customary activities to dance attendance upon him.

■ **Problems Raised by Retirement**

For most men, retirement poses three basic problems. First, they cannot move to pure sociability, because that is characteristic of women; they do not feel at home with sociability for its own sake, but require some instrumental activity to mediate their relationships. However, an age-graded society of advanced industrial technology, whose economic system has trouble consuming what it produces, does not want such men to be engaged in serious instrumental activities. Men must find some way of orienting themselves so that they develop new skills and learn to feel comfortable acting in types of role that have been considered characteristic of women. They must either compete with women for socio-emotional roles or find mediating instrumental tasks through which to relate.

The second retirement problem is loss of status identity. Men have been used to endowing their wives and children with such prestige as their occupation commanded, and for most men this is seriously weakened by retirement. Only men whose accomplishments have been accumulative, and not easily forgotten can continue to articulate their families to society through their occupational history.

The third problem retirement poses for men is the loss of a peer group. The horizontal solidarity of a lifetime is seriously disrupted by retirement, and men must integrate themselves into a new membership group and adjust to a new intimacy with their wives. In our panel, only a tiny fraction of the retired men report keeping in touch with work colleagues. No matter how solid working groups are, there seems to have to be a mediating reason for the relationship; once the reason is gone, the relationship is difficult. For most men, wives mediate; they connect men with kinship systems; in fact, a wife is often closer to her husband's kin than he is himself. When a man retires and loses his membership group, he has to spend more of his time with his wife and her companions. But as men grow older, their wives tend to become more and more engaged with groups of widows because their friends and kindred have lost their husbands. This means that a retired male has difficulty finding a membership group unless he has a large kindred, because although it is possible for a man to be integrated into a kinship group of surviving women, it is impossible for him to be integrated into a group of widows to whom he is not related.*

Townsend (74) reports that working-class Englishmen lead their social lives in pubs, with other men; retirement cuts them off from this solidary relationship because they no longer have money for beer. Thus, when they are old they are demoralized by being denied the companionship of men. Among our sample there is a small group of retired men who have very low morale. Their alienation scores are high—that is, they are out of sympathy with the major optimistic norms of society—and they have no available siblings. They appear to be suffering from a marked loss of horizontal ties, because they have no siblings to turn to in place of working companions. It is probably not retirement that has lowered their morale so much as the lack of any alternative to it. In other words, it is not the loss of work which is difficult for men, but rather the loss of the types of

---

* There may be exceptions to this among the well-to-do, where widowed men are much in demand for dinner parties, and so on.

relationships which have accompanied work and which are mediated through the performance of a task. On the other hand, women act the roles of daughter, mother, and grandmother, shifting back and forth, from helping to being helped, in mutually dependent and closely knit relationships throughout their life cycle. There is no discontinuity; only the emphasis changes. We do not have this inter-generational solidarity among women in America, as we pointed out earlier, probably because we do not have a patriarchal system, but we do have an analogous division of labor, between work and sociability with kin, which makes aging considerably smoother for women.

■ Solutions to Retirement Problems

To sum up, retirement is a visible point in the transition between engagement and disengagement, and may temporarily lower a man's morale by presenting three problems. First, he can no longer articulate himself and his family into society via the occupational structure, and hence he loses a lifelong identity. Second, his valued occupational skills probably become obsolete. Although he has withdrawn cathexis from his work, a man is not necessarily anxious to learn a new set of socio-emotional skills to replace the instrumental ones he is giving up. It is characteristic of this problem that only a temporary set of new skills is needed.* As we shall point out in Chapter XI, men and women who survive to extreme old age are, in the matter of role performance, virtually indistinguishable. The third problem of retirement arises from the abrupt disengagement from the accustomed horizontal solidarity with peers, sometimes with no alternative membership group available. In spite of these three major problems, men, according to Streib (70, 71), experience retirement as a

---

* It is at this point that we meet the "implicit theory" discussed in Chapter II, and depart from it again. The retiring man does need new roles to replace the one he is losing, but he needs them only temporarily and not as a means of expanding his life, according to our view.

trauma from which they quite quickly recover. How is it that so many men seem able to resolve these problems satisfactorily? This is not a subject we have explored directly in this study, but we have some impressionistic evidence of our own, and some data are available from other sources. Theory suggests further reasons.

The problem of losing occupational identity may eventually be self-resolving. The same process of turning inward, which removed cathexis from the occupational world in the first place, probably allows men to identify themselves not with what they do now but with what they have done.* A process of reintegrating one's own past history may produce a solid core of identity in terms of what has been. This very process may then turn back upon itself to allow the removal of still more cathexis from the present. This willingness to be disengaged

---

* The following quotation (from the Paul Hightower *Senior Forum,* daily newspaper column, syndicated and copyrighted by General Features Corporation) illustrates the adjustment to retirement very clearly and also the normative position of the columnist, acting on the assumptions of the implicit theory outlined in Chapter II.

By PAUL HIGHTOWER

"(Q) I retired three years ago from a better job than most men have. I got—and still have—more income than most retired people get.

"I chose to stay on in the nice residential community where my wife and I had lived for 18 years.

"For almost a year I watched my neighbors go to work every morning and come back at night, watched the mailman and the milkman come and go, and dwelt on the fact that I was a has-been who was now shoved aside to live in a world of women and children.

"But then I recovered.

"Slowly, it no longer mattered to me that I was not part of a workaday world. The grass in my yard grew more important to me than who got promoted today. My roses and rusting gutters were a way of life too.

"Where we would go next winter, when our grandchildren would visit us next, and the state of my rheumatism became as absorbing as my office had once been.

"I think nature has a magnificent way of conditioning us for the various ages of life. I think it has conditioned me well. I just don't care any more about business. I care instead about the chrysanthemums in my backyard. H.D.F.

"(A) Thank you, sir. You are what the psychiatrist would call a well-adjusted individual. You are not going anywhere and you'll never be President of the U.S. But you are adjusted."

may be, in psychological terms, a continuation of the readiness to disengage which adumbrates the process in the first place. Men may emerge from this process with a self-image of the "wise old man," and this may be the reason why men, as they get older and are free from the everyday normative control of the working world, often talk in broad and sweeping statements. Being able to do this without being told to either put up or shut up may compensate for the loss of the instrumental role. Finally, they may be *unable* to reintegrate into the instrumental world because their normative control is weak and their cathexis is low.

The problem of finding a suitable membership group produces a visible strain for many men. Among our panel members we see evidence of attempts to resolve this strain. Wives of retired men sometimes volunteered to the interviewer that they found their husband's leisure very burdensome. Some men, in fact, cannot stand retirement and shortly take on new work. They usually do not stay long at any one job, but it is not uncommon for men to become re-engaged with the working world more than once before they finally leave it. In a study made in Washington of healthy old men, Yarrow (82) found the same thing—retirement is not as abrupt as we have thought. Many men seem to practice for retirement by giving up work, starting again, and changing their status several times before finally retiring for good.

Some men find things to do that require instrumental skills but are not formally designated as work—some retire to country places and spend a lot of time fishing. Many of our panel told us that when they retired they would fish all day. They perceive this as a particularly fine activity because it is not only pleasurable but also provides food.* In the same vein, a newly retired panel member told how the widows of all his closest

---

* In the nature of our sample, we miss the bona-fide country-dwelling fishermen.

friends saved their chores for him. The first six months of his retirement had been spent puttying windows, planing door-jambs, and fixing screen windows. He felt that just maintaining his own and all their houses would keep him occupied quite comfortably from then on.

Many recreational programs for retired men are based on the belief that old age is a time for leisure. But they overlook the basic problem that men face: they must either learn to relate like women or find activities that resemble work. An official of a New York City recreational center tells us that men attend the program more regularly when they are made to come at nine in the morning and remain until five. Although their activities are no different, these worklike circumstances make them attend more faithfully. One recreation center * has organized its entire program around men's activities—educa-tion tours, and constructive projects—while the women are or-ganized as if in auxiliaries to the men. In such a way it is possible to attract a large number of men to the center. A worker in another center says that men enjoy learning skills they did not have when they joined the program. They do not like to "play" but to "play at work." On the other hand, they never select "serious work" skills at which they have earned their living. Retired carpenters join the pottery group, and re-tired plumbers make furniture. This anecdote illustrates an important principle. It is not the loss of the specific content of the occupatonal role which traumatizes men but the loss of *general instrumentality*. Indeed, all evidence suggests that men are pleased to disengage from specific tasks, to withdraw their cathexis from the content of work, but to change their entire manner of relating is apparently more than they are able to manage.

The problem of finding a new membership group is less

* Francis McHale, in a personal communication.

easy to solve. As Townsend (74) has said, isolation is not a serious matter for very old people because, being so self-pre-occupied, they need only someone to care about what happens to them. It is the transition period between retirement and extreme old age that we are discussing here. Although we have no quantitative evidence, it is our impression that a kind of technical reintegration with kindred is very important for re-tired men. A surprising number of them construct genealogies. This activity involves quasi-relationships, gives a sense of mem-bership, but at the same time involves very little diffuse obliga-tion. It brings into the interactional orbit sisters and cousins who have been forgotten, and they in turn are able to say where lost kindred can be found. It is like drawing a shawl around one's shoulders—a closing of the ranks against time, a preparation for extreme old age.

Apparently siblings or substitutes must exist if the morale of men is to be maintained.* *If health care and economic in-dependence are guaranteed,* those few retired men who cannot reintegrate with a membership group and cannot shift their skills are probably the only true "problem" group among old people in society. Generally speaking, our findings support those of Streib (71) and Tyhurst (75) in that retirement † in itself does not appear to be a problem for most men; it is the lack of horizontal ties and of a suitable way of relating, which retirement may carry with it, that seem to make trouble. We

---

* The morale of men in all age groups is higher if they have siblings.

† A personnel officer in a large industry writes, "We find that an increasing number of employees are voluntarily electing early retirement each year before age 65. For example, in 1959, of the 611 employees in this company who went on retirement, about 31 per cent, or 187, went on early retirement. [Another large company] finds that the average woman retires at age 57 and the man at 62. [Still another large-company experience] in 1959 showed that 80 per cent of the hourly employees retired before the mandatory retirement age of 68. With good company retirement and savings plans plus hospital benefits, most persons make a very satisfactory adjustment to retirement." Personal communication from J. C. Hurley, Employee Relations Department, Standard Oil Company (Indiana).

differ here from a substantial number of authors who consider retirement inherently difficult for all men.

■ **Widowhood**

Widowhood is to women what retirement is to men, the conclusion of the central task of adult life and, at the same time, formal permission to disengage. Furthermore, the difference in the death rate means that widowhood is a common fate of women; in our study group, it is almost as common as retirement for men. Of the 99 men and women over sixty-five for whom all data are available, there are 38 retired men, 32 widowed women, 16 married women, and 13 working men. Widowhood marks a transition state, as does retirement, and as we can see in Table VIII–1, it is a state to which women appear, on the whole, to adapt successfully.

TABLE VIII–1
Morale by Sex, Work, and Marital Status
(Those over sixty-five only)

Respondents	Number Inter- viewed	Morale			Per Cent	
		Low (0–1)	Medium (2)	High (3–4)	Low Morale	High Morale
Total	99	44	27	28	44.4	28.3
Married women	16	10	0	6	62.5	37.5
Widowed women	32	13	9	10	40.6	31.3
Retired men	38	15	12	11	39.5	28.9
Working men	13	6	6	1	46.2	7.7

Just as retirement for women is non-modal, so is widower-hood for men. However, there is a very important asymmetry between the two conditions. As we remarked above, retirement for women is without importance and does not seem to ruffle the waters. On the other hand, widowerhood is a desolating experience for men. It is not anticipated, and it leaves a man bereft of the mediator into the world of kinship and culture whom he has relied upon. We will contrast these two non-modal transition states in more detail later, when we summarize the differences in patterns of disengagement between men and women.

■ **Problems of Widowhood**

The problems facing widows are also threefold. First, they lose a highly cathected object abruptly which is most traumatic if sexual involvement is still high. Except for this intimacy, marriage is less functional as the life span progresses, because the task of socializing children is over, and there remains only the job of tension management. Once sexuality becomes irrelevant, there is some question whether the marriage bond is any more effective for this purpose than, for example, the sibling tie. Wives and sisters, brothers and husbands, all have the important quality of knowing and appreciating past accomplishments and difficulties and of sharing memories.

As we shall see in the next chapter, the very old seem to be able to relate to all comers in much the same way. Birren (11) has suggested semifacetiously that the biological organism is "programmed" only until the end of childbearing; after that, aging is essentially a random event. Analogously, marriage can be thought of as programmed until the central task of child-raising is over. At that point, a reconstitution of the relationship must occur, or the marriage becomes non-functional.

However shifting the nature of the marriage bond may be in later life, there is no doubt that widowhood presents a problem in redistribution of cathexis. As we see in Table VIII–1, the married women are significantly polarized in terms of high and low morale, although this may be partly because the items in the index are more centrally important to women than to men. We may be seeing here a high-morale group with a continuing satisfactory intimacy in the marriage, and a low-morale group frustrated by the inability to move on to the horizontal type of relationship with peers. The continuation of an active sexual relationship may be vital here. We do not know.

Besides the redistribution of cathexis, the widow faces a second problem—finding a method of integrating herself into the social systems around her. A woman is usually given her social identity through her husband's occupation, and at his death she must find a way to reconstitute her identity as a person who was once the wife of a certain man. In this, she faces the same problem as the man at retirement. The widow must also use her later years to integrate her life experience satisfactorily, and to identify herself as a person who performed her central task adequately and then terminated it through no fault of her own.

The third problem of widowhood is that of shifting from the organic solidarity of the marriage, with its divided labor and mutual dependency, to the mechanical solidarity of membership in a group of unattached women. In this, widowhood is the opposite of retirement, because men characteristically lose their peers and acquire a new close relationship with their wives.

■ Solutions to Problems of Widowhood

On the whole, the resolutions of these problems of disengagement are much easier for women than for men. Probably the most difficult hurdle for the newly widowed woman is the loss of the intimate relationship, if it has been valued, and here she faces the basically irreconcilable problem which men face upon losing the instrumental role. However, as women age this becomes less salient a problem, and although we do not know its dimensions, it is, in many cases, probably not severe.

Integrating herself into both the larger society and small social systems without a husband is a problem, but a relatively easy one for a widow. In the first place, widowhood is an honored state. There is a certain consideration afforded to widows which has no counterpart in society's general stance toward retired men. In the second place, widows are identified to a large degree with their late husbands' careers, and though they may lose financial status, they do not need to lose such prestige as their husbands had at the same time. Furthermore, women have always been the mediators of relationships with kindred, and while there is some evidence suggesting that women do not maintain close ties with their dead husbands' kin, it is probable that they quickly revive ties with their own. Furthermore, if they have children, they are able to identify with them, their careers, and their successes. Indeed, many spontaneous remarks about the gratifying success of children were made to our interviewers. Finally, widows have a ready-made peer group in other widows, and there is reason to believe that they join this very happily. There is, in fact, some evidence in our interviews of considerable frustration among some married women over being unable to join the society of widows, a frustration especially true of the wives of retired husbands.

In most respects widowhood fortifies disengagement. The transition to horizontal, less demanding ties is harmonious with reorientation to the less involved relationships of the fully disengaged person. The reintegration with kindred leads to the small, tight, supportive social system characteristic, as we saw in Chapter IV, of extreme old age. Once the shock of loss is overcome, widowhood, unlike retirement, presents problems which the disengaging process itself seems tailor-made to resolve.

Of course, not all women respond favorably to the widowed state. Some of our study group have low morale, and we know that the suicide rate is high among widows. Perhaps we are dealing, in our study group, with survivors of this transition, and have missed the depressed, despondent widows, because they did not meet our criteria of good health and economic stability.

On the whole, the women of our group respond favorably to growing old, as we have shown in Chapter VII. This may be because both widowhood and children's leaving home are harmonious with the disengagement process. In our panel we found some evidence of a desire to gallivant once the cares of middle age are over. One respondent who had raised a family of eight children declared that as soon as her husband retired she was going to be "just like a gypsy." Many women said, "I love to go," an idiom of the area, which describes any active recreation.

People who have worked with recreation groups for the aged assure us that older women love to be on the move. They enjoy bus rides and outings, just for the fun of moving around, while men, in contrast, prefer activities to be useful or educational. A disengaging dressmaker of our acquaintance wishes she had a motorcycle so that she could ride quickly to all the weddings and graduations she makes dresses for! This tendency among women seems to be the outer expression of the increase of aggressiveness that we reported in Chapter VI. Men seem to retreat gladly from active mastery with age, while women, in their new freedom, achieve a kind of activity that is a counterpoise to their life experience. Certainly our empirical observations suggest that the disengaged older man is a thoughtful, reflective, perhaps somewhat opinionated "wise man," while the disengaged older woman is an active, carefree, perhaps even frivolous "girl." In the next chapter, however, we shall see that this is only a stage. In the end, the men and women are remarkably similar; both display in their eighties and nineties the same pattern of dependency, self-satisfaction, self-centeredness, and placidity.

Finally, we can draw together the similarities and differences of retirement and widowhood as the most visible markers in the disengagement process. As we have suggested earlier, there are important psychological crises in middle age for both men and women, but they have not been nearly so carefully explored as the public shifts which occur later, and which are, in their nature, rites of passage.

On the whole, men make an abrupt transition from the engaged to the disengaged state, but it is soon resolved; women have a smoother passage, which lasts longer. Men are removed from a peer group and returned to a close relationship, and must somehow resolve this "backward" step. Women lose an intimate relationship and become free to join less demanding horizontal groupings—thereby moving in the same direction as the disengagement process. Men lose the right to exercise their chief skills and lose their lifelong instrumental roles. Women remain in their same basic socio-emotional roles and need to learn no new skills but, rather, to redirect their old ones. Furthermore, although men in many cases can practice at retiring, women lose their central role slowly. First they become unable to bear children, and then their children leave home. Finally they become widows. There is time to absorb each stage in the well-spaced transition.

The atypical aging experiences differ, too. As we have said, retirement has little meaning for women, whereas widowerhood is a serious blow for men, especially if they do not consider remarriage. Furthermore, the completely stripped condition in which the individual has no one available—no spouse, no job, and no close kin—is considerably more devastating for men than for women because women are used to the mediating role. They have mediated between their husbands and their kindred, between their children and the school, between their family and the neighborhood, whereas men have been used to conferring status on the family through their occupations, and not primarily through their ability to relate. Because of this, women are much better able than men to establish quasi-relationships resembling kinship ties, and thus fill the gap when there is no one else. Furthermore, they are much better able to live alone, because they are in command of the necessary domestic skills and it is appropriate for them to exercise them. This is not so for men; even when they are good at housework, they are ashamed of it.

We see, in summary, that the nature of the modern industrial world, which does not make use of the accumulated wisdom of men, creates an important asymmetry in old age. If we were a traditional people, there would be honored roles that old men could assume. In the soap-opera comic strips, there is no wise old man to match the widow Mary Worth. As it is, those who have special skills and knowledge that society cannot afford to lose are treated with great respect. Men like Einstein, for example, are treated in old age as all men might be in a society where knowledge, being tradition, was as valuable as Einstein's. We have modern science to thank in a very real sense for the asymmetry which makes ours, in old age, a woman's world.

CHAPTER IX

Two Cases: The Main Theme of Disengagement

IN THIS CHAPTER, we shall describe two respondents who illustrate the foregoing discussions. We will present only that material from their life stories which elaborates and enhances the meaning of the disengagement process. The first case is that of a man who was sixty-eight at the beginning of the study. He appears to be gradually working free of the demands of instrumentality. He is doing this with considerable success, and is only moderately distressed by the loss of autonomy which disengagement carries with it. He illustrates both the heightened awareness of self and the quiescence of feeling and emotion which characterize most of our male respondents. The second respondent is a woman of sixty-two, still fully engaged and, like the man, in the upper half of the morale distribution. She is beginning to loosen the mutually dependent and responsible bonds with her children and to develop less binding horizontal ties. In contrast to the increased quiescence of the man, she is beginning to develop the greater expressiveness and aggressiveness characteristic of the older women.

■ **Mr. Allen: A Study in Disengagement**

Mr. Allen was employed in a responsible clerical position when we first interviewed him, but he retired shortly afterward. Living with his wife in a pleasant middle-income home, and within reasonable visiting distance of his children, he was, during our first contacts with him, in the process of readjusting his habits to retirement. Mr. Allen's entire life had been one of fairly regular progress. His parents valued schooling, and aided their son as much as they could. Mr. Allen subscribes to their regard for education, and has passed it on to his own children. After working at two or three interesting jobs without sufficient promise, Mr. Allen took a position in the organization he was about to be retired from when we found him.

Mr. Allen's scores on our engagement measures are roughly typical of our panel. His Role Count is 5, just at the median; Interaction Index is 3, also average. His total amount of actual interaction with others, however, is somewhat low, falling within the lowest third of the distribution. This score pattern derives from his way of life in retirement, in which his primary interactions are with his wife, occasionally with his children, and less frequently with his friends and his church organization.

The quality and content of this interaction pattern can be seen from Mr. Allen's response to our request for a description of his typical weekend activities. Shortly before retirement his weekend was as follows:

SATURDAY: I don't work on Saturday. I may work in the yard—plant flowers, mow grass, work on property. [How about the afternoon?] May go to the grocery with my wife. I rest quite a bit, relax, read, watch TV. [How about Saturday night?] Sometimes watch TV or have friends in for bridge. Haven't been to a movie in years.

SUNDAY [Morning]: Sunday school and church. I'm no longer active in promotion work as I used to be. [Afternoon]: We may go to visit [children]—it's usually a full-day project because of distance. Otherwise I rest, may have relatives in, or we sit on the front porch. [Evening]: Watch TV—rarely go out Sunday night.

Mr. Allen seems to find this schedule fairly satisfactory. When asked what he enjoys most, he finds it hard to specify anything in particular. "Hardly know what to say," he reports, but finally notes that he and his wife go to an outdoor theatre on Friday nights, and that they enjoy this. He repeats, however, that they "also [enjoy] the rest and relaxation." Similarly, he cannot think of anything unsatisfactory about these weekends. "I can't say as there are less enjoyable things. We may take a drive and that's enjoyable."

Three years later, and two years after his retirement, his pattern is markedly similar. As he then reports:

Well, I'm up at seven, and eat breakfast. Then I read the papers and listen to the news on the radio. Then there are various household tasks. When the weather's good, I'm out in the yard with my roses. I had forty varieties [in a former residence] and I hope I can do as well here. Then I might taxi my wife to her bridge group or downtown shopping. If I do that, I have my lunch downtown. If I've got two or three hours to kill, I come home and read. I can never get enough reading. In the evening we might visit [children] or we might play bridge with friends. And then there's always my church organization. Once a month we have a dinner meeting and there's an enormous amount of work to be done preparing for that.

There has been some shift in emphasis in these activities. Mr. Allen reports an increase in the time spent reading and gardening. Also increased is church activity. This occurred the year after retirement, but it has subsequently slackened again.

One important characteristic of Mr. Allen since we have known him has been his readiness to give up his strong bonds to work. His earlier history was one of competence, devotion, and pride in accomplishment. Yet on retiring he was able to alter this pattern with comparative ease, and with only minor twinges of guilt and feelings of loss. In common with many of our more successful male "disengagers," Mr. Allen can point with pride to a past history of instrumental success, but he does not feel still bound to these goals. The first clue he gave to this shift in attitude was his report that he could have stayed at work another year. He noticed, however, that the work was increasing, owing to fewer employees, "and I felt my health would suffer and so it was time to quit."

In the year before retirement, he was less involved with his work than his reports of his earlier career would suggest he had once been. When he was asked what part of the day he found least enjoyable, his response indicated a swing away from instrumental activity. He says, "I don't know anything I dislike particularly in the run of the day. At work there's a mental strain, so you might say the hours of relaxation are the more enjoyable."

Anticipating the gap in his time schedule, he expected no difficulty, as he points out, since he would "just substitute other activities for my work." This he has done, but with the same reduced sense of commitment implied by his ease in giving up work. As he reports a year after retirement:

No, I'm not disappointed [with retirement]. Of course, if your health fails you have a problem. But that wouldn't have anything to do with retirement—it would be the same problem under any circumstances. The main thing is to keep interested, alert and active. It's good to have time to relax to do what you please. I'm enjoying that, but I'll also have interests. I took up Spanish last year, and had to drop it because I was too busy [at work before retirement] but I think I'll start again.

Implicit in his statement is the notion that "interests" are important but can be started or dropped with ease and are, in any case, closely related to "relaxing" and "doing what you please." This emphasis on comparative freedom and reduced responsibility was restated by Mr. Allen when he was asked a year later, "What are the best things about being the age you are?" He says, "[You're] not forced at this stage to do any particular thing. Do as I please and come and go as I please. Not the responsibilities you had earlier in life."

Mr. Allen's reduced involvement was belied somewhat by his post-retirement increase in church activities. This included a variety of activities—Sunday-school teaching, adult-discussion-group work, planning for speakers and dinners, planning joint meetings with the men's and women's groups. Throughout all these enterprises, however, he seemed to focus upon those that do not demand interpersonal responsibilities. Working at home on programs, newsletters, and letters to "established" and "outstanding" people regarding speaking engagements interested him greatly, as did pure sociability. He comments in his interview on how "busy" he is kept by these productive yet uninvolving activities. He has found a "worklike" activity as a temporary solution to his loss of instrumentality. When he is directly involved with others in a joint church venture, his interest is in sociability more than in religion. Though he is a sincerely religious man, he remembers the pleasant people he met, not the things he did. "I've led men in the church and have made hosts of friends. . . . There's an association [in the church] that elderly people enjoy. . . . There's an inward feeling, loving your fellow men." He comments further on certain dogma and rituals in his church and indicates he is completely liberal about them. "If we change our form of [rituals] it would be all right with me. I would prefer that people choose their own form. . . . It's only a matter of form—and either way doesn't get you any place—Heaven or Hell—it's the people, not the form, that matter."

The striking aspects of Mr. Allen's post-retirement behavior have been his desire to have something to keep him busy, his short-range planning, his revised sense of time, and his inner satisfaction with his past accomplishments. His increased, generally pleasant, but not binding, sociability have aided him in this transition. Illustrating one of the points in Chapter VIII, he finds sociability more comfortable if it is in a joblike context. His orientation blankets his slight resentment at loss of autonomy. Commenting further on retirement, Mr. Allen says:

[It] gives you time to do the things that interest you that you didn't have time to do while you were working. Of course, some people don't have anything that interests them. I feel sorry for the man who's going to retire and can't figure out what he's going to *do*. My wife and I, we go a lot, and I haven't had to worry about finding things to occupy me.

He illustrated this statement with a review of how he had spent the previous day—designing a bulletin announcing a church dinner, typing the stencil, stuffing the envelopes, mailing them out. As he says, "this gives me a little something to keep myself occupied."

These activities also reflect an important aspect of Mr. Allen's time perspective. The interviewer comments that Mr. Allen thinks from day to day, working out daily routines, but seldom plans beyond a month ahead. As he himself reports about one of his major activities, reading, "I don't wolf down a book any more. I piece it out, a little at a time."

This pattern seems to be successful for Mr. Allen and for many other men like him. One indication of this is his morale score, which is in the upper half of the distribution. The score, described in Chapter VII, is not necessarily equated with adjustment in the psychological sense but reflects, at the least, a personal feeling that life is going fairly well and, all in all, probably couldn't have been very different. This view is found in many places in Mr. Allen's comments beyond the answers to the questions composing the index. He describes how satisfactory he finds his community. He likes a large city, as opposed to a rural area or small town—"You have more opportunities—the best of schools, teachers, the best of ministers." He specifically likes his own town. "Our city has everything it takes to make a great city. It has schools, churches, excellent amusement, and in general, I'd say, a fine class of people." He sees in it "no more special problems . . . [for older people] than they used to have. Today, if they're in good health, social security, however meager, lightens their load."

In reviewing his own life, he says that he has achieved his goal. Beyond work, "Naturally your goal is to feel secure in old age and to give your children an education. I think I've done both." He has a kind of halo of satisfaction around his own life. He might appear to be almost a meaningless stereotype were he not moderately active intellectually, interested in travel and in fairly wide reading, and if he did not conduct his personal relations in a manner harmonious with a genuinely felt satisfaction.

When he was asked if he wanted to live his life over again, he replied, "No." This might show a general disenchantment, and reflect a general pessimism, but when questioned about his response, he remarks, "Life has been kind to me. I've taken it as it comes and I've enjoyed it. If I lived it over, it might not be as good."

We have indicated that Mr. Allen sustains himself well in retirement because he has softened his demands on himself, has turned to less emotionally binding activities, has provided himself with a diffuse set of responsive, but not demanding, personal contacts, and because he evaluates his own condition positively. There are additional important elements to this process, however, some of which indicate the strain he feels in making this transition to the disengaged state, and some of which show other strengths of Mr. Allen.

Mr. Allen's TAT responses are characteristic of a group of subjects who maintain the outer forms of achievement orientation while showing strong concern with retreat from all action. This ambivalence is suggested by Mr. Allen's preference for leaving the majority of his stories unresolved. In three of the six stories he told, he raised issues of achievement which he was unable to complete. His first story displays some of the indecision he sees in others. To the picture of the boy with the violin, he says:

Well, that's a violin. I don't know what's laying out here. It's a child at a table with a violin. Well, he is in deep reverie—probably he's a lover of music and the violin means a lot to him. He visualizes mastering the violin and the study of music. He may already be a student. Maybe that's a toy laying at the edge.

Mr. Allen muses about the issues of instrumentality. He is in a reverie; he visualizes the boy as a lover of music. He moves toward action—the child *may* be a student. But then his lingering concern with quiescence takes over, and he ends on a distracting note: "Maybe that's a toy laying at the edge." In the card depicting a family scene, he again phrases the conflict without resolving it—one woman seems "resigned to the tilling of the soil," but the other, "in deep thought, in reverie," is thinking of a better life without hardships.

Two cards seem to hold sufficient appeal for Mr. Allen to treat them more fully. One, showing a young man with an older one, raises the issue of wisdom. He suggests that an older man should not be asked to act, nor should there be any unpleasantness or disagreement between the two men. Rather, the older man should be consulted—youth should seek the advice of age. The second card that engages him raises the issue of receiving love. One woman is in sorrow and is receiving loving sympathy from another.*

These stories, whether describing unresolved instrumentality or love, sympathy and wisdom, illustrate what we have called Passive Mastery—the gentleness, softness, and lack of assertive energy. For this group, however, these elements of low energy involvement are still in proper perspective, and are told without too much hesitation. The storyteller seems to be in charge, and is retreating in good order.

We infer that Mr. Allen is indeed in some conflict over his reduced instrumentality. He fusses too much without doing anything about it. He prefers passive, caressing imagery. He likes to describe deep reverie, fantasies, sympathy, and friendship; he eschews disagreements. But he sets these stories in a context of rational objectivity, and he states ideal abstract goals. More than some other respondents, equally preoccupied with retreating assertive powers, Mr. Allen stresses a kind of compensatory reidentification of himself as wise and just, above the fray of battle. This is not an easy image for retired men to maintain in this society, but he has succeeded.

Much of Mr. Allen's concern with "busy" activities serves his image of himself as the wise counsellor. So do his easy generalizations to our interviewers on modern education, delinquency, segregation, housing, and child-rearing. They serve

* Card 10 of the Murray set.

him well, in the sense that they represent a useful integrating device of abstract and ideal values, while at the same time permitting him to "do" many little things; the combination softens the blow of his reduced autonomy.

This recent refocusing of his values has probably been the reason for several of his wife's comments and for some of the interviewers' observations. One interviewer commented on his being "vaguely feminine." Another reported, somewhat more precisely, that "his manner was more languid and relaxed than before." At another time an interviewer was impressed by his "narcissistic" concern with himself. None of these attributes overrides the clear statement of Mr. Allen's views and experiences, or his willing co-operation with the research, but they do suggest the effort to reorganize himself in a more self-centered and non-assertive way. That his wife has also noticed this is suggested by various comments during the interviews. She sometimes seemed irritated by his self-involvement, and offered comments like, "Oh, don't make so much of it . . . You know that was only an accident." His wife is clearly more active, and "always on the go." She seems to be rather constrained by Mr. Allen's present behavior, suggesting that he has increased his dependency on her, or at least demands more of her time and attention. "Do you know where I can find a husband-sitter?" she asked the interviewer, only half in fun.

Mr. Allen's perception of this situation differs somewhat from his wife's. Others view him with a mixture of love and esteem, he believes. He says with pride that his children telephone every day to ask how he is. On the list of relational rewards described in Chapter V, Mr. Allen describes himself primarily as a person who is loved. This image of himself as the loved object who cherishes others conflicts somewhat with his desire to be viewed with esteem. In a series of paired comparisons of the four rewards, Mr. Allen always checks "love" as his preferred style. He would want to be "loved" more than enjoyed, approved, or esteemed, but his second choice is always esteem. His concern with receiving esteem from others may reflect his desire for recognition of his past successful instrumentality. It is also entirely consistent with another important characteristic of Mr. Allen—his firmly held optimistic, liberal and egalitarian value system. Mr. Allen has a high Conformity score, standing for high adherence to cultural values. His low F-scale score means democratic orientation, and his very high Religious Piety score underlines his stance. In these terms, Mr. Allen is formally tolerant of the rights of others, and in accord with most dominant cultural values, which, in turn, he integrates firmly with his religious values. The attitudes represented by these scores serve him as a kind of protective coating, mediating many of his interactions with the outer world, and acting as a buffer during his shift from an active, full engagement into a self-focused, nonassertive disengagement. His engagement with society's norms has outlasted his engagement with society.

■ **Mrs. Brown: The Threshold of Disengagement**

Mrs. Brown, our second case, is a fully engaged woman of sixty-two who is beginning to wonder about the alternatives to a life of intense family and church involvement. She represents the threshold of the disengagement process; she shows signs of readiness for a reorientation away from intimate family responsibility toward greater freedom of action. Like many of the women in our panel who are older than she is, she has begun to withdraw energy from diffuse-affective commitments and transfer it to images of greater personal freedom. In this change, Mrs. Brown has not developed the domineering assertiveness which so effectively frees some of our women from the demands of others, but she has developed the basis for it. Thus, she has a tendency to project upon external events her own preferred interests. By putting to the fore her own self-concerns, she is implementing her desire for a change from obligatory involvement to less binding and more expressive relations.

Mrs. Brown is a woman whose morale has probably always been high. She is now well up in the top half of our distribution; that is, she displays a general satisfaction with the life areas the index covers. She appears to be generally enthusiastic about her present life. When she is asked how she likes living in Kansas City, she replies, "Oh, on vacations we have visited most states and cities and of all Kansas City is my choice. It surpasses all of them. . . . I'm used to Kansas City. I know all the streets. It just looks good to me. . . . Just gives you a good feeling to get home."

Her enthusiasm carries over to many other areas of her essentially home-centered life. If she could live anywhere she chose in the city, she'd still pick her present address: "Well, it's just the location. It's handy to the stores, schools, church. It's quiet and peaceful. We have nice neighbors. We don't have any traffic or noise. . . . We've raised [our children] right here. It's a wonderful place. It surpasses all other places we've been. I'd do it again." Young people are "wonderful. The young ones I know—my daughter runs around and her friends come here. They're just wonderful."

The focuses of Mrs. Brown's life have always consisted of home and church, and the friendly, busy activities associated with them. Her enthusiasm for her own life seems to arise from firm family stability. Her vacations, and other excursions from the home, have always been with her husband, to visit children who have moved elsewhere—a pleasure exceeded only by that of returning to home base. "It just gives you a good feeling to get home," as she says. The preference for her present city—a "smaller community," as she calls it—is partly because she sees it as undifferentiated, and partly because it is familiar to her. As she reports, "Well you get to know everybody and they get to know you. You don't meet as many strangers. Like New York—you don't know anyone and they are harder to get to know. In a smaller community, you get closer to people."

Her definition of "strangers" suggests some ambivalence, or at least some doubt as to their merit. She thinks them important, yet in the same breath she notes her own well-formulated version of the good life. When asked if she would like to live where she'd meet people pretty much like herself, or, alternatively, to "live among different kinds of people," she votes, in effect, for many different kinds of people, all of whom are pretty much like herself. She answers this question by saying, "Oh, no, I'd prefer different people than me. I like to meet all kinds of people. When you meet a stranger you like to find out all about them, their lives and what they do." But she continues this praise of difference with the statement, "I prefer quiet home-loving people, no rowdy drunkenness, ones who live a religious life. We are religious and I want people who raise their family in the church."

Her own life certainly documents this latter preference. Alternatives have never interested her. When asked if she ever thinks of taking a job outside the home, she is quite clear in her rejection: "No [shaking her head], no, I haven't thought about taking a job. I just don't have any desire to take a job. I never did think I would like to work and get away from my home. I can find plenty to do [here]."

Because of her strong involvement in home and the demands of children, husband, and grandchildren, Mrs. Brown has lived all her life very close to home. At the time we found her, she was living with her husband and one child, who was visiting temporarily. Thus, her Lifespace score is low, reflecting this limited arena of action. Her interactions, however, are highly "condensed," as seen in her high Interaction Index. She spends almost all her time with other people, but her roles are only moderately varied: housewife, friend, mother, and church worker. Mrs. Brown's high Perceived Lifespace score shows that she views herself as much more active, involved, and busy with interaction now than when she was forty-five—in spite of the fact that her eight children were at home then and are now gone. This high score probably comes partly from her feeling, not too well documented in her reports of actual activities, that she must see more people now because she is not bound to home by children. We are inclined to interpret this score as reflecting a desire for a broadened and less home-bound life pattern as much as it does an actual present extension into this kind of activity. As we saw in Chapter IV, some women have a burst of activity in their early sixties, before the disengagement process begins. In a sense, Mrs. Brown seems to us to be spinning her wheels a bit, re-enacting in her own mind her earlier life of high intensity and involvement, and not quite knowing how to fill her life now with a comparable degree of non-family activity or, alternatively, how to reduce her sense of urgency. This inner disharmony seems to have developed in the past few years and is portrayed in part by the difference between her report of her daily activities at the beginning of the study and her response to the same question three and a half years later. Her earlier report reads:

I get up at 6:30 every morning and prepare breakfast for my husband and daughter. I'm free to go back to bed. Some mornings I do because I like to rest in the early morning. Every morning I read my Bible as soon as my husband leaves. I get quite a number of phone calls. I call for my groceries. I do the chores. Tidy up the house, do the washing and ironing. Sometimes I go out on the back-porch swing and relax or I do some sewing. Sometimes I just sit and read.

[Noon] I prepare lunch. Most every day I have a hot lunch, scrambled egg or just whatever I want to eat. I always wash my dishes. I don't want dirty dishes staring me in the face. I generally bake a pie and prepare for the evening meal. Then I generally take a shower and always rest an hour. Sometimes I have odd chores to do. We are very active and go a lot for the church, so I may press a dress or wash hose or put my hair up for the evening. I always get cleaned up before preparing the evening meal. I get presentable. I get fixed up for my husband just like I'm ready to go out. I put on my cosmetics and things like that. At 6 I have the evening meal ready to set on the table and we eat immediately. A lot of times when it's hot we go downtown to eat. We always decide earlier whether we will go out for supper or not.

[Evening] We sit and pass away the time. My husband tells about work. I do the dishes, he reads the paper, or gets dressed if we're going out. If we stay home, we watch TV or sit out on the porch. We are usually in bed by 11 o'clock.

Three and a half years later, she reports:

[Morning] I take care of my granddaughter and do housework. Listen to stories at about eleven o'clock and sit for about one hour and a half. Do my baking.

[Afternoon] when [daughter] gets home we go to the store and get the groceries. Go to shopping and any running around.

[Evening] Go out once or twice a week. We lost one of our very good friends about four months ago. We don't go out quite so much. That [death of friend] seems to do something to us.

At the time of the more recent report, she may be suffering from some temporary malaise, although this is not apparent elsewhere in this same interview. She seems to us both less active and more depressive. Her earlier enthusiasm for her morning time to "go out on the back-porch swing . . . or do some sewing" seems to be converted to "[I] sit for about one hour and a half." Similarly, she no longer calls our attention to her cosmetics or her dressing up for her husband. Their loss of good friends has indeed done something to her; it has called her attention to the fact that life has changed and that she has hardly realized it. Even her report of caring for children and grandchild has taken on a different character. Just before this second interview, her daughter came home to live, bringing two grandchildren of whom she is very fond and around whom her earlier life had been so pleasurably structured. When we asked her on the second interview, "On the whole, do you think grandparents really enjoy baby-sitting with their grandchildren, or do you think they find it annoying once in a while?" Mrs. Brown ventures the cautious comment, "I have heard grandparents say that [they find it annoying once in a while]." When asked specifically how she herself felt, she says, "Oh, I haven't done much of it. Could become annoying if I did much of it." In a less guarded moment, she phrases this attitude much more directly. When asked what things tend to annoy her now, she says, "Well, one thing, because I'm getting older, the children and the noise. I get to where you can't take it any more like you used to." The contrast between these statements and her earlier, happier reports of child care and the joys of motherhood is striking.

This disenchantment with life and with what has been her major involvement in it—children and home—is presaged by her Thematic Apperception Test responses. There are three TAT cards to which she responded * that can be considered family-oriented cards. In all three, Mrs. Brown sees conflict, which she never reports about her actual family life. In Card 2, the rural family scene, she goes so far as to propose a rather cold mother in whom a daughter could not be expected to confide. She resolves the conflict in two of her stories by having the mother "give in" in one of them, and by an appeal to wisdom and authority in the other. Neither solution is in accord with parental attitudes expressed by Mrs. Brown. On Card 10, the two adult faces, she sees two parents consoling each other now that the children are all gone. These stories

* Card 2 is the rural family scene, Card 6-BM the mother and son, and Card 7-BM the father and son.

probably reflect attitudes Mrs. Brown has not recognized overtly—that diffuse-affective bonds can chafe, and that there are substitutes for family life. The remaining two cards portray specific, as opposed to diffusely-affective, relations.* In both, her stories show no conflict and tend to be rather bland and unresolved, but they also contain one notable element lacking in the diffuse-affective situations—the tendency to personalize and externalize inner states which appears to accompany successful adjustment in many older women. In these cards she tells the stories in the first person; in the violin card she makes the entire story a personal reminiscence about her own violin-practicing days and her difficulty getting her son to learn how to play the violin. For the picture of the man on the rope, she tells the story in the first person, and at the same time portrays a character, earlier identified as a son, as "just coming down from a big act." Mrs. Brown, too, is coming down from a big act, and her landing has not been too easy. It seems to us a positive sign, however, that these projections of highly personalized inner states upon the impersonality of the TAT cards occur in connection with the specific-affective stories. It suggests an increasing realization that she is now able to conceive of more personal, more selfish, less normatively bound ideas and activities.

It is in part because of these indications from the TAT that we do not consider the depressive tone of Mrs. Brown's most recent interview as permanent. As Blenckner (12) has pointed out, this is an age period in which a decline of morale is fairly common. Mrs. Brown's interviews show direct evidence that she recognizes the change, and partially adapts to it. In telling us what she finds best about being her age, she reports that while her daughter now lives nearby, and she (Mrs. Brown) is, of course, "glad to help," the main thing is that, with the family now gone, "We are on our own and free to come and

* Card 1 is the boy and the violin, Card 17-BM the man on the rope.

go." In anticipating her husband's retirement in a few years, she is even more specific. As she says, "Well, sir, we both like to travel. He says he's going to get a trailer. *We'll be gypsies.* We always wanted . . . we have two friends who go to Florida every winter. [My husband] wants to go to Florida in the winter. He likes to fish. I enjoy it, too, when you catch anything." *

In characterizing some of their present best friends around whom an alternative life pattern might be constructed, some of the positive, useful elements of aging are on her mind. One of the women is "well dressed . . . wears lots of jewelry . . . goes a lot." In passing, she notes that this woman's husband is "quiet, hardly says anything." In describing another couple, she says, "We have a lot of fun with them. They like to go. Their main thing is to eat."

When asked to check a list of various activities that had given her most satisfaction when she was forty-five, Mrs. Brown checks: (1) Just being with your family at home, (2) Keeping house, (3) Church work with fellow church workers.

Now, however, she ignores these family-bound activities and instead checks those reflecting lessened responsibility and "going": (1) Spending time with close friends, (2) Going downtown and shopping around, (3) Going out to eat, (4) Keeping up with the news and what's going on in the world.

Noting the indications of changed orientation in her TAT and in these newly valued interests, we see Mrs. Brown's readiness to disengage and her partial shift into an early stage of disengagement. Her over-all personality type, a form of Active Mastery with externalizing but not aggressive properties, seems harmonious with this mode of adaptation. In her transition,

---

* It is relevant to note Mrs. Brown's distinction in this last sentence. Her husband, like our other successful males, likes quasi-instrumental activities. "He likes to fish." But she, like our other women, prefers it when something active happens—"I enjoy it, too, when you catch anything." Here we see the tendency of the woman to prefer activity, the man tending instead toward passivity and quasi-instrumentality.

she will probably be aided by her firmly held, but flexible, normative value system; her low Alienation Score suggests majority values and the sense of "belonging" these provide, and her low F-scale score suggests a flexible democratic orientation. Her high Religious Piety score implies the sustaining value of religion.

In the next chapter we will describe briefly an older, more disengaged woman, a young, engaged man, and some less typical cases.

CHAPTER X

Variations on the Theme – Alternate Modes of Aging

IN THIS CHAPTER we will describe an engaged man and a disengaged woman to complement the two cases of the last chapter, and deal briefly with some major variations on the central theme of disengagement. The first respondent is a woman who is fully disengaged and of good morale, similar to Mr. Allen. The second is a man who, like Mrs. Brown, is of high morale, still engaged, and showing signs of readiness for disengagement. The next two cases will deal with apparent failure: a man of seventy-two with low morale and incomplete disengagement, and a woman in the same situation. The final group illustrating continuing engagement in old people is chosen as atypical of our total group, but they illustrate the fact that disengagement can be postponed for a very long time.

■ Mrs. Clark: A Study in Disengagement

Mrs. Clark is a widow, sixty-nine years old at the beginning of the study, who displays full disengagement, low energy, and high morale. This state is well portrayed by her disengagement measures. Her Lifespace is small, her Interaction Index, Role Count, and Perceived Lifespace are all low. Her interaction is limited in amount and lacking in variety, and her interest in greater interaction minimal. Her personality type is a form of Passive Mastery marked by low assertive energy and a preference for interpreting external events to suit her own convenience, while not actually distorting them. Mrs. Clark is in good spirits—in the upper half of the morale distribution.

Her interaction pattern can be seen in outline from her description of daily activities. She lives alone and reports:

[Morning] I get up about seven in the morning. Then I fix a little breakfast and have my breakfast. Then I clean the dishes and start in cleaning the house. Dust, scrub, wash and just general housecleaning. Sometimes I wash or iron and do things like that.

[Afternoon] A little before noon I prepare a little lunch. I usually have lunch about noon. I clean the dishes, and if I can, I gad about. I usually visit [a relative]. Sometimes I just watch TV or sometimes I straighten up things around the house.

[Evening] I usually prepare a little supper to have it ready by about five. Then I wash the dishes and usually watch TV the rest of the evening.

Her weekend-activity list is essentially identical, except that she often goes "with my son to the grocery store." On Sundays she doesn't "go to church like I should because it's too hard for me to walk the long distance. I either visit my son, go riding with him, or stay at home and watch TV."

Her limited interactions are largely with her son and daughter, her husband's cousins, a few neighbors and the grocery-store clerk, all of whom are mentioned elsewhere in her comments. While she notes that she saw more people when she was younger, she seems quite content with her present reduced life space. Her preference is clearly for relatives. As she comments, "When a woman lives by herself, relatives are very important. Others just say 'Here comes that old woman again.'" However, this does not seem to be said in resentment. She thinks that having a few neighbors and friends around is "very important . . . [because] I'm here by myself and if anything happened to me, I'd want them to know." Friends and neighbors thus serve in fairly specific roles for her—"keeping an eye on me" and helping her to get groceries. She does not want obligatory relationships with them. In fact, she visits spontaneously with only one neighbor, pointing out that "if I visit with the kinfolks that's all I can get done." Other neighbors and friends are perceived quite neutrally by her. When asked about having old friends or making new ones, her interest lags. "No, [there was a] lady down the corner who moved away, but she wasn't a real close friend. I don't get too close to any of them. You can't, you know, and stay on good terms with them. A lot of our neighbors . . . are friendly and that's all I care."

Non-kin are pretty much of a mystery to Mrs. Clark. She says that seeing a person fairly regularly wouldn't make her a friend. The distinction between friend and neighbor doesn't impress her either. When asked how they differ, she said, "Well, I don't know just what that would be, because they both do just about the same, I think." New contacts are of little interest. When asked if she agreed with people who say that you need new people to get new ideas, she demurs and answers, "It may be all right for other people, but it doesn't seem true to me." She'd rather do business with strangers, in fact, than friends. "I think I'd have more luck with a stranger, because a friend will *do* you sometimes." Her situation is, as she reports, "O.K. as is. I don't like to get too thick with anyone because if you gossip around the neighborhood the first thing you know you're in trouble." At the same time, she "hardly ever" gets lonely, certainly not more than she ever did, and she can't think of a thing when asked what makes her feel bored.

This low degree of interaction has developed over the past few years. She reports that all her activities were greater when she was forty-five, but she has moved to this degree of non-involvement in a fairly active way. She is not an unwilling disengager. Part of this active process has probably been a reflection of her increasing tendency to please herself as much as possible and to snap back at situations that don't meet her requirements. She told a friend off about some issue of child training and they didn't "speak to each other for a year." She likes Kansas City because "it's convenient, you can get most anything." What she doesn't like is that "there's a lot of politics goes on that shouldn't. They are not very honest with the people." The nice things, it is clear, are functionally specific ("You can get most anything") and the worst are the infringements on personal interests and energies. She likes a larger town, because in a small one "everybody knows your business." In her area of town, the stores are convenient, the street lights are better. "Out at my sister's [in a suburban area] it was so dark you didn't dare go out after dark."

One reason for Mrs. Clark's general sense of satisfaction is the extent to which she has allowed her own indulgences to grow. When we asked her what things are really less interesting and less enjoyable, she put us in our place by reporting, "I don't know. I don't *do* anything that I don't want to." When asked what things tempted her that she knew she shouldn't do, her response was hardly in the moral-restraint area anticipated. She says, "Eating, right now." Later on, when asked what she did when she was tempted, she reported that she attempts self-control, but resorts to substitutions: "I take a piece of apple instead of a sweet." She anticipates little change in this life style. Her responses to the question of what she would be doing five years from now are consonant with this general focus upon the immediate. She says, "Oh, I suspect I'd be a little older. I hope I'll be the same, but that's too far to count." When she was asked to reflect upon the issue, so intriguing to middle-aged persons, of what they would do if they only had six months to live, her response is entirely in keeping: "Well, really, I don't know. I'd like to help people. For myself, I might just gad about."

Mrs. Clark's Alienation score is fairly high, as are her Piety and F-scale scores. In younger persons of higher interaction, we take these high scores to reflect both religious involvement and constricted and authoritarian views. In particular, the high Alienation score suggests a real disharmony with major societal values. However, at seventy Mrs. Clark answered these items in a situation of full disengagement. The high Alienation and F-scale scores seem to us to reflect a more general increased rigidity about the unknown world beyond her small life space (see Chapter V). Although Mrs. Clark is not an actively religious person or churchgoer, her Piety score does reflect her fairly direct, naïve view on religious questions and her belief in a personal salvation in Heaven.

In our terms, Mrs. Clark is a successful ager because she has competently disengaged from the bonds of earlier relations and has done so in good spirits. She displays attributes which are an integral part of this process—reduced energy and cathexis to persons, shift from obligatory to gratifying interactions, and an overall reduced desire for interaction. At the same time, she is neither lonely nor disenchanted, pleasing herself by increased small indulgences and not doing "anything that I don't want to."

■ Mr. Duncan: Readiness for Disengagement

Mr. Duncan was a fully engaged man at the start of the study showing signs of readiness for disengagement. His morale was good and his plans for retirement—and for disengagement—sensible and in keeping with his basic life style. His Lifespace score is high, as are his Role Count, his Interaction Index, and his Perceived Lifespace.

His TAT response reflects his sense of competence and active mastery of life, although it shows some indications of the strain of continued activity.

Mr. Duncan's description of his daily round, when he was fifty-eight, is typical of someone who interacts fairly heavily and is fully involved with work, family, organizations, and friends. He says:

My wife has the bathroom from 6 to 6:30. At 6:30 I'm in the bathroom. I listen to the radio at five to seven. At seven o'clock, breakfast is ready. We listen to the newscast. I wash my face, wash my glasses, put on my coat and get in the car at 7:16. Get to work at 7:45. On the way down, I pick up three or four people, it gives me contact with new ideas. Then on the way home I bring home a different set of people. That way I have contacts with a different set of people. I enjoy mixing with different people and getting their ideas. Get home at 5:30 and do yard work, water every evening.

Dinner at 6:30. Club meeting one night a week, Tuesday evening the Starlight [Theater]. In winter I take a class at [work]. I bowl on Thursday. On Friday I bowl with [another group from work]. On Saturday, go to [another club group]. We talk, play cards.

Go to bed at different times. Read for an hour after I get home, get paper and read it. I am not a book reader. Keep up on *Kiplinger's Letter, Reader's Digest* news articles on stocks and bonds. Listen to radio. I have a portable radio so don't miss out on [favorite program]. I'm stubborn about that.

His life is marked by a large number of pleasurable inter-actions, though apparently not by very deep ties. He says that he probably knows a thousand "people who are friends but not really close friends," but can think of no one who is "really close." He describes himself as a person who "meets a lot of people and makes a lot of friends." When asked what difference he saw between a friend and a stranger, he responded, "I never saw a stranger— Well, I suppose if I start a conversation and they don't want to speak back, they are a stranger."

Mr. Duncan's life of extended easy sociability might to some persons appear shallow. He enjoys meeting new people and getting their ideas. He believes that he is enjoyed and respected by his friends at work and in organizations. The positive, affective tone of his interactions is reflected in radio and TV participation. As he comments about one of his favorite programs, "I live right along with the story. If it's sad, I shed a tear. Now my wife thinks that's silly. She says it's just a story and there's no need to cry. But I live the story."

Of the list of sixteen activities we asked people to check for the things that gave them enjoyment, he checks fourteen items. This contrasts sharply to the small number of checks most people made. Furthermore, he feels that all fourteen gave him pleasure at forty-five as well as now. This eclectic attitude toward pleasurable activity seems to parallel his attitude to friendship and association membership. His interests are broad in range, and widely, if not intensely, enjoyed.

In spite of his full engagement with many aspects of life, Mr. Duncan is anticipating retirement and a life of lessened activities and decreased commitments. He proposes to the interviewer a plan for retirement—essentially a form of tapering off. He recognizes that work roles must be made available for younger people, but proposes that the retiring individual should have an increasing number of days off, beginning with one day per week at age sixty and progressing to full retirement at sixty-five.

His readiness for disengagement shows in other areas of his life. He has some hesitancy about committing himself to new projects. As he says about a contemplated change of residence, "My wife would like [another section of town], but I can't see going out there and going in debt to buy a house. We've got this one all paid for." Contrasting himself with his wife, he says:

It is, seems like, a nice neighborhood. [But] my wife and I disagree. I'm quiet, easygoing; she heads up organizations. I never wanted to be president of anything, but I want to be on the committee. I don't want to be the leader, but I don't want to sit back and do nothing, either. My wife joins an organization and the first thing you know, she's president. . . . If I say something that might hurt someone's feelings, it bothers me, but she says, "It's done, it's past, that's all there is to it." She gets into wrangles in her clubs but it doesn't bother her.

In our second interview with Mr. Duncan, about nine months after he told us of the retirement plan he had invented, he responds to our question about what has happened to him since our last visit by saying:

Nothing more than these friends being ill. My wife hasn't even argued with me as much as usual. Now I'm getting out of more activities instead of taking more on—and at the same time I encourage my wife to go ahead without me. I don't know how she likes it. I'm getting her to do more of those things. She has more get-up-and-go than I have. I don't have the energy. Oh, course, she says I talk too much—after you left before, she said, "Now what did you want to go and tell her all that stuff for?" But I told her that I just said whatever I thought of and if it wasn't what you wanted, you didn't need to write it down.

He also comments that he has reduced his church involvement:

I don't want to be on boards. I don't want to get involved in things. But if I take anything on, I work at it. . . . I just don't attend [organizations] as much as I used to. . . . I will go over [to a club] and play cards and attend the meeting, but I don't play cards afterwards. I don't stay around and lock up the doors like I used to. . . . If there's a committee you want me to be on I'll do it, but I won't be chairman. . . . Oh, I can relax. I'm not a drinking man at all, but for the past six months, I've been drinking a small bit of red wine before my evening meals. Now my food tastes better to me.

As retirement has come closer, he seems to have taken some steps toward lessened activity. He describes the best thing about being his age thus: "Well . . . I'll be sixty-two next week. It's looking forward to retirement. I can spend a lot of time doing nothing and I like to do things my way. I'll fool around in the yard and go over to the club. There's a lot of tension about my work."

This process, however, is not as easy for him as it sounds. He notes that "it's hard for me to cut out activities" even though he has a real interest in doing so, and actually appears to have reduced them somewhat. He also comments that one of his difficulties is that "I can't slow my wife down, and she has no patience with slowness." As complex as this transition period may be for him, he is making progress, and during it, his spirits remain high. During our last interview with him, when he was sixty-four, his Morale Index was still high. Furthermore, he notes that he is "very satisfied" with his present way of life, that things are "better" than he thought they would be as he gets older. He finds "almost no unhappiness" in his life today. Thoughts and fears about death "almost never" occur to him, though they did occur to him "more" when he was forty-five.

He is still interested in activity, however. He says that there are "two or three organizations that have wanted me to head them up. If they want me when I retire, I'll tell them I will." When asked if he thought this would really happen, he modified the statement by saying, "I don't know whether I will or not. Maybe I'm just using [my present] work as an excuse. Maybe when I retire I won't feel like that." Possibly his basic attitude comes out when we ask him what kinds of things he most often thinks about when he's by himself. He says, "Bringing more harmony into things and less controversy. I want to be an arbitrator and not a stirrer-upper—at work, in the home, and everywhere."

In the approaches to disengagement, he has by no means forgotten his basic orientation to pleasurable sociability, an attitude which may well become an important buffer for him in his transition. When asked how he'd spend his time if he had only six months to live, he reports, "Oh, I think I'd call on everybody, see everybody I could. [I told my wife about this] and for once she didn't tell me it was a bad idea. She said she thought that would be nice."

At the beginning of our contact, Mr. Duncan showed intimations of his readiness for change, and had actually taken several steps away from full engagement by the time of our last contact with him. This process was reflected in his suggestions of decreasingly instrumental interests, in his gradual reduction in activities, and in his conceptualization of the ideal retirement plan. It became more prominent in the later interviews, in his doubt about continuing all his present affairs, in his minor indulgences—a little wine, wanting to do things his own way—and in particular, in his own words, in wanting to be "an arbitrator and not a stirrer-upper."

■ **Postponing of Disengagement**

We have seen four examples of disengagement proceeding in a modal fashion. Our next case is of a man who is having difficulty making the transition.

Mr. Everett was seventy at the beginning of the research. He has been unwilling to consider himself retired, and has entered and left a series of jobs or businesses since his initial retirement. Although "semi-retirement" is not too unusual, for Mr. Everett it has reflected a continual struggle between his firmly held belief that continued work is important—"inaction is difficult," as he says—and a lowered cathexis for persons and interactions. This conflict, together with his increasing sense of losing the battle, produces his Morale score of zero, and has led us to see him as a case of continued engagement that has not been successful.

Mr. Everett's Lifespace score is high, as is his Role Count, suggesting a fairly active and involved life, more characteristic of younger working males. However, his Interaction Index and his Perceived Lifespace are both low. Mr. Everett's interactions take place primarily in non-normatively governed circumtances; that is, in short-lived and functionally specific exchanges. This is a pattern appropriate to a salesman, which was Mr. Everett's job at the time. We would anticipate greater success and higher morale if his Perceived Lifespace did not reflect a lowered cathexis. He is thus highly involved in interactions that do not in themselves have sustaining properties, and for which he lacks the energy and personal resources. This, we propose, accounts for his zero Morale Index.

His pattern of interaction emerges in his responses to our request for an account of his daily activities. He answered this question during the first interview, when he was working at one of the businesses he has been variously engaged in since selling his own business a few years previously. He responds:

Get up in the morning at 7. Go down to the offices. Get there about 8:30. Eat breakfast at home. Just a light breakfast, cereal and orange juice. I don't use tea or coffee. I don't miss them now. My doctor said I'd be better off without them.

Open mail and then about 9:30 or 10 I get out and call on customers. Of course I'm selling mostly. Go to lunch about quarter to 12. Get back in about an hour. Then in the afternoon I make additional calls. We leave the office about 4:30. Get home about 5:00. Read paper for an hour and then have dinner.

Then of course we have certain programs on TV we like. We watch TV or call on friends or they call on us. I usually retire about 9:30. I've always had to have nine hours' sleep.

Since his first retirement, Mr. Everett has made repeated efforts to remain active. As he explains about this first new job, "I sold my business and we have just started this [new] business. We aren't making any money yet but we hope to." The continued nagging need to keep occupied started when he sold his primary business. As he explains it, "I had a —— business in the X building for years but they needed the space and it was too expensive to move the machinery so I just sold it." Seven months later, he reports that "things haven't been going too well." He has just "gotten out of" the business he had started seven months previously, and is now working as a superintendent in another man's business.

During this contact, we asked him if it might not be possible for him to "ease off" work a little and what he thought it would be like to retire completely. His response reflects his basic attitude: "It's either a full-time job or total retirement. . . . I don't know [what full retirement would be like]. I haven't the slightest idea. I don't know what I'd do, just sit here in a rocking chair. I'll be active as long as I live." Nine months later he was "playing with the idea" of another new business. During our final interview he had started this new enterprise but reported, "I am an economic loss in the present circumstances." Following each of these ventures, he repeats his conviction that "it was a great mistake to have sold my business with the idea of getting out. . . . It is hard for a man my age to find a job. It never entered my mind. . . . I'd never have sold my business if I had realized. No, I never thought I'd have any trouble." In spite of these unsuccessful efforts, he is still trying. When we asked him what he thought he might be doing five years from now, he exclaimed, "Five years from now! I think I'll probably be doing what I'm doing now—working."

It is conceivable that this drive for continued activity, in spite of little success or satisfaction, stems from some pressure on the part of his wife. During part of one interview, his wife was present and occasionally interjected remarks. At one point when he said he was visiting friends "about the same" as previously, his wife interjected, "Whatever *that* was!" and added, "He isn't a visitor. It is wrong for a man not to have social contacts." "Maybe so," Mr. Everett responded, "but I haven't been feeling well." His wife went on, with some exasperation in her voice, our interviewer felt, "You get nothing out of a thing unless you put something into it. But you have to be pushed into it." Later in the same interview, we asked him what he felt to be the most important thing in his life right now. He said, "It is to have a little security—to know I'll be able to make it the rest of my life." He then reiterates his complaint of the difficulty a man his age has finding a job. His wife comments here, "Surely you feel some security. If I thought you really felt like that, *I'd* go out and get a job"—a remark hardly helpful to a man driven to work and already worried about his ability to hold a job.

Whether or not this pressure from his wife is crucial in Mr. Everett's need for continued activity, his own sense of a "wasted" earlier life probably is. Mr. Everett picks forty-five as the age he'd most like to be, "when a man is most efficient and has had considerable experience." When he was asked how he might live his life over if he had the chance, he has several comments to make. "Well, I'd be much more conservative, and I would save, retire, and quit. If I had half a million dollars, I wouldn't work." He also reports that he regrets "wasting time playing golf and poker. I could have accomplished a lot if I had used my time better and planned for the future." The worst thing about being his present age is "looking back and realizing that I didn't take advantage of all the opportunities I've had. Instead of having the money I have I could have had three times as much. . . . Think of all the time I wasted playing poker three times a week."

In spite of this sense of time wasted, and perhaps in spite of needling by his wife, his work, temporary and without notable success though it has been, is a pleasurable and welcome break. It reminds him of his earlier instrumentality, and distracts his attention from his low morale. However, there is little indication that these activities give him a sense of either pleasure or productivity. Nor does his present pattern of personal interactions suggest any compensatory enjoyment or a softening of his sense of malaise. His daily activities, reported toward the end of the study, have in them little flavor of either competence or confidence. As he reports:

[Morning] Half the time for the last three years I've been working. Haven't had much work lately. Now I work around the house, minor repairs, basement foundation, painting and that type. Help my wife take care of house. We had a woman help, but she wasn't satisfactory.

[Afternoon] In afternoon, do the same; cement work, painting, cutting the lawn. Occasionally I take a rest, seldom take a nap.

Daughter takes my wife downtown about twice a week and [my wife] gardens a lot.

[Evening] Read and listen to television, go to bed about 9. We do this together. Occasionally we have friends in, very seldom.

Mr. Everett's choice of interaction styles stresses neutral and specific orientations and no affect, the choice more appropriate for older and pleasurably disengaged men. In a list of various things that give him satisfaction now, he chooses (1) Keeping house—working around the house and yard, (2) Doing a good job at work, (3) Keeping up with the news and what's going on in the world.

The interesting thing about this list is the absence of any recreation, even though many forms of it are available on the list he was given. Furthermore, when asked which of the full list would have given him pleasure when he was forty-five, he checked the identical items. Thus he concedes no change in the last thirty years and indicates no choice, at his present age, of the quasi-instrumental or recreational roles so commonly chosen by our more successfully aging males.

More crucial, perhaps, in evaluating this pattern as a less successful one are Mr. Everett's remarks about his own sense of dissatisfaction and incompleteness. In his most recent interview, his responses to a series of items inquiring about current personal evaluations are concordant with his low Morale Index. His own present work worries him. As he said, "I've had about one and a half years of work in the last three. . . . I'm not nearly as efficient as I was twenty-five years ago. I receive $120 per week for work I do now and I honestly don't think I'm efficient enough at my age to earn that much money. That's what I worry about." In evaluating his own life goals, he feels he has "fallen short." He finds his present life "pretty monotonous," and frequently considers "trying to think of some useful thing I could do to get back into useful activity. Being out of business has been a tragic thing." He specifically rejects the suggestion that he might occasionally think, "Why am I breaking my neck? Why don't I just take it easy and enjoy myself?" by responding, "No, it's a mistake to become inactive. Inaction is difficult." Unlike most of our respondents, he says that he never feels "joyful and on top of the world for no particular reason," and often gets "blue or depressed for no particular reason." While most respondents say (on a rating scale) they never or hardly ever get bored, Mr. Everett checks "Sometimes but not often." He adds, "[I] have certain friends that are a bore. The things they talk about—themselves or tell the same story over and over again. . . . [I] get nervous and like to get away." He has already told us that he finds life "pretty monotonous."

Most respondents claim that they never or hardly ever think about "what death would be like" or "find myself feeling afraid of death." Mr. Everett follows the general tendency to say nothing about death. However, the others report a lessening in the frequency of thinking fearfully of death between their present age and when they were forty-five. Where most respondents say "less now" or "no difference," Mr. Everett reports more thoughts of death now, and more fear of dying. We also asked if our respondents agree or disagree with the statement "A person starts dying the day he is born." Most of them find this statement meaningless and either say "don't know" or "disagree." Mr. Everett seems to find it a meaningful item for he checks agreement with it and volunteers, "Each day that passes you are nearer the end." Of all of the items referring to self-evaluation, the only one he answers in a positive, non-depressive way is a question asking how he would spend his time if he had only six months to live. In what sounds suspiciously like too little relief, too late, he responds, "Go to some delightful resort and finish my life there."

Mr. Everett's TAT responses also reflect a sense of dissatisfaction. His stories are seldom resolved, even stories about the work he claims to be so important. He sees disharmony in close personal ties and sees the card of the two adult faces (usually seen as a man and woman in some positive intimate situation) as two unpleasantly gossiping fellows. He is inconsistent and contradictory in some stories, which suggests that he has some reason for worry about work inefficiency. In short, Mr. Everett is aging unsuccessfully, primarily, in our view, because of the discrepancy between his level of cathexis and his desire to remain fully engaged. He may be a "late bloomer"; that is, in a stage of disengagement characteristic of younger men. On the other hand, his inability to let go may be a continued problem to him.

Occasionally we find aging people who have remained remarkably firmly engaged. These people, we expect, will eventually disengage. However, there is a rare kind of very old person who has lost neither cathexis nor skill, and who may be especially endowed biologically. We will here describe briefly the only aged member of our study group who presents this picture of energetic full engagement. Afterward, we will describe a less exceptional case of continuing engagement. Both have high morale scores.

Mrs. Elton is a woman in her early eighties who lives with her daughter, her son-in-law, and their three children. She is physically active and alert. As she says, "[I] don't think of myself as getting older. Feel a little old since I had this accident [broken hip]. Feel a little older last five years. I do the washing, ironing, cooking, housekeeping. My daughter works. Doctor says I'm fine." Her daily round would exhaust many women half her age:

Get up at 6:45 or a little earlier. Get my daughter's and her husband's breakfast and she goes to work. Others, three girls, get their own in the summer. When going to school, we all eat together.

Do up the work. Tidy up the house. Wash on Monday, iron on Tuesday, do daughter's and her husband's ironing. Girls do their own.

I'm usually the only one here [during the day]. If they are here, make dinner. My daughter got to come home today, so I had dinner for her.

Have quite a lot of writing to do to my family and friends. Take a day to get that off. Do mending and take care of my shrubs and flowers.

5:15—have supper. Get bawled out every day because I cook so much. They don't like to put on weight. I've had a big family and have always done the cooking.

We used to go to a study class on Monday. Wednesday our prayer-meeting night, and we go.

Watch TV [in the evening] and read a lot. Daughter has a lot of church work. I taught a group of young married people for a while. Since my eyes got bad, cataracts in my eyes, can't see very well. Not ready to remove yet. Go to bed to 10:00 P.M.

This description summarizes Mrs. Elton. Not only does she perform the function of housewife and integrating figure but she also maintains contact with her more distant kin, through writing letters. Furthermore, she has an active role in the church, and reveals by her function there that she still remains well enough in contact with the norms to teach them to others. The only indication that she will inevitably disengage lies in her comments on her physical impairment, cataracts. But these are curiously bland and lacking in frustration. She says, "In the afternoon, I can go sit down and read, write, or visit if anyone comes in. Used to enjoy visiting, but don't have any way to go now, unless they come and get me." Her comments on religion suggest that she has considerable inner support from her faith. She says, "It [religion] has helped me in every way. It has helped me to realize why I'm here. When I put God in it, I knew why I was here." With her solidly rooted religious and moral values, her large kinship system, with which she keeps in close touch, and her friends—all church-connected—she appears to be one of those few people who have stayed engaged because they have such a high level of vitality, place a high value on activity, and tolerate obligatory contact excellently even when very old. When they are forced to dis-engage, however, through physical impairment, their inner resources and outer supports sustain them. We do not know whether Mrs. Elton has special biological or psychological characteristics that account for her continuing full engagement, but as we will point out when we mention her again briefly in the next chapter, her kind is extremely rare among old people.

Mr. Bradford does not show quite the same picture as Mrs. Elton, although he is still fully engaged at seventy. He works, has immense enthusiasm for his many activities, and is rated by the interviewers who saw him as extraordinarily energetic and "young-looking." However, beneath his euphoric descrip-tion of a busy life there lies a kind of anxious fear that he will lose control of events.

Mr. Bradford lives with his fifty-year-old sister and still works as an insurance salesman. This means that he has numer-ous contacts with people, but that he can to a large extent con-trol the hours of his work. Furthermore, he appears to view his work as recreational. He enjoys the responsiveness of his customers, and does not seem to be particularly concerned with the amount of business he transacts. He says, "[I] spend the day calling on and talking to interesting people . . . in con-nection with my business. I drink coffee with customers. Have one customer who likes soup, so we have soup together. Don't go to office regularly. Telephone in and handle business through office. Eat lunch anywhere I may be . . . take a customer to lunch." Then he adds, "I don't think there is anybody who enjoys their work more than I do."

Mr. Bradford appears to be fundamentally different from Mrs. Elton. Where she remained engaged because her cathexis on outside objects was still strong, and no tendency to self-centeredness seemed to have appeared, Mr. Bradford has found himself in an occupation that, because it depends upon expressiveness for its execution, can be satisfactory long after inner changes have taken place. He uses his instrumental role partly as a form of self-indulgence. But it is working well for him, and his continuing engagement with the occupational world appears to be keeping his morale high. The interviewer reports that it is hard for him to remain on the subject, and apparently his tendency to a kind of narcissistic rambling makes the interviewing situation difficult.

Mr. Bradford is a "tither" at the church, and active in its affairs. He also likes to shop. Buying a television set means canvassing all of the dealers and then choosing at leisure. He says, when asked what he enjoys most about the weekend, "I enjoy the whole weekend. Unless it would be our dinner meal that I like best. We read articles to each other and discuss them. If the next world is better than this it will be something. This has been a honey." When he is asked which parts he likes least, he replies, "Nothing." When the interviewer probes, and asks, "What about working around the house?" he says, "We painted these rooms, had fun talking, radio, drinking coffee—like a holiday."

This euphoric description of life has a tone of overprotest. When we look at his TAT cards, we see that all the stories are concerned with disharmony among the people pictured. The boy with the violin outwits his parents and does not learn to play it. In the farm scene, there is conflict between the mother-in-law and the daughter. In the scene between a mother and her son he sees conflict over whether or not the recently dead father will be buried or cremated! When he is shown the picture of the father and son he sees strife between them over the son's career, and the father prevailing over the son. The picture of two ambiguous figures he interprets as a scene of bereavement, and the man on the rope is seen as escaping from a sexual escapade. His impulses are pressing him fairly hard, and depression is not too remote a possibility.

The consistency of this conflict theme suggests that Mr. Bradford has a strong undercurrent of anxiety. He wonders, apparently, about how well the world will continue to treat him. It is possible that his perception of other people's response to him is impaired to some extent, and he has a constant nagging worry about how well he is being received.

Mr. Bradford appears to be able to sustain engagement with life through his occupational contacts, because they are of a kind that can continue even though his cathexis has turned inward. Apparently, society still expects—or tolerates—from an insurance salesman the kind of *bonhomie* through which Mr. Bradford expresses his increasing interest in his own reactions and sensations. It would be impossible to call him anything but a successful ager by our criteria, but we do not know whether he can make a successful transition from his current situation to one in which he has a smaller audience. Only time will tell. Compared to Mrs. Elton, however, we would call him only quasi-successful. Unfortunately, our instruments are still too unrefined to distinguish between these two except on the clinical, intuitive level.

CHAPTER XI

The Very Old

with MARY LOU PARLAGRECO

IN THIS CHAPTER we will discuss very old respondents—those in their eighties—and compare them with both the panel and people in their seventies. Many observers have commented on the special qualities of the very old. Riesman draws attention to Bertrand Russell and Toscanini; others talk of Bernard Baruch and Bernard Shaw. There is some evidence that living to be over eighty, whether or not you are famous, is associated with being a member of a biological, and possibly psychological, elite. Furthermore, very old people often have a surprisingly high level of social competence and seem able to maintain high spirits.

Cosin (15), talking of aged people with whom he works in Oxford, says that such physical insults as broken hips, common among the elderly, are less traumatic for the very old than for the moderately old. There may be a group of people who, more than being merely survivors, have a special biological invulnerability to such things as hardened arteries and failing senses. Even their learning ability appears not to decline inevitably with age. Arnhoff (5), among others, reports that there is a separate group of very old people whose learning processes resemble those of younger people.

When we turn to our interviews, we find a marked difference in tone between the respondents in their seventies and those in their eighties. Through the interviews of the seventies there runs a thread of pessimism which sometimes broadens into irritability and self-pity. These people do, of course, have more illness than those younger and older. It is during this decade that illnesses that prove fatal are taking their toll of the less sturdy. Among the eighties there is less complaining and more chirpiness, sometimes a mood of using up the last days of life in tranquility and sometimes a genuine carefree quality. Furthermore, eighty-year-olds take pride in their longevity; to be seventy-five is to be old in an undistinguished way, but to be eighty-five is to be old in a notable way.

All lives appear to have plateaus between periods of unrest and change. It is during change that the demands on the individual are heaviest. Havighurst (33) and his co-workers feel that there is a plateau from about forty to about seventy. According to them, before the period of old age there is one of settled, mature adulthood. Our findings, like Blenckner's (12), suggest that, following a plateau in the late forties and through the fifties, there is a crisis, marked by anxiety, between sixty and sixty-five. After this, most people become more contented. Again, in the seventies there is a restlessness and irritability that, if not resolved by death, may lead, for the special few survivors, to a period of tranquility and satisfaction in very old age. As Table XI–1 shows, these eighty-year-olds have higher morale than the seventy-year-olds, who, in turn, are better off than the panel. Our morale score may reflect a kind of contentment with the status quo more likely to occur when the need for changing and learning and achieving becomes

TABLE XI–1

MORALE OF THE VERY OLD COMPARED WITH THE
SEVENTIES AND THE PANEL

Age Group	Number Interviewed	Per Cent with Low Morale (0–1)
Total	*186*	*41.9*
Panel	117	48.7
Seventies	41	34.1
Eighties	28	25.0

NOTE: A smaller percentage of those in their eighties have low morale than of those in their seventies; and a smaller percentage of these, in turn, have low morale than of those in the panel. $\chi^2 = 6.7$, d.f. $= 2$, $.05 > P > .02$.

less pressing, and new adjustments are not so necessary. As we shall see, some of our respondents recognize a difference in the kind of contentment they are now experiencing.

■ **The Period from the Seventies to the Eighties**

Our 38 very old respondents ranged in age up to ninety-six years. Their interviews differ from those of the regular panel not only in tone but also in content. These old people have less illness, probably because the attrition process has left only healthy *ambulatory* people in this age bracket. Although quite a number (nine out of 38) * were impaired, they seem adjusted to the impairment. There is more acceptance of old age, but less social activity. There is also among this group a rather high number with good incomes. This in itself might be reason enough for high morale and content-

* See Appendix 1 for details about health status.

ment, but more careful examination, while showing that those on relief and social welfare had lower morale, also shows that adequate income is not in itself sufficient to insure high morale. Our oldest respondents are probably unrepresentative of the universe of eighty- and ninety-year-olds for another reason. Owing to the "bush-fire" technique of choosing them, we found ourselves with a markedly religious group because two retired clergymen had led us to their friends.

Despite all these biases, we are comparing these old people with our quasi-sample of seventy-year-olds and with our panel because the striking quality of the differences seems useful for the development of our theory. These very old people seem inwardly directed; all their energy is spent in one form or another on self-concern, without interference from the social norms that once forced them to consider others. On the other hand, our seventy-year-olds still seem to be in the process of being freed from these norms, and they reveal it by giving normative responses resembling those of the general panel. They declare less often than the panel members that they are friendly, don't get angry, don't fear death, and love their grandchildren, but do so more often than the very old group. Much of the difference between the various respondents in the seventies seems a result of their different stages in aging, but in those over eighty, the differences seem related to different personalities; there is no feeling, as there is with the seventies, that they will change or are in transition. In fact there is so much change and crisis among the seventy-year-olds that when the first interview has a cheerful or carefree tone, the reader half expects some drastic, negative change before the fifth interview. The eighty-year-olds showed great stability throughout the interview series (nearly three years). A typical eighty-year-old response gives this feeling of stasis, "I have done a day's work and have finished [my] job as near as [I am] able and am ready to go when [the] end comes."

The seventy-year-olds still tend to describe their friends as people with whom common interests and activities are shared. Among the eighty-year-olds, friends are people who "do things for you," and therefore, conveniently, they are often neighbors and younger people. At this stage horizontal solidarity has given way to vertical dependency, to the organic solidarity of childhood. Friends come to visit, to clean house, to arrange transportation to the doctor, to cook meals. It is very common to read in these interviews that neighbors are intimate friends and that there is no difference between a neighbor and a friend. Typical descriptions are "That's the woman I worked for and [she] took care of me when I had a broken leg," and "She and her husband come every Saturday and take me to buy my groceries. I also go riding and visiting with them once in a while." The emphasis is upon what friends contribute to comfort and convenience. There are, of course, comments more characteristic of middle age, but the over-all effect is one of receiving what is only one's due: "Mrs. F., my next-door neighbor and minister's wife, looks after me when I'm here alone," or "I like her because she looks after me and gives me gifts and does nice things for me." The rewards for those who look out for these old people are, one imagines, similar to those for taking care of children; they are both important parts of the social fabric.

Very few of these respondents describe kin as friends, and those who do so tend toward low morale, although the difference is not significant. Relationships with kindred may have come to involve too much responsibility and too much affective return. Friendship with neighbors, who help but demand nothing, is much easier.

For a similar reason, probably, living with intimates seems associated with low morale, as we see in Table XI–2. The one person who lived with a sister was an exception. Sibs were often available, but in all except this one case, the old person chose to live with children. The low morale associated with living with children is compounded when there is financial dependence upon the children. Those who were financially independent had the highest morale, but those on public welfare were better off than those dependent on children, although the difference does not reach significance. All of these influences on morale are the same for men and women; there are no differences by sex among the very old.

TABLE XI–2

MORALE BY LIVING ARRANGEMENTS

FOR RESPONDENTS OVER SEVENTY-SEVEN

Respondents	Number Interviewed	Per Cent with Low Morale (0–1)
Total	25[a]	*32.0*
Living with spouse, children, or sibs	12	58.3
Living with distant kin, non-kin, or alone	13	7.7

[a] Both Morale scores and living arrangement are known for only 25. $P = .0095$ by Fisher's Exact Test.

There is one highly engaged respondent, an eighty-two-year-old widow who lives with her daughter and son-in-law and is financially dependent upon them. She keeps house all day, says she feels less carefree than before because of her many responsibilities, goes out socially a good deal, and has considerable affect toward others. She does not appear to be disengaged either in tone or in terms of any of our quantitative measures. Her morale score is 4. The only other score of 4 is that of a widow who is the picture of complete disengagement, both in tone and in terms of our measures.

An examination of daily and weekend activities showed that 21 of our 38 respondents did not go out on weekdays, and

that 19 of 38 didn't mention seeing people in the evening.
There are only five who see no one at all on weekends, and
three who didn't go out at all on weekends. Going out or seeing people was not associated with morale. These people seem
to have settled comfortably into a style of life that suits them.
They tell us, "[The] evening meal is about 6. I do the dishes,
I just think, I watch TV, and my niece often watches with me.
I go to bed I think maybe about 10." Another respondent says,
"[I] work in garden about two hours a day, mostly late in the
evening. [At] 9 p.m. [I] go to bed." Another says, "I go to bed
about 7 o'clock and spend [the evening] very pleasantly in
bed." This is nicely in balance with the fact that their favorite
activities were without interaction. When people are necessary
to them, they prefer intimate kin or familiar neighbors. It is
certainly very clear that, even though living with intimates
has a depressing effect upon morale, these people are still more
willing to be with them than with strangers. Twenty-four respondents (63 per cent) said they preferred activities like
thinking and watching television alone at home. Another thir-
teen (34 per cent) liked walking and gardening and outside
activities which did not involve other people. Twenty people
(53 per cent) expressed pleasure in spending time with intimate kin, and eight (21 per cent) enjoyed formal activities
like church, which took them out among others. One woman
showed her freedom from the need for people when she said,
"Well, it would be rather tiresome to see a great swarm of
people. [I] don't need people—[I] don't mind being alone. [It
is] kind of restful. [I am] glad to get home from church to
where it's quiet."

Generally speaking, these eighty-year-olds are a group of
disengaged people who differ from those ten years their junior
in the degree of their disengagement and especially in their
lack of change, or movement toward a new state. The static
feeling of a completed adjustment—a nearly finished course,

a marking time—contribute to the feeling of tranquility these people display.

When reading the protocols of the panel members, we could usually guess the morale *score*, but never the questions that contributed to it. However, this was not true of the eighties; the individual questions seem to have a more literal meaning for them. Whereas discontent with the area of residence, for example, might stand for a more general discontent with life style in the panel, it represented, among the eighty-year-olds, a highly specific complaint about living arrangements.

There are four general factors, as we see it, that influence the morale score and the general tone or mood of the interviews with these old people. These are certainly not the only determinants, but they seem, intuitively speaking, to be the most important. First, these men and women seem to have found an agreeable stability between the inner and outer aspects of disengagement. Second, they seem to have integrated their own past lives into an acceptable whole. Third, they seem to have accepted the closeness of death. And, fourth, a certain "carefreeness," a freedom from pressing worries or responsibilities, seems to be necessary for the maintenance of morale. The following responses to the question "What is the most important thing in life?" typify the last two elements:

"Preparing for the future, if you can put it that way. [I] have a bright hope of the other world. If [I am] fortunate enough to get to Heaven, I expect to stand by God and see Him create something. An ambition and hope. [It is] up to me to get there." Another says, in the same vein, "Just living as good as I can until I pass over to the other side." These are people who are waiting quite comfortably for the curtain to drop. Freedom from care shows up in the following: "Having good meals. I can't give a better answer than that. Most important, my morning and evening paper—[I] get more pleasure out of that." Only four cases mentioned kindred in response to this question. None mentioned non-kin.

The factor with the greatest bearing on morale seems to be the ability to disengage. This is absent in all the respondents with low morale. Those unsettled in disengagement sound like seventy-year-olds; they often have immediate, serious problems and responsibilities, leading to unsettling changes. The illness of a wife or husband, the need to care for a house or to work hard, the necessity of worrying about money—all these things were forcing an unwilling engagement. As we have said, this holds for all those with low morale; only one respondent with high morale had such a situation. This woman, described at some length in Chapter X, may resemble the disengaged oldest people in having freely chosen her style of life. Perhaps the essence of good morale is such a free choice rather than ability to disengage *per se*. The latter may appear to be the cause because most choose it.

Finally, then, our group is favorably disposed toward disengagement. They say that they are not so happy as they were in earlier life, but they don't much care, and they recognize that each period in life brings its own kind of happiness: "Well, in some ways I'm a whole lot happier—I don't have to work so hard," or "A different happiness. I just feel happy. Spiritually happy." There are some who complain, but almost always the complaint is specific rather than diffuse, and thus does not pervade the tone of the whole interview.

To sum up, we suggest that, given an adequate income, the very old enjoy their disengaged existence. They have reduced their ties to life, have shed their cares and responsibilities and turned to concern with themselves. They lead static, tranquil, somewhat self-centered lives, which suit them very well and appear to provide smooth passage from a long life to an inevitable death.

CHAPTER XII

A Formal Statement of Disengagement Theory

with ERNEST DAMIANOPOULOS

IN THIS CHAPTER we will draw to-
gether, and articulate into a formal theoretical statement all
the crucial concepts we have used throughout this book. In
this way, the logical relationship among the various concepts
comprising the theory will be clear, and in "working order"
for the development of new hypotheses.

Our statement of theory is, of course, provisional, not final.
Hypotheses generated from it, and data gathered to test them,
will contribute refinements and necessary revisions. As we have
said before, the evidence offered here has been selected for its
accord with the theory, although no available negative evidence has been omitted. We have outlined below the main
postulates of the theory and their corollaries, omitting co-
ordinating definitions. The empirical material necessary for
such definitions is readily available in the previous chapters.

■ Definition

Disengagement is an inevitable process in which many of the relationships between a person and other members of society are severed, and those remaining are altered in quality.

Postulate 1: Although individuals differ, the expectation of death is universal, and decrement of ability is probable. Therefore a mutual severing of ties will take place between a person and others in his society. *

When most of the relationships connecting a person to his social system are severed, disengagement has occurred. Death itself is, of course, the only total disengagement, but the fully disengaged condition of the living can be considered to exist when only those bonds necessary to sustain life remain.

Corollary 1: Because people differ in physiology, temperament, personality, and life situation, disengagement occurs earlier for some people than for others. Furthermore, the precise number of bonds broken, and the number remaining, differ from person to person.

Corollary 2: Because of the differences among people, qualitative changes that occur in relationships with the people to whom the aging individual is still bonded will vary from person to person.

Postulate 2: Because interactions create and reaffirm norms, a reduction in the number or variety of interactions leads to an increased freedom from the control of the norms governing everyday behavior. Consequently, once begun, disengagement becomes a circular, or self-perpetuating, process (Chapters IV and XI).

---

* The word "society," here and throughout, refers to those concrete cultural groupings and social systems to which the individual belongs, actually or symbolically.

All social interaction is rooted in norms, and reaffirms those norms. If interactions become sparse, the control of the individual weakens. Thus, elderly people who have become eccentric in their style of interaction, because they have few normatively governed relationships, find it hard to relate to people who did not know them before they became eccentric. They cannot find common ground with new acquaintances. This means that since they find it difficult to replace friends and acquaintances lost through death, their society becomes even smaller, they turn more into themselves, the normative control over them weakens further, and they are even less able to relate to strangers—or even their own kin, if they have been at a distance—and the disengagement process, once started, becomes self-perpetuating.

Postulate 3: Because the central role of men in American society is instrumental, and the central role of women is socioemotional, the process of disengagement will differ between men and women.

The characteristic role of men requires mechanical skill or technical knowledge, and it carries them away from home into the occupational world. The task of husband-father-worker with regard to the family is *primarily* that of preventing it from disintegrating because of inadequate economic relations with the environment, even though his occupational obligation is only the appropriate technical performance of his role. He articulates the family to the community by endowing it, through his occupation, with a status in the class structure.

The characteristic role of women requires skill in creating a tension-free environment, and knowledge of the norms and values of society. The task of a woman with regard to the family is *primarily* that of reducing among the members tension developed in the course of instrumental activity under conditions demanding considerable control, and of reinforcing the family values and norms. She maintains the integrity of the family against disrupting tensions developed from within, and she reinforces the norms governing the attainment of family goals.

Disengagement from the central life task will differ because the relinquishing of *all of* an activity—one carried out in a particular place, under specific rules of conduct, and judged by definable criteria of performance—is qualitatively different from relinquishing the *main burden* of an activity, while keeping a style of interacting that remains appropriate until the very end of life.

Postulate 4: The life cycle of the individual is punctuated by ego changes—for example, aging is usually accompanied by decrements in knowledge and skill. At the same time, success in an industrialized society is based on knowledge and skill, and age-grading is a mechanism used to insure that the young are sufficiently well trained to assume authority and the old are retired before they lose skill. Disengagement in America may be initiated by either the individual because of ego changes or by the society because of organizational imperatives, or by both simultaneously.

The ego is a product of experience. Because experience changes in quality and in amount, the ego also changes. It is also possible that there are some inevitable ego changes "programmed" into the development of the organism, which occur regardless of any but the most extreme experiences. Maturation is one such change; disengagement may be another.

In modern industrial society, positions in the occupational world are allocated on the basis of universalistic criteria of performance, and not on particularistic criteria of either biological or cultural heredity. This means that the young must be trained and the old retired before their knowledge is obsolete. Age-grading is one of the mechanisms through which this is accomplished. To say that someone is "old enough to retire" is not to comment on the obsolescence of his particular skill but upon his membership in an age echelon.

The individual may initiate the disengagement process because he has experienced ego changes that rob him of motivation for maintaining some of his bonds with others. On the other hand, society may initiate disengagement because the individual belongs to an age grade that is considered, on the whole, to be trained in skills too obsolete for adaptation to modern conditions. This avoids invidious comparisons between individuals, but sometimes retires valued members with usable skills. In the case of a woman, once her family is grown, some of her skill at homemaking, cooking, and baby care may, in American society, be considered obsolete.

When the individual's readiness for disengagement coincides almost exactly with society's readiness to release him from his main commitments, the ideal case of simultaneous disengagement occurs. (See the case of Mr. Allen, Chapter IX.)

Postulate 5: When both the individual and society are ready for disengagement, completed disengagement results. When neither is ready, continuing engagement results. When the individual is ready and society is not, a disjunction between the expectations of the individual and of the members of his social systems results, but usually engagement continues. When society is ready and the individual is not, the result of the disjunction is usually disengagement.

Inner ego changes may occur before the individual reaches the age where his echelon is normally retired. More commonly, in affluent American society, the echelon reaches retirement age before the individual has experienced sufficient inner change to prepare him for disengagement.

Corollary 1: If society is ready to disengage from the individual before he is ready to give up his central role—more the case for men than women—or if the individual is ready and cannot get permission—more common among women than men —lowered morale can follow.

Corollary 2: If society dispenses with the skills of an individual, but he is not, himself, ready for disengagement, he may re-engage himself through a different set of skills. Bertrand Russell is an excellent example; he has been engaged with the world consecutively as mathematician, logician, educator, social philosopher, historian of philosophy, moral and political philosopher, and, finally, as a writer of fiction.

Corollary 3: If the individual is ready for disengagement before society is, and if he has disengaged himself "prematurely," then society may try to re-engage him. During a national crisis, such as war, many disengaged individuals re-engage, some reluctantly, because of an appeal to their duty to country.

Postulate 6: Because the abandonment of life's central roles— work for men, marriage and family for women—results in a dramatically reduced social life space, it will result in crisis and loss of morale unless different roles, appropriate to the disengaged state, are available.

Corollary 1-A: Men face three problems of disengagement (Chapter VIII): membership in a peer group is lost, instrumental tasks through which to relate themselves to society are lacking, and status identity is lost. The first problem arises, in an age-graded society, because men have depended upon work for peer relations, the second because they have no purely sociable skills and must mediate relationships through instrumental activity, and the third because they have acquired their socioeconomic status through their occupational identity.

Corollary 1-B: The solutions to all of these problems will eventually arise from ego changes leading to preoccupations with inner states and to the narcissism of the very old

(Chapter XI). Temporary solutions to the first problem are provided by certain recreational groups and by kinsmen; to the second problem by voluntary instrumental activity, by temporary, short term, or part-time, re-engagement with the occupational world, and by recreation that has instrumental aspects. The solution to the third problem resides in Passive Mastery, described in Chapters VI and IX, which leads to satisfaction with what has been, rather than a pride in what is (Chapter VIII).

Corollary 2-A: Women face three problems of disengagement (Chapter VIII). Upon being widowed, they lose a highly cathected—whether negatively or positively—spouse, they lose the status derived from their husband's occupation, and they shift from obligatory to voluntary relationships.

Corollary 2-B: The solutions to all problems, as with men, need to be temporary only, because none of them remain problematical for the very old. To the first problem there is probably no true solution short of remarriage, although cathexis can, perhaps, be distributed among a group of kin. To the second problem, the solution is usually automatic; widows are given enough special consideration in this society to compensate for loss of status. The third problem is also easy to solve for women, because the higher death rate among men leaves an available peer group of widows. Furthermore, after the shock of bereavement has passed, membership in such a group allows a kind of non-obligatory, horizontal, peer relationship compatible with the process of disengagement (Chapter VIII).

Postulate 7: (a) *If the individual becomes sharply aware of the shortness of life and the scarcity of the time remaining to him (Chapter XIII), and if he perceives his life space as decreasing (Chapter V), and if his available ego energy is lessened (Chapter VI), then readiness for disengagement has begun.*

It seems probable that disengagement would be resisted forever if there were no problem of the allocation of time, and thus no anticipation of death. Questions of choice among alternative uses of time lead to curtailment of some activities. Questions of the inevitability of death lead to introspective reflections on the meaning of life.

(b) *The needs of a rational-legal occupational system in an affluent society, the nature of the nuclear family, and the differential death rate lead to society's giving echelons of people its permission to disengage.*

The requirement of specific skills (Chapter VIII and Postulates 3 and 4) leads to the retirement of groups of men, regardless of the skills of any given man. The self-limiting characteristics of the socialization process mean that children grow up, leave home, and relieve the mother-wife of half of her role. The preponderance of male deaths over female deaths means that many women finally disengage from their central role through widowhood (Postulate 6).

Postulate 8: The reductions in interaction and the loss of central roles result in a shift in the quality of relationship in the remaining roles (Chapters V, VIII, and XI). There is a wider choice of relational rewards, and a shift from vertical solidarities to horizontal ones.

As mutual, obligatory relationships decrease, the affectively neutral orientation necessary in the working world can be abandoned, and the diffuse, emotional, but responsible attitude necessary for the socialization of children can be abandoned.

Horizontal solidarities, being composed of similar units, are less interdependent, less demanding, and more optional than vertical solidarities, which, because of differences in role specifications, ability, and power, require mutual responsibility.

Corollary 1: In American society, those people who have high prestige and considerable power associate their image of their own success with the taking of responsibility and the management of hierarchical relationships. Therefore, the shift to the non-obligatory, egalitarian horizontal relationship is a serious disjunction for them; for this special class, retirement is a trauma.

Postulate 9: Disengagement is a culture-free concept, but the form it takes will always be culture-bound.

In American society, disengagement is more difficult for men than for women (Chapter VIII). In societies like classical China, which was traditional and patriarchal, and therefore valued wisdom, the role of the men merely shifted with age, and they became, in some ways, even more engaged as they became older. In some non-literate societies, especially those with scarcities of food, disengagement is coincident with the loss of instrumental ability.

In the next chapter we will discuss the connection between disengagement theory and four other concepts—intergenerational tension, the structure of the life span, time, and death.

CHAPTER XIII

The Relationship of Disengagement Theory to Some Other Concepts

WE WILL END this book by discussing briefly the connection between disengagement theory and intergenerational tension, the structure of the life span, and, finally, time and death. These are examples of the way in which this theory can be used to elaborate other sociological and psychological concepts.

■ Intergenerational Tension

All societies must handle tension between generations. Disengagement can be viewed as a phenomenon that functions to soften the rivalry between generations. A society whose organization depends partly on the assumption that science yields the only sure knowledge must somehow train its young in competence and retire its old, at the same

219

time avoiding wastefulness as well as rivalry. It is hard to keep the generations from stepping on one another's heels; the young are often ready for authority before the old wish to abandon it. Direct competition between the young and the old for powerful and instrumental roles would be highly disruptive, because it would cut across many important alignments, especially the family. If the young must wait and the old must withdraw, it is important that there be specifications for the attitudes appropriate to each age grade. We have observed already how sensitive we are to age-grading. This, in itself, may be part of our concern with "readiness" for tasks, and with specifying when full engagement may begin.

There are many mechanisms for reducing intergenerational conflict. Parsons (50) has suggested that the rather flamboyant youth culture in America allows the rebellious adolescent to free himself from his family before he engages himself fully with society and presents himself as a serious competitor for adult roles. Many other mechanisms are no doubt in use. An interesting analysis of intergenerational tension among the ladies of the W.C.T.U. (27) shows how the structure of the organization guarantees that the old women retain the power, and the young women develop solidarity among themselves while they wait their turn to run the show. The stability of the pattern is reminiscent of age-grading in some primitive societies. Bureaucracies, like families, have numerous ways of maintaining the balance between age and youth, experience and energy. These are all institutionalized expressions of society's specifications for when the young may become fully engaged and the old disengaged.

The dominant pattern of retirement at a fixed age, as we have pointed out in Chapters VIII and XII, is another such expression, and it operates even when it does not seem particularly appropriate. For example, in the lay leadership of a traditional organization like the church, there are norms that say that older men should disengage themselves from positions of authority and let younger men take over (69). Because these norms are subscribed to by these older men themselves, intergenerational tension is avoided.

The difference in the satisfactions available for each generation is probably directly related to the value placed upon it in relation to the other generations. We are said to devalue the old, and indeed, compared to the young and middle-aged, we no doubt do. But seldom, if ever, in the history of mankind have the old, as a group, been dealt with more sympathetically than they are in modern industrial society. Perhaps because we fall short of an ideal of perfect humanism, we are often dissatisfied with ourselves.

■ The Structure of the Life Span

There are some interesting parallels between the young and the old in their levels of engagement with society. The human life span can be thought of as rainbow-shaped, in the sense that the two ends are more similar to each other than either is to the middle. People have always been sensitive to the similarities between childhood and old age, and poets have found a piquancy in this symmetry. Psychologists, too, sometimes describe the very old in terms of "regression to infantile behavior," and anthropologists tell us that grandparents and grandchildren address each other by the same term in many societies, and that this means a symmetry of role. Durkheim, talking about suicide, describes a similarity in relation to society between the young and the old. "Suicide is known to be rare among children and to diminish among the aged in the last confines of life; physical man in both tends to be the whole of man. Society is still lacking in the former, for it has not had the time to form him in its image, and it begins to retreat from the latter or, what amounts to the same thing, he retreats from it (21)."

The level of this interpenetration of person and society marks the degree of engagement. Very small children, like very old people, are weakly engaged. They have few ties, although those they have are solidary and organic. Both ages are marked by egocentricity, idiosyncrasy of behavior, and indifference to all but the most intimate aspects of the environment. The developing ego of the child has not had time to incorporate much of society, or learn to master it; the aged ego has turned inward, relinquishing its former mastery.

The child is only beginning to learn to be bound by the expectations of others, and therefore mistakes are tolerated; the old person, slipping out of the web of normative control, is allowed almost as much freedom. The important difference between them is in the accumulation of values and beliefs which still anchor the behavior of the old person, but have yet to be acquired by the child. Because of this, there is a major difference between them; the child is usually spontaneous and expressive, the old person perhaps opinionated and fixed.

The roles assigned to very early childhood and to old age are predominantly socio-emotional rather than instrumental, and relatively weak in power. The old and the young are expected to seek response and pleasure, to assume a minimum of obligation. Both have solidary relationships with those in responsible, instrumental middle age. As a very old respondent says, "I have as much fun as children." *

The young, unlike the old, are expected to change their behavior because of the direction of movement. The child is expected to learn to be instrumental where it is appropriate, and to be guided by the major norms of society. The very old person, if he can still perform some tasks, is rewarded, but primarily he is expected to *be* rather than to *do*, to maintain

---

* It cannot be stressed too often that this is a sample of healthy people with reasonably adequate means. There is no implication that old people enjoy life if they are not well cared for physically and economically.

his equilibrium, to symbolize the past rather than to change and learn and create a new history. The *status* of childhood and old age are similar, but the *direction of movement* is opposite.

Adolescence and late middle age have a similar symmetry; the youth is beginning to move toward a firm engagement, the aging person is moving away from it. The adolescent is learning to master himself in order to master the world. He conforms as closely as possible to the ideal of his peers. He is seeking an identity. The aging adult gives up mastery of the world in favor of conformity to it, in order to free himself for introspection and in order to consolidate his identity. Both prefer solidarity with their peers, are often intolerant of vertical, binding, obligatory ties. The adolescent resents the authority of his parents; the aging person is setting aside an authority he has grown weary of.

Society permits a certain indulgence of both adolescents and aging adults. The one echelon has its fads, the other its foibles. Both may be prone to the sweeping generalization, the one because they are beginning to test, through doubt, the values they have always accepted, and the other because it views itself as the repository of them. But the adolescent is not so free as the aging person because of his direction of movement. He is having a last fling before entering the long period of full engagement with society. He must increase his responsibility for others, learn to put off his gratifications, and begin to affirm society's values. For the aging person, all these things lessen.

Middle age differs typically from adolescence and the aging years in four important ways: ego involvement must be with the outer world, responsible instrumental roles must be played, and a tight organic solidarity with less competent people must be undertaken, and, finally, the norms and values of society must be embodied and protected by this most highly engaged of groups. The middle-aged are at a period of their lives when it is hardest for a man to be an island unto himself.

■ Time and Death

The certainty of death brings the question of the allocation of time into sharp focus. It is possible that there are two points at which this allocation is related to the process of disengagement: first, when the knowledge that time does not last forever presents itself urgently to the mind, and, second, when the feeling comes that time is nearly over.

It is said that no young man believes that he will ever die. The young know *about* death but do not seem to feel its inexorability. However, everyone seems to reach a point at which both the mortality of life and its briefness come into clear focus. Wallach and Green (76) have explored the different perceptions of time in the young and the old. Old people describe time in images that suggest it is short and swift, while young people choose images that suggest that it is slow and long. It is commonly believed that filled time flies and empty time crawls, but old people with empty time find it fleeting, and young people, with filled time, feel it crawl. When time first begins to fly, and to become precious, readiness for disengagement may have started.

We do not know when this shift in perception of time takes place, but we can speculate. Perhaps it is between thirty-five and forty, the halfway mark, the point at which we cease to measure our age by the distance from our birth and start to measure it by the distance from our death (22, p. 7). Perhaps the shift begins when we wonder for the first time whether we are wasting the time we have left. With our days numbered, as it were, we may discard some activities we have never valued much. We may start to read books we have long had on the agenda, or we may decide that we have no more time to spend reading. The first awareness of the shortness of life is often caught vividly in literature. There is a story of a man who, watching the ice skaters at Rockefeller Center, realized, suddenly and sadly, that he had always harbored a belief that "someday," when he had time, he would learn to skate.

There is a comic side to the discovery that time runs out. Stephen Potter describes waking on his fiftieth birthday with a stiff back: "Up to that moment," he writes, "I had always privately assumed that if I really put my mind to it, I could not only take twelve strokes off my handicap, I could win the Golf Amateur as well, and it indeed was only just this unfortunate business of the clash of dates, which would make it impossible when I really get down to it as I had intended, to win the Golf Open and Wimbledon in the same year (56)."

Perhaps in all minds there lurk schemes that are one day abandoned. Perhaps they are planned during the long years of youth, when we are learning the art of putting off today's gratifications in order to invest in tomorrow's. The first stirrings of a willingness to disengage from the peak involvement of the middle years may be the feeling that there is not time to do everything we had meant to do.

The beginning of discrimination among all the possible uses of the time we have left is probably tied to the beginning of the shift of cathexis from outside achievement to reflection on the meaning of the past. If this is so, we have a conceptual overlap with Erikson's developmental stages, for he characterizes "ego integrity," his eighth and most mature phase, as "acceptance of one's one and only life cycle as something that had to be and that, by necessity, permitted of no substitutions (24)." Such an acceptance may have to be preceded by an apprehension of mortality. Children do not have this apprehension; even intellectual clarity about death comes quite late in childhood (2), and emotional clarity not until much later. One respondent told us that until he had a heart attack, at the age of fifty-nine, he felt that his life was "just practice." After his illness, he realized that it was not, and that his life was nearly over. We do not know, however, if everyone experiences such a sudden and poignant shift in perception.

The thought that time is finite may sharpen until it becomes "Time is running out; life is nearly over." This realization may herald the severing of all but the most intimately needed ties with others; it may be the point at which disengagement becomes as complete as it can get this side of the grave. We do not know when this feeling comes, and it may never come to some. Others may have such a feeling, but still be subject to demands upon them that override it.

The apprehension of death as a not-so-distant goal may be a time of redefinition of the self as less bound to the surrounding network of interaction. The anticipation of being apart from those nearby may accelerate withdrawal of cathexis from them, and hasten the turning of all cathexis inward—to the self for its own sake and the past for its memories.

The anticipation of death frees us from the obligation to participate in the ongoing stream of life. If there is only a little time left, there is no point in planning for a future, and no point in putting off today's gratification. Thus, the ego-centeredness of old age, rooted in the withdrawal from normative controls, has this second important source. Furthermore, society, recognizing the scarcity of time at the end of life, gives even its most illustrious men and women permission to disengage, if they wish to, from all interactions but those most necessary for their survival. When a middle-aged man dies, he is torn from the fabric of life; when an old man dies, he has already unravelled the web of interaction so much that he can slip from life almost unnoticed.* Old people thus feel ready

* A newspaper reporter tells us that, as a cub writing obituaries, he could guess the age of the deceased from telephone conversations. When young people die, even when there has been some warning, there is devastation; old people leave a composed sadness. It was not, he felt, because they were less loved, but because there is "a time for living and a time for dying."

to die, and this may be why, as we have said in Chapter VI, they discuss death with considerable poise.

If the very old person faces a final developmental crisis, it may be the outer aspect of the crisis of accepting his past identity and his one and only life cycle. It may be the crisis of holding on as against letting go. If he can accept what his life has been, he may be happy to spend its short remainder almost totally preoccupied with himself—with his ruminations, with instantly gratifying and undemanding contacts. His last pleasures seem to reside in good meals, an occasional outing, short naps, and long dreams. By the end of his life, his bonds have been all but severed—disengagement is complete, he is free to die, and death is the last logical step in the process of living.

In this book we have developed an inductive theory of aging to fit our data. We have presented the theory logically, and have illustrated how it can be related to other concepts. If it is a good theory, it will be used to develop new hypotheses and to generate solutions to problems; in the end, there is nothing so practical as a good theory.

The Study Population

The panel studied in this research is a sample of men and women between fifty and seventy years of age, augmented by a quasi-sample of men and women between seventy and ninety. We will discuss the panel first.

■ **The Characteristics of the Panel**

The universe the sample was drawn from was a random 8700 dwelling units in the urbanized area of Kansas City, both in Missouri and Kansas. However, our panel departs from randomness in several ways, as follows:

1. *Health:* The dwelling units of our sample base had been drawn originally for a study of the chronically ill (54). All of the members in the 8700 dwelling units between forty-five and

seventy-four had been asked to fill out a health questionnaire. Those respondents who had chronic disorders serious enough to render them unable to perform in their usual capacity at work or in the home were discarded.

Each respondent's health status was assigned by a group of medical judges to one of the following categories:

1. Reporting no chronic conditions.

2. Reporting chronic conditions but no activity limitation.

3. Limited in secondary activities.

4. Limited in amount and kind of primary occupational or domestic activity.

5. Unable to engage in primary occupational or domestic activities.

Table 1–1 shows the distribution of health status among the universe, the panel, and the losses from the panel. At the time these health data were collected, the universe was aged forty-five to seventy-four, while our panel was aged forty-eight to sixty-eight. We do not know what effect excluding the oldest and youngest members of the universe may have had upon the distribution of health statuses.

TABLE 1–1

HEALTH STATUS OF THE PANEL [a]

Health Category	Universe (Ages 45–74)	Panel (Ages 48–68)	Losses (Ages 48–68)	Total
1	5,172	55	20	5,247
2	6,762	95	16	6,873
3	678	10	5	693
4	1,422	12	2	1,436
5	640	0	0	640
Total	14,674	172	43	14,889

[a] This information was kindly supplied by Warren A. Peterson of Community Studies, Incorporated, Kansas City, who surveyed the health of this group.

When the chronically impaired are excluded, and Health Statuses 1 and 2 (unimpaired) and 3 and 4 (impaired) are grouped, the distribution of impairment among the universe, the panel, and the losses from the panel is no different from chance distribution.

Losses are, however, heaviest from those reporting no chronic conditions. Although the respondent who does not report any health impairment may be healthy, it is also possible that he resents being asked about his health and withholds information. People who refuse to take part in research panels may be healthier than those who comply, or they may have a tendency to refuse giving out any information about themselves. Some may have illnesses they are ashamed of.

In its health status, our panel is significantly different from its universe only in its lack of persons chronically ill and impaired. Within the health statuses themselves, however, error is introduced by the fact that the respondent did not always answer the health questions on his own behalf.* We cannot estimate the extent of the error introduced through this fact, but from this panel study we get the impression that it is not great.

2. *Rural-Urban Residence:* The universe was drawn from the metropolitan area of Kansas City, which, according to the census definition, includes all the counties that contain part of a city or are "metropolitan in character." We excluded all farmers from our panel by drawing a boundary around an "urbanized area" within the metropolitan area. Although this resulted in

*We are not convinced that better data are gathered from the respondent himself. Examining our own experiences, one of us found that when she gave her own medical history she excluded many symptoms she had recently complained of, but her husband included all of these when he described her health history. However, her own description resulted in a health status that matched her own subjective feeling of good health, and her husband's description resulted in a status of chronic illness. In general, refinements of judgment about such health data are unwarranted, for this and other reasons.

a loss of 5 per cent from the universe, the gain in ease of interviewing and homogeneity of the sample was considered sufficient compensation for this loss.

3. *Age:* The period from fifty to seventy appeared, from previous work, to represent middle age (33). For this reason we excluded everyone under forty-eight and over sixty-eight from the universe. By the time this panel was first approached, its members were between fifty and seventy. As we have pointed out in the text, this age range was too narrow, and it had to be augmented.

4. *Race:* Negroes were excluded because including them was perceived as compounding interviewing problems, and because the small size of the panel required a restriction of the number of variables.

5. *Socioeconomic Class:* We originally decided to use three discrete class groupings, but we have used class as a continuous variable or selected a cutting point which divided the population in half. We have not used class often in our analyses, preferring to use its four components individually, and preferring to seek differences which transcend class.

When we had eliminated the chronically ill, Negroes, and those over sixty-eight and under forty-eight years of age, we were left with a base of 1,236 people from whom to choose our panel. These people were each assigned an Index of Social Class (78, Ch. III) by a modification of Warner's method. Three elements were used: education, location of the household,* and occupation. In 130 out of the 1,236 cases, either education or occupation was not available, and therefore a score for house type was substituted. Each of the three ele-

---

* A status-reputation map was kindly supplied by Warren A. Peterson, of Community Studies, Inc.

ments was scored from 1 to 7, and a weighted total was obtained by multiplying each such score by 4 and then adding. The range of resulting scores was 12 to 84. The distribution of these 1,236 people by ISC was normal.

We decided to eliminate the lowest and the highest layers of the class structure. Lower-class people are difficult to communicate with and require special interviewing techniques. Furthermore, they are often mobile and therefore hard to keep in a panel. Upper-class people are hard to reach for different reasons. Accordingly, all those whose ISC scores were higher than 68, and those whose scores were as low as 12, were discarded. This left approximately half working class and half middle class. From this residual group we drew a panel of 216 names, half women, half men, and a third from each of the age groups: 48-54, 55-61, and 62-68. These people were then reassigned ISC scores based on a 7-point rating of occupation, education, income, and area of residence. Education scores for the older half of the panel were increased by half a point to credit them with higher status for less education than the younger half. The total was multiplied by 4, giving a possible range of scores from 16 to 114. The range of scores actually found was 24 to 102. As a result of our method of selection, we have a strong middle-class bias. Our panel is better educated, wealthier, and of higher occupational and residential prestige than the universe.

6. *Losses:* The initial health questionnaire suffered a 5 per cent loss, of which 2 per cent were refusals. We have no information about these people. After the controlled reduction of the universe on the basis of health, class, residence, and race, we made our initial contact with the 216 people chosen. At this time, 172 people agreed to join the panel and 37 refused. Seven more people were unobtainable because of removal or

death, or because of error in the recording of their ages or the data pertaining to socioeconomic class.

Thirty-seven refusals (17 per cent) are high, but our interviewers had been warned that because it was important to secure continuing co-operation with these people, high-pressure techniques should be avoided. Nevertheless, all refusals were pursued until there was no possible hope that they would capitulate; often there were four or five contacts. To this end, new interviewers were assigned, letters written, and phone calls made. Few gave in, and one threatened to sue. In short, we feel that no one who could have been persuaded to join the panel was lost from it through lack of effort.*

Because so many had refused, we felt it important to find out something about them. Recalling that these people had been approached a number of times, once with a health questionnaire and several times with our initial interview, we sent out a staff member who engaged them in conversation about their television-viewing habits. He allowed them to believe that he was a commercial interviewer, without telling them this. He asked them whom they watched television with, how often, what other recreation they customarily engaged in, and so on. Most of these people resented his questioning and he was able to interview only fifteen of the refusals, the other twenty-two remaining adamant. These fifteen did not differ from the panel in their household composition, in the duration of their residence in Kansas City, or in their church attendance. However, they did appear to be less involved with friends than the panel, and our general impression was that they were people who were either much too busy to grant the interview or much too isolated and suspicious.

In subsequent interviews, more losses were sustained. The

* The interviewer with the lowest refusal rate on Interview 1 had the highest rates on Interviews 2 and 3, and this suggests that we had been right in avoiding extreme pressure the first time around.

people who willingly remained in the panel impressed us as being more narcissistic than those who dropped out. As Table 1–2 shows, there were significantly more drop-outs from the married men between sixty and sixty-nine than from the other men in the panel, but not from the women. Table 1–3 shows that working-class women of high morale are the big drop-out group. Finally, when we look at Social Lifespace scores, we

TABLE 1–2

PER CENTS REMAINING [a] AT EACH INTERVIEW BY
AGE, SEX, AND MARITAL STATUS

Respondents	Number Interviewed	Interview				
		1	2	3	4	5
Total Panel	172	*100*	*91.3*	*81.9*	*73.8*	*66.2*
Married men	75	*100*	*90.6*	*82.6*	*74.6*	*67.9*
50–59	39	100	92.3	84.6	76.9	76.9
60–69	31	100	90.3	80.6	70.9	54.8
70+	5	100	80.0	80.0	80.0	80.0
Nonmarried men	13	*100*	*92.3*	*84.6*	*84.6*	*84.6*
50–59	5	100	80.0	80.0	80.0	80.0
60–69	5	100	100.0	80.0	80.0	80.0
70+	3	100	100.0	100.0	100.0	100.0
Married women	50	*100*	*92.0*	*86.0*	*72.0*	*60.0*
50–59	29	100	89.6	82.7	75.9	58.6
60–69	19	100	94.7	84.2	68.4	63.1
70+	2	100	100.0	100.0	50.0	50.0
Nonmarried women	34	*100*	*88.2*	*73.4*	*67.6*	*61.7*
50–59	11	100	81.8	81.8	81.8	81.8
60–69	20	100	90.0	75.0	65.0	55.0
70+	3	100	100.0	33.3	33.3	33.3
Total quasi-sample [b]	107	—[c]	—	*100.0*	*83.1*	*64.4*
70–80	69	—	—	100.0	76.8	59.4
80+	38	—	—	100.0	76.3	71.1

[a] Deaths account for about 15 per cent of the losses, moving for another 10 per cent, and the remaining 75 per cent were refusals. Deaths do not occur significantly more often in any category, even the oldest.

[b] There is no difference between men and women in the quasi-sample.

[c] The quasi-sample started at the third interview.

TABLE 1–3

PER CENTS REMAINING AT EACH INTERVIEW BY SEX AND
MORALE AND SOCIOECONOMIC STATUS

Respondents	Number Interviewed	Interview		
		3 a	4	5
Total	*211*	*100*	*86.2*	*73.9*
Total Men	*107*	*100*	*86.9*	*75.7*
Lower morale,b lower status c	21	100	85.7	71.4
Lower morale, higher status	24	100	87.4	75.0
Higher morale, lower status	31	100	87.1	70.9
Higher morale, higher status	31	100	87.1	83.8
Total Women	*104*	*100*	*84.6*	*72.1*
Lower morale, lower status	20	100	95.0	80.0
Lower morale, higher status	34	100	79.4	70.5
Higher morale, lower status	26	100	80.7	61.5
Higher morale, higher status	24	100	87.4	79.1

a Morale Scores are not available until Interview 3.
b Lower Morale, scores 0 and 1; Higher Morale, scores 2, 3, 4.
c Lower Status, ISC, 70 and over; Higher Status, under 70.

find that isolated people, both men and women, drop out (54 per cent losses by Interview 5) significantly more often than do busy and involved people (25 per cent losses by Interview 5).

■ The Characteristics of the Quasi-Sample

During the early part of the analysis, it became evident that we needed to extend the age range of our panel, because a cutting point at around seventy years of age occurred "naturally" in many of the tables. It would have been expensive and difficult to get a stratified random sample of healthy old people "continuous" with the panel, because of the scarcity of such people in the population, because it is hard to assign an ISC score to them—one must decide whether the retired person should be judged by his past occupation and income or by his present situation—and because it is hard to equate the health status of old people who may have chronic disorders but are nevertheless basically "tough," with that of middle-aged people.

For all of these reasons we used a "bush-fire" technique for gathering this quasi-sample. Three interviewers were selected on the basis of their socioeconomic class—one was upper-middle class, a professional; one lower-middle, a grade-school teacher; and one working class, a clerk. They were asked to gather a group of respondents between seventy and ninety from their own neighborhoods and from among acquaintances who were ambulatory and not obviously ill.

The resulting group of old people differ from the panel in several ways.

1. *Area of Residence:* From Table 1–4, it is clear that the older people live in more depressed areas than the panel. We

TABLE 1–4

AREA OF RESIDENCE OF THE PANEL AND QUASI-SAMPLE

Comparison Groups	High Status					Low Status		
	1	2	3	4	5	6	7	Total
Panel	3	31	38	53	28	14	5	172
Quasi-sample	0	2	17	22	28	35	3	107

might infer that these are of a different socioeconomic class, but because old people frequently prefer to stay in their accustomed homes even though the neighborhoods have deteriorated, it would be a mistake to assume this too certainly. Especially is the attachment to residence important when we consider that the respondents' average length of residence in Kansas City is more than thirty years. However, we do know that inasmuch as area of residence is a prestige and status symbol, the old people are deprived relative to the middle-aged people.

2. *Sex:* As Table 1–5 shows, the sex ratios do not represent the sex distribution in the general population. We have, as a result

TABLE 1–5

Sᴇx Rᴀᴛɪᴏ ᴏғ Pᴀɴᴇʟ ᴀɴᴅ Qᴜᴀsɪ-Sᴀᴍᴘʟᴇ ᴀɴᴅ Gᴇɴᴇʀᴀʟ Pᴏᴘᴜʟᴀᴛɪᴏɴ

Comparison Groups	Per Cent Male	Per Cent Female
Panel	51.2	48.8
General population (white) 1950 Census (50–69)	48.5	51.5
Quasi-sample	46.7	53.3
General population (white) 1950 Census (70 and up)	44.7	55.3

of the distribution of our initial refusals, a greater proportion of men in our panel than the general population would predict for us, and similarly, in our quasi-sample, we have more men than we could reasonably expect. The difference from expectation is about the same in each case; neither is very great.

3. *Religion:* The slight excess of Catholics in the quasi-sample (Table 1–6) may indicate that there is a genuine, if small, class difference between the panel and the quasi-sample.

TABLE 1–6

Rᴇʟɪɢɪᴏɴ ᴏғ Pᴀɴᴇʟ, Qᴜᴀsɪ-Sᴀᴍᴘʟᴇ, ᴀɴᴅ Gᴇɴᴇʀᴀʟ Pᴏᴘᴜʟᴀᴛɪᴏɴ

Comparison Groups	Per Cent Protestant	Per Cent Catholic	Per Cent Jewish
Panel	80	16	4
Quasi-sample	81	18	1
Kansas City area (1947)	81	13	6

4. *Health:* The quasi-sample cannot be directly compared with the panel because the former did not have the same inten-

sive health interview. However, during the interviewing, they were asked about their recent illnesses and general health, and their responses were classified into those complaining of no ill health, those complaining but evidently little impaired, and those seriously impaired by illness. Table 1–7 shows that there is little difference between the younger and the older members of the quasi-sample, except for a greater percentage of the older group being seriously impaired. Impairments include

TABLE 1–7
HEALTH STATUS OF QUASI-SAMPLE

Health Category	70–79		80 plus	
	Number	Per Cent	Number	Per Cent
Number interviewed	69		37 [a]	
Uncomplaining	33	47.8	16	43.2
Complaining but unimpaired	26	37.7	12	32.4
Impaired	10	14.5	9	24.3

[a] This information was lacking for one respondent over eighty.

blindness and deafness as well as arthritic crippling and heart conditions.

If the uncomplaining are roughly equated with Health Category 1 of the panel, and the complaining but unimpaired are equated with Categories 2, 3, and 4, the quasi-sample differs from the panel in having more in the extreme categories. The chronically impaired are excluded from the panel, but 19 members of the quasi-sample were included even though they were seriously impaired. The quasi-sample had a significantly higher proportion of uncomplaining people than the panel. This may be a reflection of the biological toughness of very old people, or a reflection of their decreased preoccupation with health matters.

In general, the quasi-sample appears to be sufficiently like the panel to warrant combining both populations for the purposes of analysis, although there is some reason to believe that the panel has a greater upper-middle-class bias than the quasi-sample.

There are three basic totals which are most commonly used throughout the tables. In a few tables there is a slight reduction in number from these totals because of one or two people refusing particular questions in the interview. The largest total is 279 which is the number of panel and quasi-sample members who furnished Wave I of the interviewing program. This includes 172 panel members of whom 88 are men and 84 women, 69 quasi-sample members in their seventies, 34 men and 35 women, and 38 in their eighties, 16 men and 22 women.

The second total is the 211 respondents who finished Wave III. This includes 142 panel members of whom 73 are men and 69 women, and the original 69 members of the quasi-sample seventies who were picked up later than the panel and given an interview which was a composite of Interviews 1, 2, and 3. However, the eighty-year-olds are not in this total because many of the questions analyzed were not asked of them owing to the difficulty in maintaining their interest in the subject matter.

The third total is 156 who finished Wave V and is made up of 115 panel members, 62 men and 53 women, and 41 in their seventies, 19 men and 22 women.

The psychological analyses were performed only on cases in which TAT protocols were suitable, and sometimes only on samples of the whole group. In some cases respondents from the earlier Carnegie Study are added.

■ **Reliability of Respondent's Information**

In general, we have observed that the more normatively governed an area of inquiry, the more likely we are to get stereotyped answers to our questions. It has been demonstrated by others, for example, that information about sexual practices reflects the cultural norms (77), and this is probably true for many areas of behavior. In our panel, for example, we tend to get highly similar responses to questions about religion. Occasionally it is possible to be reasonably sure that a normative response is replacing a "truthful" one; that is, that the respondent is telling us what he thinks he ought to believe or what he thinks we want to hear. We have two types of questions for which it is possible to say, with reasonable certainty, that the respondent is telling us not what he does but what he thinks he should do and what he thinks we expect him to do. For example, the respondents were asked, "Would you say that you're a fairly regular voter, or don't you vote so regularly? I mean all kinds of elections—local, state, and national?" In our panel, 71 per cent claimed that they always voted if they were physically able to, 12.7 per cent said they voted occasionally, and only 3.6 per cent admitted they never vote.* However, the fact is that in this area only Presidential elections produce a vote as heavy as our panel claim. The usual figure is about half or fewer of the eligible voters, depending upon the election. Obviously our panel is composed of people who feel they ought to tell us they vote, probably feel they ought in fact to vote, but, equally probably, do not vote so regularly as they claim.

A second type of question that yields normative answers concerns food. Part of the panel was asked, in the course of a series of questions about their daily round of activities, to describe their meals. Our panel members reply to this questioning as if they were reading from a textbook on dietetics. Almost no one admits to eating desserts; almost everyone declares that he eats cottage cheese and salad for lunch; almost everyone eats a well-balanced, high-protein, low-calorie diet. However, our panel contains people of various degrees of obesity, and it seems most improbable that their descriptions of their daily diet tell us much more than the norms about ideal eating habits in America today. Closely related to the norms about eating are

---

* The remainder were not asked this question for administrative reasons.

the norms about early rising. We have found that rising as early as 5 A.M. to 6 A.M. is almost universally claimed. No panel member boasts of lying abed during the day, but here, of course, we have no evidence, even inferential, that they do.

There are ways to circumvent this tendency toward normative responses. If the questions asked are very specific and concrete, they are less apt to receive a stereotyped reply; for example, the respondent is more likely to give an account of his wife's shortcomings if he is asked to select from a check list her irritating personal habits than if he is simply asked to tell us her faults.

Finally, ideological material is by no means a loss. We may be disappointed when a question turns out to be a "sleeper" and produces the same response from each respondent, but it gives a useful picture of the norms prevailing among our population.

APPENDIX 2

The Measures of Engagement

■ Interaction Index

This variable is a subjective judgment based on detailed responses to the questions "I would like you to tell me what a typical day is like for you," and "What is a typical weekend like?" Two scorers assigned scores from 1 to 5 to each respondent on the basis of the amount of each day spent in situations where others could exercise normative controls over his behavior. The two scorers had a reliability of .8, using the statistic "C", or Contingency Score. The Interaction Index is essentially an indication of the saturation of the daily life with interaction and says nothing about variety of roles or numbers interacted with. An aged couple who live alone and are together all day might get as high a score as a person who worked in constant interaction with others and had a busy

243

social and recreational life, but lived alone. The range of scores was from 1 to 5; 58 per cent scored 1 or 2 and are called low scores throughout.

■ **Lifespace Measure**

Because this is a pilot study, some hypotheses and concepts have grown out of the data, and the operational use made of these concepts has had to be based on data already collected and available. This is true of the Lifespace Measure. Although the interviews were developed around the concept of "social life space," the operations for its measurement were not developed until after Interview 3. The following questions were analyzed:

1. When you were last interviewed, there were $\overline{\text{(no. in household)}}$ living here. Are the same number of persons living here now? ___

2. Last time, you mentioned $\overline{\text{(whoever mentioned in Interview 2)}}$ as the relatives you feel closest to. Is that right? ___

3. How often do you get together with these relatives?

    0___ (every day)
    1___ (at least once a week)
    2___ (a few times a month)
    3___ (about once a month)
    4___ (a few times a year)
    5___ (about once a year)
    6___ (almost never—haven't seen in years)

4. How many people that you know do you consider close friends— that is, people you can confide in and talk over personal matters with? (Get Respondent to give you a specific *number,* if possible.)

5. Now take the friends you're closest to—about how often do you get together with any of them?

   0____ (at least once a week)
   1____ (a few times a month)
   2____ (about once a month)
   3____ (a few times a year)
   4____ (almost never—haven't seen in years)

6. Now, about people you see for certain specific purposes—like storekeepers, bus drivers, waiters, salespeople, and so on. About how many of these do you see fairly regularly, would you say? (Try to pin Respondent down to a number, even if only approximate.)

7. Last time, you mentioned $\overline{\text{(whoever was mentioned in Interview 1)}}$ as the neighbors you know best. Is that right?

8. How often do you get together with these neighbors? *

   0____ (every day)
   1____ (at least once a week)
   2____ (a few times a month)
   3____ (about once a month)
   4____ (anything less)

9. In the course of a day's work, about how many people do you see and talk to?

The following questions about church and voluntary organizations were omitted, because they do not *necessarily* imply interaction. Furthermore, if interaction takes place in such a context with any regularity, the people interacted with are usually listed as friends or neighbors.

* Sometimes respondents list the same people under several categories; thus, a neighbor may also be given as a friend, or a relative as a friend. It is important to make sure in the analysis, therefore, that the interaction or frequency score is not artificially increased by counting the same person more than once.

1. How often do you attend church (temple)?

    1＿＿(twice or oftener per week)
    2＿＿(once a week)
    3＿＿(once or twice a month)
    4＿＿(2 or 3 times a year)
    5＿＿(on very special occasions)
    6＿＿(never)

2. Do you belong to any committees, auxiliaries (teach Sunday school), or anything like that? *[If yes, get list of all activities.]*

3. Now, I'd like you to think over very carefully and tell me if you belong to any groups, clubs, or associations, or anything like that. Do you belong to any such groups?

    Yes ＿＿ 1
    No ＿＿ 2
    [If yes, ask A and B.]
    A. What are the groups and how often do you attend each?
    B. What do you do at each of the groups?

The unit of time selected for scoring was arbitrarily set at one month, because that was the smallest unit in terms of which we could score the questions without doing violence to the responses. The questions were weighted according to the following criteria in order to yield the rate of interaction per month in each role. Consideration was given to the relative amount of normative control generally expected in the situation when the weighting was worked out. Thus, friends and relatives were weighted more than neighbors.

1. *Number in household*
    Frequency Score: Assuming daily interaction with each other person in the household, each person (other than the respondent) listed is multiplied by 30 (days).

2. *Relatives*

Frequency Score: Each relative mentioned is given a score as follows:

If seen every day . . . . . score 30
If seen once a week . . . . score 4
If seen a few times a month . score 3
If seen once a month . . . score 1
If seen anything less . . . . score 0

3. *Friends*

Frequency Score: Each friend mentioned is given a score as follows:

If seen every day . . . . . score 30
If seen once a week . . . . score 4
If seen a few times a month . score 3
If seen once a month . . . score 1
If seen anything less . . . . score 0

4. *Neighbors* (based on neighbor seen most frequently)

Frequency Score:

If seen every day . . . . . score 30
If seen at least once a week . score 4
If seen a few times a month . score 3
If seen once a month . . . score 1
If seen anything less . . . . score 0

5. *Fellow Workers*

Frequency: Number stated × 20. (This assumes daily interaction, approximately 20 days per month.)

6. *Specific People*

Frequency: Number stated × 4. (This assumes that when asked this question, the respondents thought in terms of number seen per week. There is some empirical evidence for this assumption.)

The Lifespace Measure produced by summing these six elements was markedly Poisson in distribution. We anticipated using Lifespace as a continuous variable, and therefore we transformed the scores $\sqrt{A} + \sqrt{n+1}$ where A is the raw sum of the six items. The resulting distribution was still Poisson, but much improved.

TABLE 2–1

DISTRIBUTION OF LIFESPACE SCORE

Lifespace Score	Per Cent of Panel and Quasi-sample	Lifespace Score	Per Cent of Panel and Quasi-sample
0–4	.5	55–59	1.0
5–9	1.5	60–64	1.5
10–14	6.5	65–69	2.5
15–19	26.5	70–74	3.0
20–24	15.0	75–79	1.0
25–29	6.0	80–84	1.0
30–34	5.0	85–89	0.0
35–39	5.0	90–94	2.5
40–44	6.5	95–99	2.5
45–49	6.5	100 +	1.0
50–54	5.0		

The Lifespace Measure has the desirable quality of being an actual estimate of the reported interactions and not an index of them.

The relationship between the various interactional elements in the Social Lifespace Measure and the Total Score are shown in Table 2–2. As far as we are able to verify in interviews, the heavy weight of work which Table 2–2 shows is a true reflection of reality.

■ **Role Count**

This score was developed by summing the following elements:

1. Number in Household: If only one person other than the respondent who lives in the household, count 1.

TABLE 2-2

DISTRIBUTION OF RESPONDENTS BY CONTRIBUTION OF EACH LIFESPACE ITEM TO TOTAL SCORE
(PANEL AND SEVENTIES, WAVE III)

Per Cent of Contribution to Total Score	Item					
	Household Members	Relatives	Friends	Neighbors	Specific People	Fellow Workers
Total respondents	211	211	211	211	211	211
Total workers	100	100	100	100	100	100
No contribution	14	36	34	43	6	0
1–29% of total score	82	63	66	57	89	1
30–59% of total score	4	1	0	0	3	23
60–100% of total score	0	0	0	0	2	76
Median number interactions per month	30	4	6	3	36	400
Range of interactions per month	0–180	0–180	0–75	0–30	0–400	30–10,000
Total nonworkers	111	111	111	111	111	111
No contribution	31	37	34	52	7	111
1–29% of total score	21	58	70	51	39	0
30–59% of total score	43	12	6	8	37	0
60–100% of total score	16	4	1	0	28	0
Median number interactions per month	30	8	8	3	16	0
Range of interaction per month	0–150	0–60	0–40	0–30	0–220	0

For two or more people, count 2.

2. Relatives: For each category of relatives mentioned in Interview 1, count 1. If none, count 0.

3. Friends: Count 1 if any friends are mentioned, 0 if none are mentioned.

4. Neighbors: As for friends.

5. Fellow Workers: Score 1 if employed, 0 if unemployed.

6. Specific People: Score 1 if any mentioned, 0 if none are mentioned.

In addition to the above elements which are also in the Lifespace Score, the following roles which may not require interaction are counted.

7. Church: Score 1 for membership, 0 if not a member.

8. Organizations: Score 1 for each attended, 0 if none.

The distribution of roles is shown in Table 2–3.

TABLE 2–3

DISTRIBUTION OF RESPONDENTS BY NUMBER OF ROLES
(PANEL AND SEVENTIES, WAVE III)

Number of Roles	Number of Respondents	Per Cent
1–2	8	3.8
3–4	60	28.4
5–6	93	44.1
7–8	46	21.8
9	4	1.9
Total	*211*	*100.0*

■ **Authoritarian Personality**

The following items were adapted from the original scale developed by Adorno and his co-workers (1):

1. The most important thing to teach children is absolute obedience to their parents.

2. There are two kinds of people in the world: the weak and the strong.
3. Any good leader should be strict with people under him in order to gain their respect.
4. No decent man can respect a woman who has had sex relations before marriage.
5. Prison is too good for sex criminals. They should be publicly whipped or worse.
6. Familiarity breeds contempt.

■ **Perceived Lifespace**

This measure was developed from the questionnaire items that asked the respondent to compare his present interaction pattern with his remembrance of his interaction pattern at age forty-five. The items used and the scoring technique follow:

1. Did you see more or less of (the relatives you feel closest to) when you were forty-five (than you do now)?

Answer	*Score*
more now	4
about the same	3
more then	2

2. Did you have more close friends whom you saw regularly when you were forty-five, or more now?

more now	4
about the same	3
more then	2

3. Would you say you are more or less of a churchgoer now than when you were forty-five?

more now	4
about the same or never went . .	3

	Answer	*Score*
	more then	2

4. Would you say you're more or less active in clubs and organizations now, or were you more active when you were forty-five?

	more now	4
	about the same or never went . .	3
	more then	2

5. How about when you were forty-five? What was a typical week like for you then in terms of the people you saw and talked with?

	more now	3
	same	2
	more then	1

When these scores are summed the possible range is 9–19; however the actual range was 9–18. The score 14 indicates no net change is perceived; 1–13 means smaller, and 15–18 larger Perceived Lifespace. The question regarding a typical week has a very slightly lower weight than the other questions because answers to it were not precoded and hence were more ambiguous. Furthermore, the type of interaction was judged to be slightly less relevant. Distribution of the panel and the quasi-sample on this index are shown in Table 2–4.

TABLE 2–4

DISTRIBUTION OF SCORES ON PERCEIVED LIFESPACE MEASURE
(PANEL AND SEVENTIES, WAVE III)

Score	Per Cent of Panel and Quasi-sample	Score	Per Cent of Panel and Quasi-sample
9	7.1	14	13.7
10	11.8	15	7.6
11	18.5	16	10.0
12	15.2	17	1.4
13	12.8	18	1.9

■ Ego Energy Scores

This score (62) was developed from responses to Cards 1, 2, 6-BM, 7-BM, and 17-BM of the Murray TAT set (47). The responses were scored for four items: (1) the introduction of non-pictured characters, (2) introduction of conflict into the story, (3) activity-energy level ascribed to characters, and (4) affect intensity. Each respondent was rated from 0 to 5 on each card, and these ratings were summed.

The Ego-Energy Score is related to Perceived Lifespace. Forty-five per cent of those with low ego-energy scores had stable or increased life spaces, compared to 70 per cent of those with high ego-energy scores among the 144 respondents for whom both measures are available. Although this difference is significant, it is not impressive, and might arise as an artifact of both measures being related to age. Furthermore, there is the usual bias of the 144 people compared to the total. We deal with these variables, however, as if they were related, although this must be treated as a hypothesis.

■ Orientation to Interaction

Orientation to Interaction was determined on the basis of responses to the following question:

"Here are four general types of people we see around us in our daily lives. Look these descriptions over carefully, then tell me which two of these descriptions resemble you most, as you actually are. First tell me the one you think resembles you *most*, then the one that resembles you *second* most."

A. A person who is *esteemed* by others, and takes a continuous interest in human welfare in general. (Diffuse and neutral set to interaction)

B. A person who is *enjoyed* by others, and takes his joys and sorrows as they come, from day to day. (Specific and affective set)

C. A person who is *loved* by others, and takes a continuous inter-
    est in the personal welfare of all those who are dear to him.
    (Diffuse and affective set)
D. A person who is *approved* by others and attends to his affairs
    conscientiously, from day to day. (Specific and neutral set)

The respondent is then asked to say which two he would
prefer to resemble. This gives him four choices, two of how he
actually perceives himself and two of how he would like to be.

■ **Religious Piety and Religious Activity**

A Religious Piety Index was developed for
the panel and for the members of the quasi-sample who were
over eighty by analysis of their answers to the following questions:

a) Could you tell me a little about what religion means to you to-
    day?
b) In what ways has religion helped you?
c) In what ways do you think religion helps people—especially older
    people?
d) Have there ever been periods in your life when religion was par-
    ticularly important to you?

The members of the quasi-sample who were between
seventy and eighty were not asked the same questions, but
a Religious Piety Index was assigned to them on the basis of
their answers (probed in considerable detail) to the question:

"Do you believe in life after death?"

It was felt that the scores assigned to the two groups were
roughly comparable and that a score of 4 or 5 by either system
represented high Religious Piety.

The scores and the bases for their designation follow:

Score	Analysis of answers of Panel and Quasi-Sample 80–90	Answers of Quasi-Sample 70–80
1	Atheist.	No life after death.
2	Agnostic with regard to the existence of a Diety. Philosophic or secular approach to living.	Didn't know, and not very concerned.
3	Belief in a Diety, but not dogmatic. More interested in religious ethic than religious doctrine. Secular orientation. Often conformity appears to be the main element in the answer.	Belief in personal survival but not much interest in it.
4	Firm belief in the Diety. Prayer mentioned throughout. Religion a source of help and hope.	Belief in personal survival and anticipation of it.
5	Whole life organized around faith. Strict adherence to doctrine and dogma.	Vivid and absorbing belief in personal survival. Highly concrete imagery.

The distribution of the two groups is given in Table 2–5.

TABLE 2–5

DISTRIBUTION OF RELIGIOUS VALUES
(PANEL AND QUASI-SAMPLE, WAVE I)

	Panel		70–80		80–90	
Score	Number	Per Cent	Number	Per Cent	Number	Per Cent
Total	*172*	*100.0*	*69*	*100.0*	*37* [a]	*100.0*
1	1	0.6	7	10.1	0	0.0
2	8	4.7	22	31.9	3	8.1
3	57	33.1	20	29.0	11	29.7
4	65	37.8	18	26.1	17	46.0
5	41	23.8	2	2.9	6	16.0

[a] One respondent did not give this information.

The differences in these distributions undoubtedly arise from the fact that the seventy-to-eighty-year-old group were scored on the answers to questions about the afterlife. It is interesting that this concrete question gets, on the average, a more secular response than do the more general questions about religion.

The religious activities of the panel and the quasi-sample were scored according to their answers to the following questions: (1) How many times a month do you usually attend church? and (2) Do you belong to any auxiliaries, committees, (teach Sunday school), or anything like that?

The score is the sum of these two numbers and the distribution appears in Table 2–6.

TABLE 2–6

RELIGIOUS ACTIVITIES SCORE

(PANEL AND QUASI-SAMPLE, WAVE III)

Score	Panel		70–80		80–90	
	Number	Per Cent	Number	Per Cent	Number	Per Cent
Total	*139*[a]	*100.0*	*69*	*100.0*	*38*	*100.0*
0	22	15.8	29	42.0	16	42.1
Low (1–3)	57	41.0	14	20.3	8	21.1
Medium (4–7)	40	28.8	21	30.4	8	21.1
High (8–30)	20	14.4	5	7.2	6	15.8

[a] Three panel members did not give this information.

The Measure of Morale

Morale and world view are considered together because the procedures used to develop these measures are inextricable. Our original search for a way to measure "successful aging" led us to use Kutner's Morale Scale (41). Since it seemed to differ in no essential way from Srole's Anomia Scale (67), we combined the two sets of items and subjected them to the Guttman scaling technique, using a random 88 of the panel. Table 3–1 shows the result of this effort.

Several things are noticeable about this first scale. First, the error is too high, averaging, as it does, 13.5 per cent. And even this is artificially low because the distribution of responses on the last four items is so lopsided that error is minimized. (For example, if only 7 per cent of people give a low morale response to an item, there can, at the most, be 14 per cent error

TABLE 3–1
First Attempt to Scale Kutner-Srole [a]

| | Per Cent | |
Item	High Morale	Errors
1. How much do you regret the chances you missed during your life to do a better job of living? (Kutner)	42	21
2. As you get older, would you say things seem to be better or worse than you thought they would be? (Kutner)	43	19
3. How much unhappiness would you say you find in life today? (Kutner)	47	13
4. How satisfied would you say you are with your way of life today? (Kutner)	48	14
5. These days a person doesn't really know whom he can count on. (Srole)	54	13
6. There's little use writing to public officials, because often they aren't interested in the problems of the average man. (Srole)	58	15
7. Nowadays a person has to live pretty much for today and let tomorrow take care of itself. (Srole)	59	17
8. How much do you plan ahead the things you will be doing next week or the week after? (Kutner)	76	17
9. In spite of what some people say, the lot of the average man is getting worse, not better. (Srole)	81	10
10. It's hardly fair to bring children into the world the way things look for the future. (Srole)	81	9
11. How often do you feel that there is just no point in living? (Kutner)	85	7
12. Things just keep getting worse and worse for me as I get older. (Kutner)	93	6

[a] These items were originally all trichotomous, but the middle or "somewhat" alternative was classed with the more demoralized response in order to improve the distribution, so that the responses should be interpreted as *somewhat* demoralized or alienated.

in the limiting case, where all 7 per cent are misplaced.)
Second, this distribution in itself is bad because it not only
cuts down error artificially, but also produces marginals of
little value in analysis. Third, Kutner items, once the two with
the worst distributions are removed, appear to elicit more "demoralized" responses than the Srole items elicit "anomic" ones.
In this Midwestern population, very few people subscribe to
a gloomy world view.* They appear, in other words, to form
a scale in which the Srole items are on the "hard" end and the
Kutner items on the "easy" end. Finally, the frequencies of the
items are clumped together and do not all contribute to producing different "cuts" through the population.

Before amending the scale, we inquired whether the same
distribution applied to the seventy-to-eighty-year-old group.
It turns out to do so, although there is some shift in the order
of the items—notably the item "How much do you regret the
chances you missed during your life to do a better job of living?" which had a negative response much more often from
the old people. Apparently, after the time when restitution
might still have been made for past errors, regrets are abandoned.† There is a greater tendency for those between seventy
and eighty to respond "anomically," or in a "demoralized" way,
to these items than the panel members do. For this reason, we
felt justified in keeping all the items which broke better than
85–15 in the panel. Then, by eliminating the high-error items
that do not differ in their frequencies from low-error items, we
arrived at a seven-item scale containing four of Kutner's items
and three of Srole's, and were 90.7 per cent reproducible. For
the panel, these items were (the per cent demoralized or anomic is in parentheses): 1 (56.4), 4 (54.5), 3 (50.9), 5 (48.1),
9 (20.9), 10 (19.0), 11 (14.0). It will be noticed that the order

* This is not surprising, since Srole developed his items in displaced-persons'
camps after the war.
† In this regard see Chapter II, p. 17.

of the items has shifted. This happened because the frequency of the total panel differed from that of the first half on which the original scaling was done. However, the differences were slight. There are two clumps of items with almost equal marginals, and there is a gap between them. The use of the full range of items was rationalized by their function in increasing the scoring range. The scores for each item are either 3 or 1, giving a range of 7-21 even though, for most purposes, the panel and quasi-sample are divided simply into high and low. Table 3–2 shows the correlations of the items. Table 3–3 shows the distribution for the panel. It is skewed in a sanguine direction, although the seventy-to-eighty group is more nearly normal.

TABLE 3–2

YULE AND KENDALL'S Q FOR KUTNER AND SROLE ITEMS

	Kutner Items				Srole Items		
	11	1	3	4	10	5	9
11	---	.64	.62	.61	.65	.38	.35
1	---	---	.57	.33	.06	.03	.20
3	---	---	---	.70	.13	.32	.53
4	---	---	---	---	.57	.28	.22
10					---	.87	.80
5					---	---	.80
9					---	---	---

NOTE: Average Q: within Srole = .82, within Kutner = .58. K–S = .31.

Obviously, we could have invented new items to improve the marginals. We did not do this because we had decided, on the basis of our knowledge of the respondents, that this scale was not measuring morale (Chapter VII). However, we felt that the instrument was interesting in itself, and believed after inspecting the items, that they must be highly normative and reflect both a world view and an attitude toward the interviewer. We decided further that the scale tended to elicit a generalized response of cynicism about the nature of the world, as against a belief in its ultimate goodness and progress. Expressed another way, the score might be thought of as expressing the degree of the respondent's alienation from a belief in "the best of all possible worlds." This interpretation takes into account the difference between the Srole and Kutner items. A general belief that everything, even painful experiences, has a purpose and works toward a harmonious end is consonant with a world view that includes a belief in the inevitable triumph of good, or perhaps a belief that one *should* state such a belief in spite of one's doubts.

TABLE 3–3

DISTRIBUTION OF RESPONDENTS BY SCORE ON WORLD-VIEW SCALE
(PANEL AND SEVENTIES, WAVE III)

World-View Score	Panel Per Cent	70–80 Per Cent
Number interviewed	*142*	69
21 (most alienated)	2.1	2.9
19	4.9	7.2
17	7.7	21.7
15	14.1	21.7
13	19.7	11.6
11	19.7	14.5
9	19.7	14.5
7 (most conforming)	12.0	5.8

With these matters in mind, the intensive interviewer ranked ten respondents, whom she had seen for a total of from six to eight hours, according to her opinion of their morale, and then ranked them again according to her opinion of their world view, with the lower rank being the more sanguine view. As Table 3–4 shows, the world-view ranking fits the World-View score better than the morale score fits it.

TABLE 3–4

RANK ORDER CORRELATION BETWEEN WORLD-VIEW SCORE AND
DEAN'S MORALE AND WORLD-VIEW RANKINGS

Respondent	Dean Morale Ranking	World-View Score Rank [a]	Dean World-View Rank
1	1	9.5	9
105	2	2.5	4
53	3	2.5	1
115	4	6.5	5
181	5	2.5	2
121	6	6.5	7
21	7	2.5	3
93	8	2.5	6
68	9	8.0	8
5	10	9.5	10

NOTE: Rho between the Dean Morale Ranking and the World-View Score is .17. Rho between the Dean World-View Ranking and the World-View Score is .88.

[a] It is unfortunate that the ten intensively interviewed people did not represent the scoring range very adequately. Neither the highest nor the lowest scores are represented, and there are five respondents tied for the lowest rank and two tied for the next lowest.

Having developed what seemed to be a world-view scale, we attempted to develop a Morale Index. The steps in the development of this instrument follow.

1. The interview material already available was examined for items that agreed with the Dean Ranking at better than the .05 level, using the Wald-Wolfowitz Runs Test. This meant that a yes-no item could have no more than one discordant answer. Four such items were found:
   A. What age would you most like to be? Score of 1 for the answer, "The age I am."
   B. If you could do anything you pleased, in what part of Kansas City would you most like to live? Score of 1 if he prefers where he is, or plans removal if dissatisfied.
   C. Of all the things you do on the weekend . . . which are the

things that are less interesting and enjoyable to you? Score of 1 if nothing done on the weekend is uninteresting or unenjoyable.

D. Do you wish you could see more of your (*a*) relatives; (*b*) friends; (*c*) neighbors than you do, or would you like more time to yourself? Score of 1 if he is satisfied with the present amount of contact with all three categories of people. All other responses get a score of zero.

This index yields a score of 0–4, and its distribution is given in Table 3–5.

TABLE 3–5

MORALE SCORE DISTRIBUTION
(PANEL AND SEVENTIES, WAVE III)

Score	Panel		70–80	
	Number	Per Cent	Number	Per Cent
Number interviewed	*142*	*100.0*	*69*	*100.0*
0	20	14.1	10	14.5
1	48	33.8	21	30.4
2	47	33.1	20	29.0
3	23	16.2	15	21.7
4	4	2.8	3	4.3

2. Another of us, working blind for the Dean Ranking, sorted the ten respondents on the basis of replies to the following questions (the numbers in brackets after each question refer to the interview number):

A. How do you feel about Kansas City, what do you like about it, what don't you like, and that sort of thing? (1)

B. I'd like to ask how you and your family have been (since last interview)? (2)

C. I wonder if you could tell me what some of the nicest things are that have happened to you since your last interview? (2)

D. What would you say is the most unpleasant thing that has happened to you since your last interview? (2)

E. How have you been lately? Are you getting out, apart from your work, about the same as last time? (2)

    F. As far as your leisure time is concerned, have you changed it at all? I mean, are your weekends or days off different from what they were when I saw you last? (2)

    G. What's it going to be like when you retire? (2)

    H. A different kind of question I want to ask you is this: Imagine, if you will, that it's now 1962—five years from now. What do you think you will be doing? How do you expect things to be different for you from the way they are now? (2)

    I. If you had your life to live over again, in what ways would you want it to be different? (2)

    J. First, I'd like to ask how you and your family have been? (3)

Each of the ten respondents was scored on a five-point scale on the basis of the level of morale the answers to the above questions indicated. The theoretical range of scores was 10 to 50.

3. Working independently, another of us (DG) rated the ten respondents for "adjustment." He considered the following two components derived from Erikson (23) to be operative in his decision:

    A. Goal Directedness: This characteristic, closely related to Erikson's "generativity," refers to the ability to pursue productive ends above and beyond the gratification of one's own needs.

    B. Recognition and "realistic" handling of affective conflict. This characteristic allows the productive resolution of conflict between inner needs and outer demands. It involves the ability to defer gratification.

He ranked the ten respondents on the basis of these two characteristics, with particular reference to their defense system (Chapter VI), using material from the first three interviews with the panel and from personal interviews with two panel members.

4. An interviewer (Marx) who had been trained by us for struc-

tured interviewing was asked to pretest Interview 4 with the ten intensively interviewed respondents and to "rank them on the basis of their morale." No discussion of the meaning of this word was undertaken.

A summary picture of the correlations between the various ranks and the Morale Index appears in Table 3–6.

TABLE 3–6

MORALE JUDGMENT CORRELATIONS

	Dean	Newell	Gutmann	Marx	Morale Index
Dean	—	.80	.85	.78	.82
Newell	.80	—	.52	.76	.51
Gutmann	.85	.52	—	.62	.75
Marx	.78	.76	.62	—	.61
Morale Index	.82	.51	.75	.61	—

Rho is significant (at the .05 level) if it exceeds .60, except in the case of the Marx ranking where there were only nine cases because of one refusal. In this instance, rho must exceed .63.

Because these correlations, though high, are far from perfect, and because the range of the Morale Index is small and its distribution not normal (see Table 3–5), the relationships are restated in Table 3–7 in terms of High Scores (2, 3, and 4) and Low Scores (0 and 1). In other words, Dean's ranking was reduced to the upper and lower half, and the rankings of the others were re-examined to see how well they matched Dean's when they too were reduced to two categories.

5. Finally, ten cases, not those intensively interviewed, were selected, five with a high Morale Index Score (two with 4 and three with 3) and five with a low Score (all 0), and a pretesting interview was conducted with them blind for Morale Score. After Dean had seen them, she assigned them to high or low morale. She successfully sorted them without error. In fact, she ranked the two 4s higher within the high half than the three 3s.

TABLE 3–7

CONCORDANCE WITH DEAN SORTING INTO HIGH & LOW HALVES

	Number Concordant with Dean Sorting	Number Discordant
Gutmann	10	0
Marx [a]	8	1
Newell	8	2
Morale Index	10	0

[a] Marx ranked nine respondents. If the highest five are called high morale, she has a perfect match with Dean. If the highest four are called high, she has two discordant cases. The figure in the table is a compromise.

When we consider that the index is repeated three times in the course of the study, we would expect it to be more stable between two interviews close together than between two more widely spaced. When we compare the index compiled from the first three interviews with that compiled from the fifth, conducted two years later, we find that 17 per cent of the respondents changed scores by two points, 44 per cent changed by one point, and 39 per cent were unchanged. However, when we look at the scores from the sixth interview, which was undertaken between six and nine months after the fifth one, we find the scores somewhat more stable. Only 7 per cent changed by two points, 52 per cent by one point, and 41 per cent were unchanged. This suggests that the index is measuring changes affected by time, and is therefore more likely to be concerned with morale than with some quality of character.

The Relationship Among the Variables

Although an attempt to measure disengagement is premature, we have indices that give us the respondent's level of engagement, in the interactional sense. These are Role Count, Interaction Index, and Lifespace. We also have some social-psychological indices of engagement (Chapters IV and V). As the text shows, the relationships among these variables are not always direct. However, the smallness of the sample has in most cases made it inadvisable to attempt control for more than one or two variables at a time. In addition to this, some comparisons between variables have been omitted as irrelevant to the theory. Finally, some variables are so closely related that discussion is unnecessary.

The interrelationships of the main variables used in the study are given in Tables 4–1, 4–2, and 4–3. The figures shown in the body of the tables are Yule's coefficient of association (39, p. 310 ff). We are not concerned here with the absolute size or with the statistical significance of the relationship but, rather, the relative degree of relationship and its direction (i.e. negative or positive).

These tables are not age-specific, but they are consonant with the conclusions presented in the text. For example, the consistently negative relationships between *alienation* and the interaction variables are in line with expectation. The reason these relationships are smaller for women than for men is discussed, in part, in Chapter VIII.

The relationships among the interactional variables is as expected, and since these three variables were constructed from different data, the results obtained give reason to conclude that the procedures used are reasonable and valid.

The relationship between F-score and the interaction indices reflects the findings discussed in Chapters V and VIII, in which the amount of interaction was found to be a salient factor in authoritarianism for women but not for men. The moderate relationship between F-score and Alienation is reasonable in view of the fact that the items of both scales have a prima-facie dimension of acceptance versus non-acceptance of norms. The size of the relationship is reasonable.

The relationship between Ego Energy and the interaction variables is probably not a direct one, but mediated through other age-related variables. For example, we know that both Lifespace and Ego Energy decrease with age, and that both are associated with Perceived Lifespace (object cathexis). Thus, any relationship between Lifespace and Ego Energy is probably due to their mutual relationship with the other variable. It is interesting that the Qs between Ego Energy and Interaction Index and Lifespace are reversed for men and women. This raises the possibility that the Interaction Index provides a more accurate estimate of the size and quality of the life

TABLE 4–1

RELATIONSHIP [a] AMONG THE VARIABLES (MEN)

	1	2	3	4	5	6	7
1. Role count	—	.80	.82	.59	−.66	.25	−.25
2. Interaction index		—	.63	.60	−.74	.11	.13
3. Lifespace			—	.81	−.58	−.18	.80
4. Perceived lifespace				—	−.67	.11	.13
5. Alienation					—	.40	−.44
6. F-Score						—	.00
7. Ego energy							—

[a] Yule's coefficient of association Q.

TABLE 4–2

RELATIONSHIP [a] AMONG THE VARIABLES (WOMEN)

	1	2	3	4	5	6	7
1. Role count	—	.85	.59	.45	−.59	−.26	.67
2. Interaction index		—	.39	.54	−.57	−.42	.80
3. Lifespace			—	.47	−.23	−.52	.05
4. Perceived lifespace				—	−.26	.26	.67
5. Alienation					—	.30	−.61
6. F-Score						—	−.63
7. Ego energy							—

[a] Yule's coefficient of association Q.

TABLE 4–3

RELATIONSHIP [a] AMONG THE VARIABLES, TOTAL POPULATION

	1	2	3	4	5	6	7
1. Role count	—	.82	.67	.53	−.50	−.01	.21
2. Interaction index		—	.47	.58	−.66	−.17	.41
3. Lifespace			—	.61	−.37	−.39	.46
4. Perceived lifespace				—	−.49	.15	.38
5. Alienation					—	.35	−.48
6. F-Score						—	−.32
7. Ego energy							—

[a] Yule's coefficient of association Q.

space for women, and the Lifespace Measure provides a more accurate estimate of the size and quality of the life space for men.

The relationship of Ego Energy to Alienation and F-score for women, but to only Alienation for men, is in the predicted direction—they are both related to age in some manner and thus related to each other. The lack of relation between Ego Energy and F-score for men is inexplicable, but since F-score is only weakly related to size or quality of life space for men, and Ego Energy is related to the interaction variables via other factors, we would not expect to find a relationship between Ego Energy and F-score for the men.

In summary, none of the relationships among the variables are dissonant with disengagement theory; most of them are harmonious with it, and a few are explainable only on a *post hoc* basis. However, it should be kept in mind that except for alienation, F-score, and Ego Energy, the scores are not totally independent, being developed from overlapping data, and therefore their relationship is inflated to an unknown degree.

The Validity of the Psychological Measures

To make sure that the psychological types described in Chapter VI have internal consistency, and that the protocols grouped together to form types bore some consistent relation to one another, two validating steps were taken. In other words, we wished to make sure that protocols had not been grouped together merely because they were accidentally related in terms of one or another theme or story but because of general psychological similarities.

■ TAT Responses Categories

Procedure: The protocols contain stories to five cards: Nos. 1, 2, 6-BM, 7-BM, and 17-BM. In the first step all the stories to each card were categorized except those for No. 2, which contains a variety of latent stimuli, and not all respondents dealt with any one. Each card was analyzed separately, apart from the total protocol, and categories were devised that were relevant to a basic issue proposed by the card, reflecting specific modes of coping with this issue, and accounting for all responses to the card. After the stories had been analyzed, the records of the respondents were decoded.

After this, more general categories, no longer specific to the individual cards, against which *all* stories to *all* cards could be arrayed, were developed. The Response Categories, arranged on an Active Mastery to Passive Mastery continuum, follow:

Category 1—Assertive, autonomous: In these stories the hero moves assertively, directly, and resourcefully toward self-defined goals. The environment is relatively passive, and the wishes or opposition of others is a secondary issue.

Category 2—Vigorous competence in role performance: In these stories the hero brings appropriate energy, vigor, and resources to a social role. This category is distinguished from Category 1 by the absence of interpersonal aggression; the hero's actions are not carried out in the face of external opposition or reluctance.

Category 3—Externalized deference-assertion conflict: These are stories in which the hero struggles against agents who would force him to be passive, obedient or dependent. If the hero submits to such pressures, he does so sullenly and resentfully, without abandoning opposition.

Category 4—Internalized assertion-passivity conflict: In these stories the hero is in conflict over taking assertive roles. Other individuals may be involved but the final decision—usually in favor of achievement—is made by the hero.

Category 5—Ambivalence concerning aggression: Here are found stories in which the hero "undoes" or abandons an initially assertive attitude. Though external pressures do not usually cause the change, the hero moves to nurturant or deferent positions. In some cases, disastrous outcomes follow competitive success.

Category 6—Deference, succorance, in the service of achievement goals: Grouped here are stories in which the hero is given friendly advice or support by an older man. This allows the hero to mobilize his own resources, and a good outcome follows.

Category 7—Conforming, constricted: Two logically different kinds of stories are grouped here, one defined in terms of content, the other in terms of formal qualities. In the former stories, the hero blandly and without affect defers to the judgment and direction of an authority, and outcomes are not specified. In the latter type, the major details of the stimulus are specified, and some minimal interaction is proposed between them. The story does not move beyond this bare recognition and delineation of the stimulus, and little or no personal elaboration is introduced. These two classes of stories are grouped together since they are judged to be dynamically similar: in the first case the hero defers and conforms to whatever structure and direction are presented by an authority, and in the second case the respondent accepts without personal involvement or alteration whatever structure is offered by the immediate environment. Both approaches point to the respondent's need for outer structure and impersonal direction.

Category 8—Externalization of aggression (rationalized projection): In these stories agents in the environment either contain threatening qualities which are directed toward the hero (The rope climber is fleeing from a fire.), or outside agents are made responsible for the hero's action. (The young man leaves his mother in answer to a draft call.) What is involved here is the placement of aggression, or the responsibility for aggression, *outside* of an otherwise difficult interpersonal situation, or outside of a usually powerful agent.

Category 9—Guilty, abasive: In these stories the hero is abasive and inadequate in the presence of an achievement press, or guilty and deferent in the presence of an authority.

Category 10—Distorted responses: These stories involve gross distortions and misperceptions of the stimuli, in the service of strong personal needs (the rope climber is asleep or is a "sex peeker," the older man is trying to lead the young man into evil ways, and so on).

Though the TAT stories were categorized without reference to the interview, the distribution of individual TAT stories by age and category in Table 5–1 parallels the distribution of total protocols by personality type. Accordingly we see here an internal consistency in the direction of change indicated in the distribution of personality types. That is, the individual

TABLE 5–1

PERSONALITY TYPES BY AGE

(MEN ONLY)

Response Categories	Responses	Per Cent of Responses by Age		
		40–49	50–59	60–69
Total	*563*	*100.0*	*100.0*	*100.0*
Categories 1–5		*56.5*	*52.9*	*41.5*
1. Assertive, autonomous	37	6.5	9.0	3.5
2. Vigorous competence	58	9.3	9.8	11.5
3. Externalized deference-assertion conflict	72	20.4	11.8	10.0
4. Internalized assertion-passivity conflict	49	8.3	8.2	9.5
5. Ambivalence concerning aggression	63	12.0	14.1	7.0
Categories 6–10		*43.5*	*47.1*	*58.5*
6. Achievement through deference	41	9.3	5.9	8.0
7. Conforming, constricted	61	4.6	11.8	13.0
8. Externalization of aggression	89	17.6	13.3	18.0
9. Guilty, abasive	71	9.3	11.4	16.0
10. Distorted responses	22	2.8	4.7	3.5

NOTE: The responses of the men under sixty are more frequently in the first five categories. The responses of the men over sixty are more frequently in the last five categories. $\chi^2 = 7.2$, d.f. $= 1$, $P < .01$.

TAT stories, like the total protocols, show a shift with age from attempts at active mastery to versions of passive mastery.

■ Relation of the Personality Types to Ratings on the Draw-a-Person Test

At the end of Interview 4, respondents were asked to draw an old man and an old woman. These drawings were rated blind for age and personality type according to the fourfold criteria developed by Molly Harrower (28):

Level I: Drawings classified here are relatively formless, without clear boundaries, often without recognizably human shape, proportion, or limb arrangement.

Level II: Drawings have relatively firm boundaries, though major disproportions are introduced. The drawings are not so much chaotic and disorganized, as in Level I, but, rather, distorted in ways that might be judged to arise from unconscious images or wishes.

Level III: The drawings here are relatively well proportioned and firmly outlined. Appropriate details of feature and clothing are included. However, detail is sparse, and the figure is relatively static and constricted.

Level IV: These drawings are well proportioned, outlines are sure and precise, many reasonable details of feature and clothing are introduced, and perspective and action are included. These drawings have a clear, vigorous, and sometimes original quality.

In rating drawings that were not clearly at one level or another, a score halfway between the two levels was assigned. Total score is an average of the two drawings. Table 5–2 shows that the distribution of these scores appears to be associated with the major personality types discussed above.

TABLE 5–2

DISTRIBUTION OF DRAW-A-PERSON SCORES AGAINST PERSONALITY TYPES
(MEN ONLY)

Types	Number Interviewed	Respondents with Scores of			
		4.0–2.5		2.25–1.0	
		Number	*Per Cent*	*Number*	*Per Cent*
Total	37				
Active mastery	12	8	66.7	4	33.3
Passive mastery	13	7	53.8	6	46.2
Ego defect	12	3	25.0	9	75.0

The Publications from the Study

1. CASSETTA, RHONDDA, NEWELL, D. S., and PARLAGRECO, MARY LOU. "Morale Changes in Women During Aging." Paper read to the Midwest Sociological meeting, St. Louis, April, 1960.
2. CUMMING, ELAINE. "Social Change and the Aging Process." Paper read to the 13th Annual Conference on Gerontology, Ann Arbor, June, 1960.
3. ———, DEAN, LOIS R., and NEWELL, D. S. "A Disengagement Theory of Aging." Paper read to the Gerontological Society meetings, Philadelphia, November, 1958.
4. ———, DEAN, LOIS R., and NEWELL, D. S. "Measuring Successful Aging—A Validity Problem." Proceedings of the Committee on Human Development Symposium, Chicago, February, 1958.
5. ———, DEAN, LOIS R., and NEWELL, D. S. "What is Morale?— A Case History of a Validity Problem," *Human Organization*, XVII, 2 (1958), p. 3.

6. ———, DEAN, LOIS R., NEWELL, D. S., and McCAFFREY, ISABEL. "Disengagement—A Tentative Theory of Aging." Paper read to the American Psychological Association meetings, Cincinnati, September, 1959, and *Sociometry*, XXIII, 1 (1960), p. 23.

7. ———, and McCAFFREY, ISABEL. "Some Conditions Associated with Morale Among the Aging." Paper read to the annual meeting of American Psychopathological Association, New York, February, 1960.

8. ———, and SCHNEIDER, D. M. "Sibling Solidarity: A Feature of American Kinship." *The American Anthropologist*, to be published in June, 1961.

9. ———, and UDELL, BESS. "Interaction Patterns in Normal Aging." Paper read to the Gerontological Society meetings, November, 1957.

10. ———, and UDELL, BESS. "Patterns of Normal Aging." Paper read to the American Sociological Society meetings, August, 1957.

11. DEAN, LOIS R. "Aging and the Decline of Instrumentality." *Journal of Gerontology*, XV, 4 (1960), p. 403.

12. ———. "The Pattern Variables: Some Empirical Operations." *American Sociological Review*, XXVI, 1 (1961), p. 80.

13. ———, CUMMING, ELAINE, NEWELL, D. S. "Interaction Style and Success in Aging." Paper read to the American Sociological Society meetings, Seattle, August, 1958.

14. GUTMANN, D. L. "The Aging Man." Paper read to the Illinois Psychological Association, March, 1960.

15. ———, HENRY, W. E., and NEUGARTEN, BERNICE L. "Personality Development in Middle-Aged Men." Paper read to the American Psychological Association meetings, Cincinnati, September, 1959.

16. HAVIGHURST, R. J. "Successful Aging, Definition and Measurement." Paper read to the International Research Seminar on the Social and Psychological Aspects of Aging, August, 1960.

17. HENRY, W. E. "Personality Changes with Age." Paper read to

the Gerontological Society meetings, Philadelphia, November, 1958.

18. ———, and CUMMING, ELAINE. "Personality Development in Adulthood and Old Age." Presidential Address of the Society for Projective Techniques at the Convention of the American Psychological Association, Cincinnati, September, 1959, and *Journal of Projective Techniques*, XXIII, 4 (1959), p. 383.

19. LORTIE, D. C. "Middle-Aged Men and Their Work." Proceedings of the Committee on Human Development, Symposium, Chicago, February, 1957.

20. ———. "Social Space and the Meaning of Social Participation." Paper read to the Midwest Sociological Society meetings, March, 1957.

21. NEUGARTEN, BERNICE L. "Personality and the Aging Process." Paper read to the International Research Seminar on the Social and Psychological Aspects of Aging, San Francisco, August, 1960.

22. ROSEN, JACQUELINE L., and NEUGARTEN, BERNICE L. "Ego Functions in the Middle and Later Years: A Thematic Apperception Study of Normal Adults." *Journal of Gerontology*, XV, 1 (1960), p. 62.

23. WILLIAMS, R. "Styles of Life and Successful Aging." Paper read to the International Research Seminar on the Social and Psychological Aspects of Aging, Berkeley, California, August, 1960.

References

1. ADORNO, T. W., *et al. The Authoritarian Personality.* New York: Harper, 1950.
2. ANTHONY, SYLVIA. *The Child's Discovery of Death.* New York: Harcourt, Brace, 1940.
3. APPLE, DORRIAN. "The Social Structure of Grandparenthood," *American Anthropologist,* LVIII, 4 (1956), p. 656.
4. ———. Unpublished Ph.D. dissertation, Harvard University.
5. ARNHOFF, F. "Adult Age Difference in Performance on a Visual-Spatial Task of Stimulus Generalization," *Journal of Educational Psychology,* L, 6 (1959), p. 259.
6. ———. "Concepts of Aging." To be published in Hoch, P., and Zubin, J. (Eds.), *Proceedings of the American Psychopathological Association,* New York, 1961.
7. BALES, R. F. *Interaction Process Analysis,* Cambridge, Mass.: Addison-Wesley, 1950.
8. BECKMAN, R. O., WILLIAMS, C. D., and FISHER, G. C. "An Index of Adjustment to Life in Later Maturity," *Geriatrics,* XIII, 10 (1958), p. 662.

9. BELLIN, S. *Family and Kinship in Later Years*, Syracuse, N.Y.: Report of Mental Health Research Unit, 1961.

10. BERGER, B. M. "How Long is a Generation?" *British Journal of Sociology*, XI, 1 (1960), p. 10.

11. BIRREN, J. Address to the American Psychopathological Association, February, 1960.

12. BLENCKNER, MARGARET. "The Research Design and Some Preliminary Findings," *Experimental Research in Social Work: A Report of a Study in Services to the Aging*. New York: Mimeographed Document, 1959.

13. BRITTON, J. H., and MATHER, W. G. "Factors in Criterion Measures of Adjustment of Older Adults." Paper read to the Annual Meeting of the Gerontological Society, Philadelphia, November 8, 1958.

14. COSIN, L., *et al.* "Experimental Treatment of Persistent Senile Confusion," *International Journal of Social Psychiatry*, IV, 1 (1958), p. 24.

15. ——. Speech to the Blue Cross–Blue Shield groups, Kansas City, 1957.

16. CUMMING, ELAINE, and SCHNEIDER, D. M. "Sibling Solidarity: A Feature of American Kinship," *The American Anthropologist*, to be published in June, 1961.

17. CUMMING, J. "Communication, an Approach to Schizophrenia," in *Chronic Schizophrenia*, Appleby, L., Scher, J. M., and Cumming, J. (Eds.). Glencoe, Ill.: Free Press, 1960.

18. DEAN, LOIS R. "Aging and the Decline of Instrumentality," *Journal of Gerontology*, XV, 4 (1960), p. 403.

19. ——. "The Pattern Variables, Some Empirical Operations," *American Sociological Review*, XXVI, 1 (1961), p. 80.

20. DURKHEIM, EMILE. *The Division of Labor in Society*. Glencoe, Ill.: Free Press, 1949.

21. ——. *Suicide*. Glencoe, Ill.: Free Press, 1951.

22. EISSLER, K. R. *The Psychiatrist and the Dying Patient*. New York: International Universities Press, 1955.

23. ERIKSON, E. H. *Childhood and Society*. New York: Norton, 1950.

24. ———. *Identity and the Life Cycle.* New York: International Universities Press, 1959.

25. FIRTH, R. *Two Studies of Kinship in London.* London: Athlone Press, 1956.

26. GRANICK, RUTH, and NAHEMOV, LUCILLE D. "Preadmission Isolation as a Factor in Adjustment to an Old Age Home." To be published in Hoch, P., and Zubin, J. (Eds.), *The Proceedings of the American Psychopathological Association,* New York, 1961.

27. GURFIELD, J. R. "The Problem of Generations in an Organizational Structure," *Social Forces,* XXXV, 4 (1957), p. 323.

28. HARROWER, MOLLY. *Personality Change and Development.* New York: Grune, 1958.

29. HARTMANN, H. *Ego Psychology and the Problem of Adaptation.* Rapaport, D. (Tr.). New York: International Universities Press, 1958.

30. ———. "The Mutual Influences in the Development of Ego and Id," in *The Psychoanalytic Study of the Child.* New York: International Universities Press, 1945, Vol. VII.

31. ———, KRIS, E., and LOEWENSTEIN, R. M. "Comments on the Formation of Psychic Structure," in *The Psychoanalytic Study of the Child.* New York: International Universities Press, 1946, Vol. II.

32. HAVIGHURST, R. *Psychological Aspects of Aging.* Washington, D.C.: American Psychological Association, 1956.

33. ———. "The Social Competence of Middle-Aged People," *Genetic Psychology Monographs,* 56 (1957), p. 297.

34. ———. "Successful Aging—Definition and Measurement." Paper presented to the International Research Seminar on the Social and Psychological Aspects of Aging, August, 1960.

35. HENRY, W. E. *The Analysis of Fantasy.* New York: Wiley, 1956.

36. HOMANS, G. *The Human Group.* New York: Harcourt, Brace, 1950.

37. HORTON, D., and WOHL, R. "Mass Communication and Para-Social Interaction," *Psychiatry,* XIX, 3 (1956), p. 215.

38. JAHODA, MARIE. *Current Concepts of Positive Mental Health.* New York: Basic Books, 1958.

39. KENDALL, M. G. *The Advanced Theory of Statistics.* New York: Hafner, 1952, Vol. I.

40. KINSEY, A. C., POMEROY, W. B., and MARTIN, C. E. *Sexual Behavior in the Human Male.* Philadelphia: Saunders, 1948.

41. KUTNER, B., *et al. Five Hundred Over Sixty.* New York: Russell Sage Foundation, 1956.

42. LANGER, SUZANNE. *Philosophy in a New Key.* Cambridge, Mass.: Harvard University Press, 1957.

43. LEWIN, K. *Principles of Topological Psychology.* New York: McGraw-Hill, 1936.

44. LORGE, I., and TUCKMAN, J. *Retirement and the Industrial Worker.* New York: Columbia University Press, 1953.

45. MILLER, W. "Cultural Features of an Urban Lower Class Community." Mimeographed document.

46. MILLS, C. W. "The Professional Ideology of Social Pathologists," *American Journal of Sociology,* XLIX, 2 (1944), p. 165.

47. MURRAY, H. A. *Thematic Apperception Test,* pictures and manual. Cambridge, Mass.: Harvard University Press, 1943.

48. NEUGARTEN, BERNICE N., and GUTMANN, D. L. "Age-sex Roles and Personality in Middle Age: A Thematic Apperception Study," *Psychological Monographs,* LXXII, 17 (1958), whole No. 470.

49. ORBACH, H. L. "Aging and Religion: Church Attendance in the Metropolitan Area," Detroit Area Studies.

50. PARSONS, T. *The Social System.* Glencoe, Ill.: Free Press, 1950.

51. ———. "Toward a Healthy Maturity," *Journal of Health and Human Behavior,* I (1960), p. 163.

52. ———, and BALES, R. F. *Family Socialization and Interaction Process.* Glencoe, Ill.: Free Press, 1955.

53. ———, and SHILS, E. *Toward a General Theory of Action.* Glencoe, Ill.: Free Press, 1951.

54. PETERSON, W. A. *Metropolitan Area Health Survey.* Kansas City: Community Studies, Inc., 1959.

55. PLATO. *The Republic*, Book I.

56. POTTER, S. "Do Try and Attend," *Punch*, July 2, 1958, p. 4.

57. RAPAPORT, D. "The Autonomy of the Ego," *Bulletin of the Menninger Clinic*, 15 (1951), p. 113.

58. RENZ, MARGARET. "A Study of Faculty and Administrative Staff Who Have Retired from New York University, 1945-56," *Journal of Educational Sociology*, April, 1958, p. 282.

59. RIEGEL, K. F. "Personality Theory and Aging," in *Handbook of Aging and the Individual: Psychological and Biological Aspects*, Birren, J. E. (Ed.). Chicago, Ill.: University of Chicago Press, 1959, p. 797.

60. RIESMAN, D. *Individualism Reconsidered*. Glencoe, Ill.: Free Press, 1954.

61. ——. *The Lonely Crowd: A Study of the Changing American Character*. New Haven: Yale University Press, 1950.

62. ROSEN, JACQUELINE, and NEUGARTEN, BERNICE L. "Ego Functions in the Middle and Later Years: A Thematic Apperception Study of Normal Adults," *Journal of Gerontology*, XV, 1 (1960), p. 62.

63. ROSENBERG, M., and THIELENS, W., with LAZARSFELD, P. "The Panel Study," in *Research Methods in Social Relations*, Jahoda, Marie, Deutsch, M., and Cook, S. W. (Eds.). 1951, Vol. II.

64. SCHAW, L. C., and HENRY, W. E. "A Method for the Comparison of Groups: A Study in Thematic Apperception," *Genetic Psychology Monographs*, 54 (1956), p. 207.

65. SIMMONS, L. W. *The Role of the Aged in Primitive Society*. New Haven: Yale University Press, 1945.

66. SLATER, P. E. "Personality Structure in Old Age," *Correlates of Anxiety*. Unpublished report from the Age Center in New England, 1958.

67. SROLE, L. "Social Integration and Certain Corollaries," *American Sociological Review*, XXI (1956), p. 709.

68. STEWART, D., and HOULT, T. "A Social-Psychological Theory of the Authoritarian Personality," *American Journal of Sociology*, LXV, 3 (1959), p. 274.

69. STONE, C. L., and SLOCUM, W. L. *A Look at Thurston County's Older People.* Washington Agricultural Experiment Stations, Institute of Agricultural Sciences, State College of Washington, Bulletin 573, May, 1957.

70. STREIB, G. F. "Morale of the Retired," *Social Problems,* III (1956), p. 270.

71. ———, THOMPSON, W. E., and SUCHMAN, E. A. "The Cornell Study of Occupational Retirement," *Journal of Social Issues,* XIV (1958), p. 3.

72. TEC, NECHAMA, and GRANICK, RUTH B. "Social Isolation and Difficulties in Social Interaction of Residents of a Home for Aged," *Social Problems,* VII, 3 (Winter, 1959-60).

73. TIBBITS, C. *A Handbook of Social Gerontology.* Chicago, Ill.: University of Chicago Press, 1960.

74. TOWNSEND, P. *The Family Life of Old People.* Glencoe, Ill.: Free Press, 1957.

75. TYHURST, J., SALK, LEE, and KENNEDY, MIRIAM. "Morbidity, Mortality and Retirement." Paper read to the 23rd Meeting of the A.A.A.S., New York, 1956.

76. WALLACH, M. A., and GREEN, L. R. "On Age and the Subjective Speed of Time." Mimeographed report.

77. WALLIN, P., and CLARK, A. "Cultural Norms and Husbands' and Wives' Reports of their Marital Partners' Preferred Frequency of Coitus Relative to their Own," *Sociometry,* XXI, 3 (1958), p. 247.

78. WARNER, L., MEEKER, MARCHIA, and EELLS, K. *Social Class in America.* New York: Harper Torchbooks, 1960.

79. WHYTE, W. F. *Street Corner Society.* Chicago, Ill.: University of Chicago Press, 1943.

80. WILLIAMS, R. H., and LOEB, M. B. "The Adult's Social Life-space and Successful Aging; Some Suggestions for a Conceptual Framework." Paper read to the Annual Meeting of the American Gerontological Society, 1956.

81. WRIGHT, V. C., and HYMAN, H. *Mass Leisure,* Larrabee, E., and Meyerson, R. (Eds.). Glencoe, Ill.: Free Press, 1958.

82. YARROW, MARION RADKE, BLANK, P., QUINN, OLIVE, YOUMANS, G., and STEIN, JOHANNA. "Social Psychological Characteristics of Old Age," *Human Aging: A Biological and Behavioral Study*. Washington, D.C.: Government Printing Office, 1961.

Index

A

achievement doubt, 114-115
adaptive responses, 111
Adorno, T. W., 250
affect-control typology, 108
  men, 109-121
  women, 121-125
age-grading, 63-64
aging, biological, 4-5
aging process, 6-7
  disengagement theory of, 14-16,
    210-218
  implicit theory of, 16-23
  panel research of, 25-26
  from seventies to eighties, 203-
    209
  social science studies of, 8-12
  successful, 128-142
  see also disengagement; person-
    ality variations
alienation, from world view, 94-96
Allegretto, J. D., xii

B

Bales, R. F., 24, 66n.
Baruch, Bernard, 201
Bellin, S., 51n., 56n.
Birren, J., 155
Blenckner, M., 142, 202
Bolgar, Hedda, xi
Britton, J. H., 17, 72
Bryant, W. D., x

C

Apple, D., 61
approval-seeking, 81-86
Arnhoff, F., 202
Arthur, T., xii
attitude changes, 75-105
attrition, problem of, 32, 34-35
authoritarianism, 87-91, 145, 250-
  251

case histories; see disengagement
Cassetta, R., xi

289